D0848146

STRONG
ADVOCATE

STRONG ADVOCATE

THE LIFE OF A TRIAL LAWYER

THOMAS STRONG

UNIVERSITY OF MISSOURI PRESS   COLUMBIA AND LONDON

Cataloging-in-Publication data available from the Library of Congress.
ISBN 978-0-8262-1997-8

♾™ This paper meets the requirements of the
American National Standard for Permanence of Paper
for Printed Library Materials, Z39.48, 1984.

Jacket design: Susan Ferber
Interior design and composition: Jennifer Cropp
Printing and binding: Thomson-Shore, Inc.
Typefaces: Minion and Apple Symbols

To the memory of my mother, Blanche Gorman Strong, who, more than all others combined, is responsible for any contribution I may have made to society.

CONTENTS

PREFACE

Why did I write a book?

It is all the fault of my daughter, Stephanie. At various times she has made suggestions to the effect:

Dad, you should record some of your stories. Many are funny, all are interesting, and they will be lost if you don't preserve them. Tell how the world has changed in your lifetime; how much of your life was before TV, interstate highways, copy machines, jet planes, birth control pills, computers, cell phones, the space age, and our nation's last six wars.

Tell what it was like growing up in a house with a roof that leaked like a sieve and an outside "two holer" for a bathroom; why you decided to be a lawyer instead of a preacher; why you were stopped by the highway patrol in 1952 because you were in a car with an African American; why you proposed to Mother on the telephone and her unexpected reaction; how you won a case in court by persuading your friend to ride on top of a car; how a fraud case ended with you owning a bank and your opponent going to prison; why Missouri's attorney general picked you to represent our state in its suit against the tobacco industry; why defective products were redesigned after you beat their manufacturers in court; why there is an award bearing your name that is given each year to the Missouri trial lawyer who best exemplifies what a trial lawyer should be; and why there is a building at Missouri State University with our family's name on it.

The idea stuck with me. I would enjoy doing it, I thought, and perhaps others would enjoy reading it. "I will do it after I retire when I will have a lot of spare time," I told Stephanie, "and the book will not be only about me. It will be about my profession." Yet when retirement came, I seemed to be busier than ever, arriving at my office at six or seven in the morning just as I had before, but now with business interests and civic work to occupy my time instead of my demanding and unrelenting master: the law. Still, I did find an hour here and there to do the necessary research for the book, reading family letters and newspaper articles; receiving ideas from my brother, children, and cousins; and reading hundreds of pages of court opinions, legal documents, and trial transcripts. When I have used full names, they are the real names of the participants. I have no interest in embarrassing or belittling anyone, so occasionally I have used first names, or simply fictitious names in order to protect the privacy of the people involved, or their families.

Others will judge whether the stories are funny or as interesting as Stephanie predicted. All I know is that I have relived many of the significant events of my life up to December 6, 2011, my eightieth birthday—some funny, some sad, some even inspiring, and all interesting to me.

ACKNOWLEDGMENTS

My daughter, Stephanie Mitchell, gave me the idea, but I had never before written a book, so I needed all the help I could get. Patty Haller typed the first drafts of some chapters and made me believe that I had a story worth telling. Linda Burns typed the final drafts and made valuable suggestions as to what was interesting and what was not. Laura Hunty, Eric Eckert, and Dr. Jonathan Groves read early versions of the book and gave me ideas as to what to cut out and what to develop. Clair Willcox of the University of Missouri Press gave me excellent instructions as to what I must rewrite and add to make the product marketable. But by far the most help came from Dr. James Giglio, who has authored several books, and whose experience, criticism, advice, encouragement, and expertise were vital in producing the final product. All of the above combined to make writing *Strong Advocate: The Life of a Trial Lawyer,* a pleasure as well as a challenge.

While not helping me put words on paper, others played an indispensable role in building the story of my life. My parents were largely responsible for establishing my character, instilling my life's values, and molding my personality. My wife, children, and brother steadied the ship and supplied encouragement throughout my practice. Two professional organizations, the Missouri Association of Trial Attorneys and the Inner Circle of Advocates, contributed indispensable instructions on how to hone my trial skills. Most of all, the lawyers, paralegals, and staff in my firm supported and inspired me to excel in every possible way. The excellence of my firm's attorneys challenged me to remain at the top of my game and, late in my career, gave me confidence that they would continue the tradition they had helped establish. Now the firm of Strong, Garner, Bauer, PC, of which I am presently just a name on a letterhead, continues to represent individuals grievously wronged, with commitment and passion.

What Is a Trial Lawyer?

Several years ago, a St. Louis attorney called to ask if I knew "X," a lawyer who had just settled a case for a paraplegic who was a passenger in an automobile collision. The client was without fault, and the insurance company was only too happy to pay its policy limits of twenty-five thousand dollars for a release. The problem was not with the client or the insurance company. "X" had charged a 40 percent fee for a result the client could easily have obtained without him. It was unconscionable. Any lawyer with an ounce of compassion would have helped the client collect the nominal settlement pro bono.

People in Springfield, Missouri, saw "Y" nearly every time they turned on their television. He told them that he was a personal injury lawyer and said he could help them if they were injured in a car or truck crash. He seemed like a person with lofty principles when he assured viewers that he gave part of his fee to Mothers Against Drunk Drivers each time he made a recovery in a drunk driving case. His various commercials proclaimed him an expert in a variety of areas in addition to highway collisions. "Y" was handsome and looked professional and trustworthy in his blue suit and red tie, and he spoke with confidence and authority. The printing at the bottom of his advertisements listed the several cities where he maintained offices. Surely, this man, with such credentials and principles, would be the ideal person to represent a seriously injured soul.

But people are not always what they seem. My partner took "Y's" deposition when he had a dispute with his former associates and made some alarming discoveries. "Y" had never appeared in a single court in Missouri; did not know how many appellate courts there were; could not name a single judge; did not know if the courthouse in Springfield (where he advertised) was wood, stone, brick, or concrete; and did not know how many jurors sat in a civil case. It is little wonder that a number of ethics complaints and legal malpractice claims had been filed against him. "Y" was a con artist of the worst kind, preying on unsuspecting clients who trusted him to obtain justice for them.

Then there was lawyer "Z," who visited the police station to scan the police accident reports. "Z" was interested in those collisions where someone was transported to the hospital. Soon a letter from "Z" would arrive at the injured person's home, expressing sympathy and offering his services. If the police report indicated a serious injury, "Z" would visit the hospital to express his compassion in person. People complained to me after being contacted by him. Not only was he unprofessional, but he was also insensitive and guilty of gross bad taste.

"X," "Y," and "Z" had one thing in common—money. It was not money for their clients that was their priority; it was money for their coffers. Insurance companies enjoyed hearing from "X," "Y," and "Z" because they knew these pretenders would sell their clients out for nearly any amount, no matter how ridiculous. Settle the case with as little effort as possible and collect a fee; that was their goal. "X," "Y," and "Z" were members of the despicable species that people call "ambulance chasers." People joke about them and ridicule the legal profession because of them. A friend once gave me a book titled *Lawyers and Other Reptiles*, full of lawyer jokes, then borrowed it before I had a chance to see if it contained a single gag I had not heard.

But a license, a mere piece of paper, does not make a person a *real* trial lawyer. "X," "Y," "Z," and their ilk are not *real* trial lawyers. They are impostors, leeches on my profession. There is a nursery rhyme:

> Jerry Hall, he's so small
> A cat could eat him
> Hat and all.

Those impersonators are too small to be members of my ancient and noble profession. My calling dates to the first book of the Bible. In Genesis, chapter 18, Abraham negotiated with God to save Sodom and Gomorrah. As an advocate for his people, he was a trial lawyer, without the title. From the beginning of written history, laws existed to protect those who were wronged by others. The code of Hammurabi, the Torah, the Justinian Code, the Theodosian Code, the Napoleonic Code, and the British Common Law are all forerunners of our unique judicial system. The United States has been a melting pot, not just of people, but of ideas and laws, selecting from history the good and discarding the bad to sculpt the greatest legal system the world has ever known.

In many societies, people who run counter to their government are treated as expendable. It is this philosophy that permitted Nazi Germany to send Jews to the gas chamber, Communist Russia to exile its citizens to Siberia, and totalitarian China to imprison protesters at Tiananmen Square. They succeeded in their oppression because their laws allowed such atrocities. In the United States, individuals have rights, which courageous trial lawyers will defend. Lawyers are the protectors of the people. When Shakespeare's Dick the Butcher in *King Henry VI* said, "The first thing we do, let's kill all the lawyers," it was not a derogatory comment. Dick the Butcher was an anarchist seeking to overthrow the government and knew that the first thing a potential tyrant must do to eliminate freedom is to "kill all the lawyers."

In addition to the right not to be mistreated by our government, Americans have the right not to be injured or killed by the wrongful act of another. Trial lawyers seek redress for such wrongs. We are the voice of the sick and injured who, otherwise, would have no voice. Because we speak for the injured, our highways, skies, workplaces, and products are safer now than ever before. Because our clients are unorganized and have no lobby, we are their advocates in our state and national capitals. We fight for the weak and wronged in legislative halls and courthouses across our land. We have courage, ethics, character, and integrity. Our wits, tenacity, talent, and sweat are our weapons. Our motivation is to obtain justice for our clients, real people, grievously wronged, who cannot speak for themselves, and whose futures are in our hands. To this end, we never tire, we never back up, and we never step down. Let the powerful and wealthy who oppose us know that we will pursue the right with all of our might. This is how it was yesterday, is today, and will be tomorrow. There is a loftier goal in life than self-promotion or the bottom line of our bank accounts. *Real* trial lawyers feel a calling to leave the world better than when they found it.

> In the world's broad field of battle
> In the bivouac of Life,
> Be not like dumb, driven cattle!
> Be a hero in the strife![1]

Unreachable as it may be, this should be every trial lawyer's goal. I am proud to have called myself a trial lawyer, to have been a member of this great profession, one who represented his clients with passion and courage. I hope my story will encourage other trial lawyers and enlighten the lay public about who and what a *real* trial lawyer is. It is my story from childhood to retirement—and beyond.

2

A Shaky Start

They say we are products of our environment. Were we raised by two parents, one, or none? Was our home religious or atheistic? Were our mentors honest or devious, criminals or saints? Were they intelligent or dull, industrious or loafers, white or blue collar? Were their examples good or bad? Did we live in luxury, comfort, or poverty? Were we taught good moral values or left to our own devices? How did any of us become what we turned out to be?

Both of my parents were college graduates, very unusual in the 1920s; my father was a graduate of the Missouri School of Mines and Metallurgy (now Missouri University of Science and Technology) with a degree in mechanical engineering, and my mother a graduate of Southwest Missouri State Teachers College (now Missouri State University) with a degree in education. Dad, an outstanding student, accepted a coveted position with the Johnson Controls Company in Boston, Massachusetts, after graduating in 1925. The couple had every right to be optimistic about their future, so joy and hope were abundant when my only sibling, John Frank (Jack), was born on October 17, 1928.

Fate was not to smile for long, however, and two nearly simultaneous calamities dashed their dreams: the Great Depression, which forced Johnson Controls to release more than half of its employees in 1930 and 1931, and a mysterious illness that struck

Dad in 1931 and rendered him a near invalid for the rest of his life. Dad developed a tremor in his arms and hands, which became stiff and partially paralyzed. He walked with a limp, and his speech was slurred. Doctors remained perplexed for the rest of Dad's life about either a name or a treatment for his incapacitation, but its consequences did have a name, "unemployment" at Johnson Controls after January 1, 1932.

With the Great Depression in full force and with an unemployed wage earner, all the family needed was an additional financial burden, which came when yours truly, Thomas Gorman Strong, entered the world on December 6, 1931. Without work or any prospect to find it, the couple and their two sons, one just two months old, moved back to the farm of Dad's parents near Marshfield, Missouri, in February 1932. With record-setting droughts that turned farms into dust bowls in the 1930s, and the Depression that made farm products worth almost nothing, the family found itself unable to make mortgage payments or even pay the property taxes. The handwriting was on the wall. Dad could not work, and the farm, which was ultimately lost to creditors in 1936, became an albatross.

Mother was our family's last hope to avoid living in one of the nation's many slums or tent cities, or as recipients of some charitable organization or agency. She hunted for a teaching position and, after one and a half years, found it at Oakland School, east of Springfield, in the fall of 1933, until moving to nearby Blackman School two years later.

In the summer of 1936, when I was four and a half years old, we moved eight miles west of Springfield, closer to Mother's new job teaching at Bennett School. Mother's first year at Bennett brought home $65 per month, $520 for the year, our only income. We were poor, even by Depression standards, but we were more fortunate than many. My experiences, still vividly etched in memory, had a major impact on the type of person I would become. Meager family finances, my home environment, my mother's values, and my father's later success as an engineer, despite his affliction, affected me in ways I neither recognized nor appreciated at the time.

The Bennett years brought stability, a time and place to establish roots. Our house, sheds, and ten acres, which we rented, were one-half mile east of Barnes' Store and one mile east of school. The rent, $9 a month, was reasonable even though it consumed a fifth of our yearly income. The L-shaped house, with three rooms downstairs and two up, was in sad shape, decaying after years of inattention and vacancy. The roof leaked so badly that when it rained outside, it rained inside—just not as hard. On a frigid winter night, when the wind whistled through the cracks in the walls, the urine in the chamber pot in my bedroom froze into ice. There was no heat anywhere in the house at night. And during the day, minimal heat was generated from a potbellied stove in the main room downstairs. On a bone-chilling winter morning, Dad would start a fire, and we would all gather around the stove. When we faced it, our backs remained cold, but when we turned our backs to it, our fronts became chilled. It was a no-win situation.

The kitchen was the L part of the downstairs and extended back from the living room. Mother cooked our meals on an inefficient stove unlike any I have ever seen. A glass container filled with kerosene and turned upside down at the end of the stove then ran down a pipe under four burners, the first two open and the last two under an oven. Wicks in the four burners, lit with a match, would ignite the kerosene and produce a fire much like a kerosene lantern. One summer, with great expectations, we planted popcorn in our garden and looked forward to a special treat when it ripened. But the stove could not get hot enough to make the corn pop. The result was a good deal of anger for Dad and frustration for me. I loved heavily salted popcorn. Our water came from a twenty-foot-deep hand-dug well across the road. I have not mentioned the bathroom in our house because there was none. A "two holer" existed outside, which became especially unpleasant in the winter, when one journeyed there as quickly as possible.

I do not know if the house was ever occupied after we moved away in 1943. The Great Depression had lost its steam with the outbreak of World War II, and people were anticipating better times. Hence, no one would be satisfied with a house that could not be properly repaired, regardless of the time and money invested in the attempt. After returning from the army, I drove by to see it. The large trees I once climbed and the yard where I rode my bicycle and played baseball with my brother looked much the same, but the house was gone without a trace. A different structure, a nicer, larger one-story ranch house, already apparently several years old, had taken its place. Somehow, inexplicably, I was sad.

In the fall before my sixth birthday I entered the first grade, there being no preschool or kindergarten in those days. Before dawn, Dad started a fire in the potbellied stove, and we crowded around it to get warm. After breakfast we milked cows, fed chickens, carried wood or coal into the house, washed dishes, and carried water from across the highway. After morning chores, Mother and I walked the mile to school on days when Dad couldn't take us. When we arrived, we carried coal and started a fire in the large potbellied stove in the middle of the room so the building would be warm when students arrived. Mother emptied the wastebaskets, swept the floors, and rang the bell calling the students to come inside. She was everything: teacher, choir director, band leader, carpenter, counselor, and janitor. Mother was an excellent teacher. Much of what I now know I learned as her pupil in grades one, two, three, five, and six. In this nondescript little school, with about a dozen students in the eight grades, we were taught history, geography, current events, science, reading, writing, arithmetic, spelling, grammar, and punctuation. I greatly benefited from what I believe are the most important "three R's" in education: "repetition, repetition, and repetition." When in the first grade, I watched and listened to Mother teach the second and third grades. When in the second grade, I learned from what she taught the third and fourth grades, and so on. Having a preview of what was to come helped when it came my time to be exposed to the subject.

Mother was a strict disciplinarian. For students, unruly conduct always brought the same punishment. Boys (I never recall Mother spanking a girl) would bend over their desks, pants would be pulled tight, and Mother would administer twelve sharp blows with a twelve-inch ruler. Invariably, tears would come not later than the ninth or tenth blow, even from the most determined children. If the offense occurred at recess, students would be brought inside for punishment. The rest of us would gather close to a window, listen to the strikes of the ruler, and vicariously feel the pain. Being whipped by Mother was an event not easily forgotten, as I can still attest. It seemed that I received this punishment more than any other student.

Each Christmas we produced a play complete with a curtain, which was attached to farm wire stretched several feet above the floor. I always wanted to play Joseph, a shepherd, or a wise man, but I was never awarded a major role—either because I lacked talent or because I was the teacher's son. Other students had parents who paid Mother's salary and were sensitive to her showing favoritism to her sons. At recess or noon, Mother could have taken a few minutes for relaxation, had she chosen, but these were our times for physical education, and she was the supervisor. We played softball, which Mother refereed, and darebase, tag, and other games in which she participated. In inclement weather, we stayed inside and played blindman's bluff or games on the blackboard.

I thought Bennett School modern because it had two bathrooms, one for girls and one for boys, and just as amazing, both were inside. A more refined eye would have seen the downside because, without running water, they were like outdoor privies enclosed in small closets at two corners of the schoolroom. Despite Mother's best efforts to restrict their odor by dumping liberal doses of lime into the toilets, any visitor would not have to see the privies to know they were there. I am sure toilet paper was invented long before the 1930s, but it was not known at our school. Sears catalogs, on the other hand, were readily available, as were a wash pan, lye soap, and towel. The human waste, paper, and lime deposited in the privies fell into concrete basins below. It was Dad's unpleasant chore, for just two dollars per privy, to empty them. Periodically, he lowered buckets into the basins, scooped up the contents, loaded it in a wheelbarrow, and dumped it in a neighbor's field to serve as cost-free fertilizer. The school building now is a portion of a barn, but some of the trees, which we planted as a school project, still live today in what is left of the school yard.

Before I entered the fourth grade, Mother and Dad explained that since Grandma, Dad's mother, no longer had relatives in Marshfield, I needed to live with her during the school year, as a helper and companion. The year was pleasant, although somewhat lonely. It was hard to make friends in a school with thirty students in my grade alone, and where I knew no one. Nevertheless, I did make lasting friends, some of whom I still know.

Once a week, Grandma gave me a nickel to buy the soft drink of my choice. I liked Coke best, but the bottles contained only six ounces, and the orange drink was twice as large. With mixed emotions and after much deliberation, I usually chose quantity over quality. After all, I had to take the soda home and split it with Grandma. Half of a six-ounce Coke just didn't go very far.

During the fourth grade I experienced a disturbing dream that would recur the rest of my life. In the dream, I was either

late to class, could not find my class, or was unprepared for it. The dream haunted me in every school I attended, including law school. As a lawyer, it took the form of my being late, unprepared for trial, not having my notes or exhibits, not being able to find the courthouse, or being incompetent in every way imaginable. Even now, years after retiring, in my dreams I still am a lawyer and I am still late, lost, unprepared, or incompetent. Less often, I am back in school taking a test for which I am woefully unprepared.

Grandma and my parents planned for me to return to Marshfield for the fifth grade, but I protested and was allowed to stay at Bennett. As a special treat for my tenth birthday on December 6, 1941, however, I went by bus to Marshfield to spend the weekend with Grandma. The next day I enjoyed my birthday present, a movie. When I came home, Grandma spoke to me solemnly: "The Japanese have bombed Pearl Harbor where Jim and Bud are stationed. Many brave boys have been killed, and we do not know if Jim and Bud are among them. This means that we will be at war with the Japanese. War is an awful thing where people kill each other. Many more will fight and die, but we are right, and we will win. The Japanese will pay for their cowardly sneak attack."

I did not fully comprehend what Grandma was saying, or how civilians and the military would partner to bring the contest to an end. Civilians did their part. Women joined men in producing ships, planes, and guns. Many planted "victory" gardens and

(Opposite top) Our rented house in 1937. Grandma is on the porch. The bed on the porch is where my brother and I slept in the summer.

(Opposite bottom) Bennett School students and teacher in 1939. Mother is in the second row. Jack is second from the right in the second row. I was in the third grade and am third from the right in the third row.

bought "war bonds." Tires, cars, bicycles, gasoline, stoves, shoes, sugar, coffee, processed foods, meats, canned fish, cheese, canned milk, and typewriters were rationed. With Dad unable to work at the start of the conflict, we were more isolated from the struggle than many. We did not need all the gas we were permitted to buy, did not drive enough to wear out our tires, did not need a typewriter, and produced almost all of our own food. Jack and I went barefoot all summer, and Mother and Dad needed only one pair of shoes. The daily necessities of life were much the same for us as before the war. Still, evil enemies had invaded us, and Grandma's assessment that we must make them pay for their cowardly actions was correct. Hitler and Tojo were mad beasts who must be stopped.

The Strong family joined others in the fight. Three cousins had enlisted before Pearl Harbor, other relatives would join or be drafted, and Jack might be old enough to serve if the war was a long one. Now we know that we won the war, but then, in the middle of the bloodshed, the outcome seemed in doubt. Hitler was sweeping through France, bombing England, and invading Russia. Italy joined Hitler, and Japan threatened us from our west. Hitler boasted of a soon-to-be-unleashed secret weapon that would bring the rest of the world to its knees. I was aware of the great struggle in a general way, but was too young to appreciate its full horror. Cousins Jim and Bud were in the South Pacific, where I thought monkeys lived. I asked them to bring me a monkey when they returned. Mother and Dad said monkeys were hard to catch and Jim and Bud might be busy fighting, but they did not ridicule my dream. Nor did Jim and Bud when they answered my letters. In my naïveté, I expected a new constant companion when Jim and Bud returned home.

At Bennett, now in the fifth grade, things were much as before. We milked three or four cows, selling the milk we did not consume, and usually had a dozen or more chickens for eggs and meat. Once, we attempted to raise rabbits. Dad built a fence

around a half acre of grassland and proclaimed it "rabbit proof."
It wasn't. With a large garden, cows for milk and butter, chickens
for eggs and meat, and a few rabbits that didn't escape for food,
we produced much of what we consumed.

On Saturdays, we washed our clothes with the aid of a fifty-
gallon iron container with a rounded bottom that Dad had designed especially for this purpose. We then carried water from
the well, filled the container, built a wood fire under it, and heated the water until it nearly boiled. Mother rubbed our clothes
on a scrub board, put them through a hand wringer, and hung
them on a clothesline in the yard. On weekends we worked in
the garden, strung beans, canned vegetables, cleaned the house,
or picked wild gooseberries and blackberries. Mother, an accomplished seamstress, made her own dresses from various colored
sacks, which once contained feed for the cows. I do not recall her
ever owning a store-bought dress while she taught at Bennett.
She also mended our clothes until we outgrew them and then
gave them to "less fortunate" children.

Christmas usually brought gifts worth about a dime, but fifth
grade was different. I wanted a bicycle, a present Dad and Mother said they could not afford. What could I do to help, I wondered? Maybe it wouldn't hurt to pray, so pray I did. It must have
worked, I thought, because on Christmas morning I discovered
a bicycle by the tree.

The bicycle was adult size, so tall that I could not reach the
peddles. The only way I could mount it was to take it alongside
the front porch where I would stand, throw one leg over the seat,
then push off and peddle standing up, wobbling until I fell over.
After many attempts and countless falls, I learned to ride. I still
had a problem, however, because the only way I could dismount
was to let the bicycle fall over on its side. I dreaded this, so I often rode in circles in the yard to delay the ultimate topple as long
as possible. Years later, I learned that the bicycle had belonged to
one of Uncle Tom's grown boys and was a hand-me-down.

The bicycle was responsible for one of life's great pleasures. Brother Jack, without consulting me, routinely rode the bike to work. This was an act I began to resent. After all, it was my bike, and I could have fun riding it at home. One morning, I waited in the yard as Jack prepared to leave. When he started to mount the bike, I told him he could not ride it unless he asked my permission and said "please." It was beneath him to accommodate a younger brother trying to exert his authority. He had a job and I did not. He needed the bike and I didn't, so he rode off despite my strong and loud objections.

When Jack returned home, Mother explained that the bicycle belonged to me, even though he had a job and needed the bicycle for work, and if he wished to ride it, he must obtain my consent. With that, I had won one of the most important battles of my life. The next time Jack went to work, he walked rather than ask for the bicycle. After a few long walks, however, Jack learned to say, "Please, may I use the bicycle today?" What a victory! I used the bicycle regularly throughout high school and occasionally until my own son, Jack, was mature enough to ride with me. After more than two decades, a more modern bike with more than one gear was in order.

The Depression years also included pets, since people often drove to the country to abandon their dogs or cats. We came upon a collie with a skull fracture in a ditch by the school. She apparently had been dumped when struck by a car. We took her home, nursed her back to health, and named her Lassie. I can still picture her anticipating my arrival from school. She could see me approaching from a quarter of a mile away and would jump, spin, and run in circles with joy until I reached her. Then we raced, wrestled, and played. She was my best animal friend until my senior year in high school when she died after a long, loyal, faithful, happy life. A more devoted dog was never born. She might have belonged to the family, but she was *my* Lassie.

Cats were everywhere, perhaps encouraged by the small amount of milk we gave them when we milked the cows. Otherwise, cats were expected to fend for themselves and, in the process, control the mice, rats, and other small rodents that were a constant plague. Unlike Lassie, who never had pups, cats seemed to reproduce in unlimited numbers. I remember one night at supper, Father remarked that he had counted twenty-three cats at the shed that evening.

Outside employment also became a part of my childhood experience. Jack led the way by working for neighbors the last summers we lived near Bennett School. He mowed lawns for ten cents an hour, except for one very appreciative lady who paid him two and a half cents extra per hour. He gathered rock, plowed fields with a team of mules, and did any kind of labor a high school freshman or sophomore could do. Perhaps to emulate my brother, I also wanted a job. There were only a few available for a boy my age, and those I attempted outside the family were not a raving success. For example, I obtained permission from Mother to pick strawberries for a neighbor for a penny a quart. After the first day, the neighbor told me that I need not come back. Upon arriving at home, my folks asked how the job had gone. I told them, "I got fired." When pressed by Dad for the reason, I claimed not to know. Dad was not going to be happy if I had been fired for no reason, so he confronted the neighbor. When Dad was told that I had talked to others who were trying to work, and in general disrupted the workforce while picking less than one quart of strawberries after a full day, the mystery was solved. Mother and Dad did not seem disappointed their seven-year-old son was unproductive but impressed upon me the need to tell the "whole truth."

Another unforgettable lesson in citizenship resulted from an incident at Barnes' Store. I was sent to buy a loaf of bread only to find I was one penny short. Mr. Barnes said he would get the penny from my parents when he saw them. I protested that I would bring a penny back to him. When I arrived home without the bread, I explained that I lacked a penny for the purchase and was going to take it back to the store. Dad was angry. Why would Mr. Barnes make me walk a mile to get a penny? Mr. Barnes's refusal to trust us for a penny was an attack on Dad's character. Back to the store Dad and I went. When Mr. Barnes explained that he had offered to let me take the bread home, my father's anger was redirected. Guess where? In the future I needed to tell him the whole truth—or else.

Fourscore years have passed since the Great Depression and I arrived in America almost simultaneously. The end of the Depression saw the beginning of change. Country roads were paved; radios, air-conditioning, television, cell phones, computers, and jet planes that fly across oceans were accepted as necessities, not matters of wonder. We exploded atom bombs, sent men to the moon, and won World War II and the Cold War, but fought five other wars to uncertain conclusions. African Americans now play on the same sport teams as Caucasians without protests and threats of harm. The whole world has changed and will never be the same. Yet my view of those early years might not be what you would expect.

If we were experiencing the Great Depression today, we would be reminded of our plight daily in our newspapers, on our computers, and on television. My world was a much smaller one. Perhaps I was like a goldfish in a glass bowl who, not seeing much of the outside world, was content with my lot in life. In many ways we were isolated. We did not even have a newspaper until Dad found employment in 1943. What I knew was my family and our neighbors, many of whom lived very much as we did. Sure, Grandpa and Grandma (Dad's parents) had lost their farm in 1936 after the Depression and droughts of the 1930s stole their income and produced no money to make mortgage payments or pay taxes. Sure, Dad was disabled and without work. But there was no complaining and no sense of panic. Mother had an income, and we had the necessities of life. If Mother and Dad felt hopeless, they hid it well from their sons. I now know that we were living in poverty, but I did not know that then and was happy in my ignorance. I now know that most nine- and ten-year-old boys are not expected to pull weeds in the garden, feed the chickens, milk cows, and wash windows. All of us were expected to work as much as our age and health would allow. That was just part of life.

Both Dad and Mother deserve great credit for making my childhood happy and rewarding. Although Dad was disabled, he asked for no favors and no sympathy. He had been an engineer with a promising future, yet would take the most menial job, even if it was just for a day cleaning human waste from an outhouse. Dad believed in making the best of things: "Take what you have, work hard, and make something of it." Like most rural Missourians, Dad was not a fan of Roosevelt and the New Deal. I remember him talking to our landlord about the evils of welfare programs that paid folks for "fill-time" work.

As I recall my youth, my thoughts return to that leaky home, that one-room school, to the shoeless summers, to the lack of toys, Boy Scout activities, organized sports, television, cell phones, and other modern conveniences. Some might think that I was deprived. Not so! They were some of the happiest times of an always happy life. On Saturday nights, we played checkers, or Dad and I would challenge Mother and Jack in pinochle. There was Sunday school and church at Elwood. There were turtles to find as pets, cats that multiplied like rabbits, and one of the best dogs in the world. There was room to play, build roads in the dirt, climb trees, slide on the ice in the winter, play baseball in the front yard with my brother, and do all the things that the imagination of a young boy could invent. We had all the food we needed, our house was filled with love, and I had one of the wisest mothers in the world. All the money in the world could not have produced a better environment.

3

Movin' Up

When Papa (Mother's father) died suddenly and unexpectedly in November 1942, Mother inherited the residence and twenty acres of Papa's 120-acre farm. It was located on Old Wire Road, which was dirt surfaced with a single lane, so when automobiles met, each had to depart from the worn tracks in order to pass. But the road had an important and proud history. Named for the telegraph lines that bordered it, it once was the main highway between St. Louis, Missouri, and Fort Smith, Arkansas. The two great Civil War battles (Wilson's Creek and Pea Ridge) that kept Missouri in the Union were fought along this road.

Papa's house was nothing to brag about, but just about anything was better than our previous home. It had three rooms downstairs and two bedrooms upstairs, and the roof did not leak. It was painted, and we had a much better cookstove. Yet our bathroom was still outside, heat still came from one potbellied stove, all of our water still came from a hand-dug well on Aunt Leona's property, and the upstairs floors sagged so badly that anything round would roll to the center of the room. Bed legs were supported by wooden blocks that made the beds somewhat level.

One giant step into the modern world came with our first telephone, on a party line with six other families. When a call was placed to one party, phones rang in all seven houses, so each party was assigned its own personal formula of long and short rings. Thus, if Mrs. Thompson wanted to eavesdrop on a call to Jack, all she had to do was pick up her phone when she heard our formula of rings. Jack, who now had girlfriends, was particularly irked when he heard "clicks," as inquisitive neighbors picked up or put down their phones during his calls. In a house as small as ours, Mother, Dad, and I also could hear Jack's half of the conversations, and I could sidle up close to hear even when he whispered. How could Jack have a romantic conversation with everyone listening? Modern conveniences came with a price.

We now had twenty acres, enough to raise animals, but no shed or barn to house them. Dad was the architect, Jack was the main carpenter, and the three of us put up a small barn with stalls for four milk cows, a workshop, a hay loft, and an area for the cows to be inside during unbearably cold weather.

Mother's new teaching assignment was at Shady Dell School on Springfield's Division Street, about five miles from our new home. The school had two rooms, one for grades one through four, and the other, where Mother taught, for grades five through eight. Great things also were in store for Dad. The Depression had ended with the US entry into World War II, and by 1943, even women, whose preferred place had been at home, were praised as "Rosie the Riveters" or as workers in other occupations that helped win the war. Engineers were particularly scarce. Dad's opportunity came when Van Frazier, an employee at Springfield Auto Works, began the Springfield Body and Trailer Company to aid the war effort and, at the same time, to make a profit. His vision was to build trailers to carry gasoline, rationed in the States, to areas where it was needed. While the idea was simple, the reality was not. The trailer became part of an eighteen-wheel tractor-trailer unit that had to meet government standards. Weight had to be distributed evenly so that no set of wheels bore more than the allowed amount. And the trailer needed several compartments in case one failed. That way, the entire load would not be lost. From a profit-and-loss standpoint, the trailer needed to be functional, attractive, and marketable and have a long life span. It took a skilled engineer to design it, and Van Frazier was no engineer.

Dad was forty-nine years old, and it had been eighteen years since he had received his degree and eleven years since his previous employment. His engineering skills undoubtedly had eroded, and to make matters worse, he had never designed anything remotely similar to a gasoline-hauling trailer. But desperate times called for desperate measures, and Dad was desperate. When he saw Frazier's advertisement for a mechanical engineer, he did not hesitate to respond.

Van Frazier must have been shocked when Dad first approached him. Dad's left arm and hand seemed almost useless; his body seemed partially paralyzed, particularly on the left side; his hands trembled; and his speech resembled that of a stroke victim. Perhaps there were no other applicants, or perhaps Frazier was insightful enough to see the keen mind that was trapped inside the impaired body. Whatever the reason, Dad was hired.

Frazier got a bargain. At last, Dad had a chance to use his considerable talents to boost his deflated ego and to contribute to society. Dad designed the trailer in its entirety, from the axles at the bottom to the method for dissipating static electricity in the middle to the hatches at the top. He did that well, but his braking system was so superior to anything else on the market that it soon became the gold standard for the industry. The system was later patented by A. J. Industries as an "Anti-Brake Hop Structure for Wheeled Vehicles"[1] and was the subject of a lawsuit,[1] decided in 1968, a year after Dad's death. Dad made no money beyond his normal salary for his invention. His pay in the early 1950s was $270 a month, the only time I heard it mentioned.

Dad, now a respected and successful engineer, remained with Frazier's company in Springfield, then in Joplin, and finally in Waycross, Georgia, until he retired. When opportunity had knocked, Dad had seized it and, in the process, had unleashed an intellect and talent that poor health and a devastating economy had almost stolen. With both Mother and Dad employed, a house to live in, a few apple trees, a garden, and some milk cows, things were looking up.

I also found ways to remain productive. The summer after seventh grade, Roy Rollings, who lived a mile up the road, hired me to help him milk his herd of twenty-one cows. I was twelve years old, five feet tall, and one hundred pounds. I had milked cows by hand for a few years, but I'd never used milking machines, which Mr. Rollings had. I rode my bicycle to Mr. Rollings's house, helped milk his cows in the morning, and returned to my home to help milk our cows. Mr. Rollings paid me a dollar a day for a seven-day workweek. With the money I earned, I soon had enough to buy a cow of my own.

Each summer I also worked in the fields for the neighbors, first for a quarter an hour and then, as I grew older and stronger, for fifty cents an hour. Shocking and thrashing wheat, bailing hay, throwing sixty-pound bails onto the wagon, stacking hay in the barn loft, picking corn, and helping put silage in a silo were some of the more common chores I was hired to do. Hard physical labor in stifling heat was not considered oppressive. It was a fact of life. Milking cows, however, remained my major source of income. Beginning in the summer after my eighth grade, I was the major worker at our farm. Jack had graduated from high school in 1945 and had enrolled at what is now Missouri State University in Springfield. He attended college during the summer and fall terms before being drafted into the army in January 1946, the last draft call of World War II. With Jack away at college and then the army, I was left to do the farmwork. Opportunity was knocking and I answered. By saving money I earned working for the neighbors and by selling milk from the cow I owned, I bought a second cow, then a third, and then a fourth.

Boxing was one of my most memorable diversions. It began after Dad brought home one pair of boxing gloves when I was six and Jack ten. They were huge, well worn, and too soft to do much harm. I got the right glove and Jack the left, and we could only hit with the gloved hand. Periodically, over the next several years, Jack and I fought and I inevitably lost, even though, as Jack always reminded me, he had the left glove and I had the right.

I made one of the greatest errors of my life when I was in the eighth grade. I told a classmate of mine, Jimmy Campbell, a Golden Gloves boxer in Springfield, that I also was a boxer. He suggested a match, and when I said that I didn't have gloves, he said he would supply them. I had no way to get to the gym, I claimed, but he volunteered to come to my house for the match. I was boxed in, so to speak, and had to either box him or take the coward's way out. Well, the latter was *definitely* out of the question. Jimmy showed up at the appointed time, we donned the gloves, and, with Jack and Jimmy's brother, Don, as seconds, the fight began. It was a short one, mercifully stopped by our seconds after a couple of minutes. I was obviously overmatched. Although I suffered no physical injuries, I received a sound thrashing, and the blow to my ego could not be overestimated.

My second "two-fisted" boxing match came when Jack returned home from the army in May 1947. It was the summer after my sophomore year, and I was in great physical shape from farmwork, doing fifty push-ups a day and walking on my hands for several yards at a time. I planned the event well in advance, forgetting that Jack, at nineteen, was four years older than I, about twenty pounds heaver, and probably also in good shape from his army service. Ignorance is bliss, they say, so I blissfully borrowed two pairs of gloves and made the challenge, which Jack accepted. Richard Carriger, next door, was the referee. Perhaps it was the frustration of losing to my brother all of my life, perhaps it was determination, perhaps Jack was overconfident, or perhaps I was just better than he. No blood was spilled, and no one was knocked down, but there was no question about who won the fight. I won decisively. The match was called after a few minutes. Oh, the thrill of victory!

Too many great champions, including Oscar De La Hoya, Roy Jones Jr., and Evander Holyfield, retired after a pivotal victory, but could not stay retired. Like drug addicts who needed just one more "fix," they chose to fight again, losing badly to mediocre fighters and tarnishing their reputations. Like those legendary fighters, I made the mistake of coming out of retirement for one more fight. If I could beat Jack, surely I could beat anyone.

In the fall of my first year in college in my physical education class, the teacher said that participation in boxing was not required, but if anyone volunteered, we could have boxing matches. There was silence for several seconds as no one spoke. With everyone so timid, I volunteered. More silence followed, this one even longer as other boys sized me up. Who was this fair-skinned and blond-haired kid, unable to reach five feet nine inches and not more than 145 pounds? He didn't look like one who had spent much time fighting in the back alleys of town. It was inevitable that someone bigger and stronger would accept the challenge. Gloves were donned and the match began. I never landed a punch, but my opponent did, and it knocked me off my feet. I jumped up to attack, but the teacher, not wanting anyone wounded during his watch, declared the match over. That ended my boxing career. After having fought some three dozen times over the eleven years since I started at age six, with a total time in the ring of less than an hour, I had never knocked anyone down and had been downed only once. No blood had ever been spilled, and no one was ever injured. With only one victory, the one against Jack when he returned from the army, and dozens of losses, it might seem like a dismal career—unless you consider the one victory. That one victory, avenging years of frustration and losses, against a brother who wanted to win as much as I, was a thrill far outweighing the combined agony of all the defeats.

More than my entrepreneurial and boxing activities, my academic successes proved most significant, beginning at Strafford School, where I attended from seventh grade through grade ten. One seemingly inconsequential event occurred there in the ninth grade when our English teacher, Miss Tunnell, instructed the class to recite the poem "How Do I Love Thee?" by Elizabeth Barrett Browning. I knew time restraints would prevent some from being called on, and I figured that there was a fifty-fifty chance that I did not need to memorize a disgusting poem about how much some mushy person loved some other mushy person.

But I was afraid not to memorize enough to get by—just in case. As luck would have it, Miss Tunnell called on me first. If I had memorized the poem well, without any interest in expressing my love for some unknown yucky girl, I probably would have recited it in a sing-song manner, as rapidly and blandly as possible, just to get it behind me. As it was, I had to carefully think of what I was saying, pausing here and there for the next phrase to come to mind, and, in the process, I emphasized some of the words and phrases. Miss Tunnell was impressed with the feeling I put into the recital and praised me in front of the class. This was the first time this had happened—and the timing was perfect. I had attended church camp the previous summer and decided that I wanted to be a preacher. To be one, I needed to learn how to speak and persuade. One short poem, halfheartedly prepared, convinced me that I could.

The stars must have been aligned that year: the summer camp, the poem for Miss Tunnel, and, in the spring of 1946, the yearly Greene County Speech Tournament, which included oratory, poetry, prose, and humorous reading. If the tournament had been at any other school, I would not have known about it, but Providence decreed that this year it would be at Strafford. Miss Tunnell asked me if I wanted to enter. Of course I wanted to enter. Miss Tunnell explained that as a freshman I would compete against older, more experienced students, even seniors, so I should not attempt to write and give an oration, or even recite poetry or prose, which would require a very dramatic presentation.

But Miss Tunnell found a place for me. Since I was a towheaded kid, with looks and a personality much like Tom Sawyer, she encouraged me to enter the humorous reading event and be Tom Sawyer whitewashing the fence. It turned out to be a perfect fit. Virgil Anderson, a professor at Drury University, the judge of all the events, not only gave me an A, the highest grade possible, but told me that I was indeed Tom Sawyer.

Still another fortuitous event occurred at the tournament: I learned that there was an event called debate, taught at Senior High School in Springfield, that pitted one team against another and required wit and speaking ability. If I was to be an effective preacher, I needed debate to improve my speech. I pondered the possibility through the summer and the first half of my sophomore year. Finally, I petitioned Mother and Dad: "I need to take debate and learn to speak well so I can be a good preacher. Dad can drive me to school on his way to work and pick me up on his way home. It is *very important* for me to go to Senior High School." I held my breath and waited for an answer.

Mother was very perceptive, always encouraging, even when I attempted to cheerlead or play the trumpet. But this was different. Early on she had told Aunt Bess, "I don't know what Tommy will do in life, but he will do it talking." This was a talent to be explored, even if it meant changing schools, imposing upon Dad, and taking time from my chores at home. "Of course you may go to Senior High and take debate. It's a good idea," she said, and Dad agreed. When I excitedly told Miss Tunnell of my plans, her reaction shocked me. "You will be lost at Senior, just a small fish in a huge pond. There are more than five hundred students in every grade. At Strafford you will be in small classes and get individual attention, but at Senior no one will know who you are. You will make a big mistake if you go."

I secretly resented the idea that I would be lost, that people would not know who I was, or that I would be a small fish in *any* pond. I could be as big a fish as anyone, anywhere. I decided that I would attend Senior High my last two years, take debate, learn to persuade, and prove to Miss Tunnell that she did not fully appreciate what I could do. So I said good-bye to Strafford. It had given me a good education the four years I had been there; I had learned how to diagram a sentence, history, and basic mathematics, and I had developed friendships that still exist today. But I left with only excitement about attending this huge, unknown school I had never seen and that held my future.

I have to admit feeling some trepidation when I first walked into the monstrous redbrick building called Senior High School. Five years before, my class had consisted of two students, and the entire school had only twelve students in eight grades. Just last year my sophomore class had only twenty-two students. Now I was starting to understand the reality of Miss Tunnell's unwelcome comments about being a small fish in a big pond. The city had many grade schools, three junior highs for grades seven through nine, but only one gargantuan high school, Senior High School (now Central High School), for grades ten through twelve, in a city of sixty-five thousand. There were in excess of sixteen hundred students, more than five hundred in each class.

Every one of those students had social advantages I did not have. In the first place, all had come from one of the three junior highs, where they knew their classmates from day one. Second, since I did not enroll until my junior year, they all had a year's head start getting acquainted with those they did not know. Third, and perhaps most important, I lived on a farm outside of town and, with chores to do and cows to milk, had little interaction with my classmates except during school hours.

I could be alone and isolated for two years, or I could try my best to fit in. Fortunately, I had been assigned David Anderson as my debate partner, and he was liked by everyone. I became David's shadow. I stuck with him as much as possible and when he met someone in the halls and said "Hi, Joe" (or whatever his or her name was), I replicated the greeting as if I also knew the person. I repeated this tactic with other friends, as I cultivated them, and in an amazingly short period of time, I had a speaking acquaintance with a few hundred people. Feeling as if I was an outcast was never a problem.

Yet I was overwhelmed that first day. Senior High seemed more like a city squeezed into one massive building. I focused on the debate classroom first, even though it was an afternoon class. All day I counted the hours, with a mixture of wonder, fear, and expectation. When the time came and I walked into the room, there was my teacher, Miss Anna B. Jefferson, a spinster in her sixties, portly, with an ugly, ill-fitting black wig. Her hands trembled slightly, and her voice cracked when she talked in her halting, uncertain style. She was anything but an impressive speaker, so how in the world could she teach me to speak? I soon learned that Miss Jefferson's reputation as a demanding, knowledgeable, no-nonsense debate coach was well earned.

Each year a new debate topic was assigned nationwide, so every school debated the same topic. The teams consisted of four members, two arguing the affirmative side of the issue and two the negative. The teams that won the most debates attended the elimination rounds and continued debating until only two remained for the championship. Before the first tournament, Miss Jefferson selected the teams. In the junior class, the first team consisted of Bob Wallace as the second negative speaker, paired with Gerald Stinson. I was the second affirmative speaker, paired with David Anderson. Bob Wallace was brilliant, knew it, and wanted others to know it. He talked of being a lawyer and entering politics. Among other things, he enlisted me in helping to push for "youth suffrage" by writing a paper on why the voting age should be lowered to eighteen.

Obviously, my life goals had changed, causing me to find the ministry less attractive. I loved the give-and-take of debate, outthinking and outarguing an opponent, and convincing people of the merits of my case. Bob's thoughts about how trial lawyers changed society made me think that I too might be a lawyer. I needed to investigate this profession first, so I talked to a local attorney and began to do research. I read about famous lawyers who represented the underdog, people who were wrongly accused and without hope but for an attorney with the resolve and talent to obtain justice for them. But if I were a lawyer, I wouldn't be satisfied to be an ordinary one. I would be a crusader, a champion for the little guy, like Clarence Darrow and others in the books I had read.

Besides debate, school politics also occupied my time and interest. This included running for office. Elections for student representatives, senators, and student body president were held in the spring of each year. Thus, candidates for the 1948–49 school year were elected at the end of the 1947–48 year. I was just completing my first year at Senior, but nevertheless I decided to run for one of the three student senate seats for the senior class.

As a newcomer running against well-known, qualified students who had grown up in the city school system, I was a decided underdog. If I had any hope of winning, I needed a plan.

David Anderson, probably the most popular student in school, also was running for the senate. He would be impossible to beat, but since three would be elected, I didn't need to beat him; coming in second or third would do the trick. I approached David with my idea: he and I should run as a team, which made no sense to David, but he undoubtedly thought he would win, even if my name was connected to his. I waged a campaign David probably did not anticipate. I prepared cards of every color in the rainbow, about three inches square, that said "With Anderson and Strong you can't go wrong!" or "Anderson and Strong for Senior Senator!" They were a hit. Soon cards were visible in classrooms and hallways throughout the school. So far, so good.

Candidates for student body president, representatives, and senators were allowed to speak at the school assembly. The candidates for senior senator were the last group to present, and since the speakers appeared in alphabetical order, I had the misfortune of being the last candidate to appear. After so many office seekers, all making about the same sales pitch, how could I be different in the three minutes allotted to me? I needed a gimmick and finally settled on one: my talk would be in rhyme. For weeks, while milking cows (a place where I did my best thinking), I composed a campaign speech, never reduced to writing, in verse form. It was unique but had substance, I thought, and would be like none of the others.

When the speeches began, however, I faced an unexpected problem. Everyone was ad-libbing something funny at the start of their talks. I needed an introduction, a clever one to get the attention of the audience. But I had to do it in rhyme, to be consistent with my message. What I had envisioned as a handicap, being the last speaker, turned out to be a blessing in disguise. It gave me time to think of an introduction:

I'm supposed to make a speech right now,
But for goodness' sake I don't know how.
There aren't many brains in my dome
And I left my speech at home.
But you can't fool me, no, not this time.
'Cause I can always talk in rhyme.

Then came the prepared poem, which told the students of my vision for the school and why I was the person to carry it out. When I had finished, I knew from the reaction of the crowd that I had been a hit. I actually might come in second or third in the voting. I did better than that. I garnered the most votes, even more than David Anderson, who finished second.

As it turned out, I never served a day as a senior senator. When school convened in the fall, Bob Wallace, who had been elected student body president, asked if I would like to be assembly commissioner. Would I? I would get to meet every speaker and entertainer and introduce them to the entire student body at the assembly. I could be witty or funny, improve my speaking ability, and everyone, even the incoming sophomores, would know me.

Meanwhile, a major improvement came to our house: inside water. We hired a well digger, installed an electric pump outside and an electric heater inside, and converted part of our porch into a bathroom with a real bathtub. No longer would our Saturday-night baths be taken in a tiny washtub with a gallon or so of water heated on the cookstove. No longer would we have to carry water from a germ- and insect-infested hand-dug well. No longer would Mother have to heat water on the stove before she could cook or wash dishes. And best of all, no longer would we have to build a fire outside and wait for hours for it to get hot enough to do our laundry.

The bathtub was great, but the inside toilet was sissy, in my opinion. I boycotted it for a few weeks, but finally succumbed to its convenience. We now were just about as modern as anyone.

Not everything moved in a positive direction, however. Jack brought home a less-than-stellar report card from his first term at Rolla's School of Mines, feeling that he didn't have what it took to be an engineer. Common forms of parental encouragement —"You can do it if you try" or "Go back and study harder"— might have been employed for most college students, but not for Jack. He was not like most college students, as Mother, a superb psychologist, knew. One comment, just the right one, spoken to Dad in Jack's presence, was enough. "Perhaps we have overestimated Jack's abilities," she told Dad in a solemn, serious voice. The statement pierced Jack's psyche like a dagger to the heart. Jack, the supreme competitor, who had not backed down from any challenge, returned to college determined to prove his mother wrong. By carrying seventeen or eighteen credit hours per term and attending school in the summers, he graduated as a civil engineer in January 1950, less than three years after enrolling—an impressive accomplishment.

Jack worked in Sydney, Ohio; Pittsburgh, Pennsylvania; and Cleveland, Ohio, before being employed in 1975, by the May Company, a department-store holding company in St. Louis that owned as many as eighteen subsidiary corporations. As vice president of the May Company and chairman of its subsidiary, May Design and Construction, he spent as much as four hundred million dollars some years building or renovating stores, always finishing on time and within budget. From the humblest of beginnings, he ended his career at the top of his profession. Mother would have been pleased with her eldest son, had she lived to see his accomplishments. Dad, who lived long enough to share vicariously in Jack's success, was as proud as when he bragged at Jack's birth, "He is the best-looking kid in the hospital."

Mother's health problems began several months after moving to Papa's farm in 1943, when she noticed a small lump in her

(*Top*) Ready to buy a cow at age twelve.

(*Middle*) Brother Jack, early in his professional career.

(*Bottom*) Mother, when teaching at Shady Dell.

breast. She saw a doctor, who told her it was an innocent mass. "Go home and don't worry about it," he advised. "If it gets bigger, come back." Over the next several months the lump grew and became painful. It was cancer, diagnosed too late to save its victim. A mastectomy of the left breast followed by radiation treatments arranged by Aunt Bess (always a great supporter of our family) at Case Western Reserve Hospital in Cleveland were apparently the only known treatments at the time. But they were too little, too late.

In retrospect, Mother faced the inevitable gracefully, just as I would have expected. Although she must have grown weaker as the months and years passed, especially after undergoing radiation treatments in Cleveland, which left her left armpit horribly burned, she never complained, never asked for favors, continued to teach until the end, and never mentioned that there was but one inevitable, tragic destination to the journey she was on.

A few days before senior graduation day, Mother was admitted to the hospital. I visited her daily, after school and farm chores were completed, still believing that her stay would be temporary. Mother seemed at peace, giving words of encouragement and expressing confidence in my place in the world. These were unusual statements, it seemed to me at the time. Why was Mother talking about my future in such a serious way when she was so sick? "Let's discuss this after you come home and feel better," I thought. Later, I understood.

Two days before she passed away, Dad told me that Mother would not return home. "The doctor said your mother has only a few days left," he told me. I was shocked. Why hadn't anyone told me Mother was going to die? This just couldn't be true! But it was true. Mother died early on the morning of May 24, 1949, three days before my graduation ceremony. She was fifty-one. I was seventeen.

It was only many years after Mother's death that I realized why she had kept her fate from me. If I had known that her condition was terminal, I might not have pleaded to attend Senior, or taken debate, or run for the student senate. In her characteristic way, silently and stoically, she made her sons' aspirations the ultimate priority. And in my naïveté, I thought Mother was winning the battle and would be fine.

Immediately following Mother's death, Dad was distraught, shaking and sobbing. I remained calm externally and discussed the final arrangements with Uncle Doolin, whose funeral home conducted the services. Within a few hours Dad was able to function. Soon after, it was my turn to come unwound. I drove us home, went to the barn, ostensibly to do the chores, and poured out my pent-up, indescribable heartache, no longer controllable, to the animals. "Why did this happen to the best person who ever lived?" I cried. "It's so unfair!"

4

I Want to Be a Lawyer

Everyone in the family knew that I was deeply affected by Mother's death. Great-Uncle S. M. Sewell, concerned that I might not continue my education, gave me a dictionary and urged me to enroll in college immediately. He need not have worried. Even in grade school at Bennett, when not one penny could be wasted, there was no doubt that I would go to college. After all, as Mother reminded me, I lived in a nation where a person born in a log cabin could become president of the United States. I was smart, she said, and could accomplish anything I set my mind to if I just applied myself.

The school year at Southwest Missouri State College (SMS), now Missouri State University, was divided into four equal terms: fall, winter, spring, and summer. A student earned 2.5 credit hours per major course, and it took 124 credit hours to graduate, so a degree could be earned by taking a "full load"— four major courses plus a one-hour course each term, except the summer term, for four years. However, students could earn 3 credit hours in a course, instead of the normal 2.5, if they made an E, the highest grade awarded. Thus, by attending two summers and receiving extra credit for good grades, I graduated at the age of twenty in three calendar years, after attending eleven terms instead of the normal twelve.

When I enrolled for the summer term a few days after Mother's funeral, still somewhat in shock, I was thinking only of signing up for some courses to get the new experience started. When the adviser asked about my intended major, I replied, "I don't know." "What do you want to be when you graduate?" she asked. "A lawyer," I replied, completely surprising myself since I still had been telling those who inquired that I was going to be a preacher. But I did not correct my statement because it felt comfortable and correct. I did want to be a lawyer, I finally admitted to myself, and I wanted to be a good one.

My decision surprised not only me, but everyone in my family, for I had never mentioned the legal profession as one that intrigued me. From 1630, when Elder John Strong landed in what is now Massachusetts, to the present, I know of no lawyer in my father's lineage. On Mother's side, only ancestor Patrick Henry, some two centuries before, had been an attorney. I doubt if Mother and Dad ever consulted a lawyer. On the few occasions I recall them being mentioned, it was in an uncomplimentary way. I recollect Dad's often repeated joke about the gravestone inscribed "Here lies a lawyer and an honest man." "When did they start burying two men in the same grave?" was the punch line. After I made my decision, Grandma always introduced me, "This is my grandson Tommy. He is going to be a lawyer, but we hope he will be an honest one." No one had encouraged me to enter the profession. No one had spoken of it in a laudable way. I had made the decision on my own, and I was excited and proud of it.

After explaining to the adviser that I wanted to be a *trial* lawyer, one who needed to speak persuasively, she suggested that I major in speech. I could change my major later if I desired, she said. Instead, speech was the perfect choice. I took Fundamentals of Speech, Argumentation, Advanced Argumentation,

Orations, Extemporaneous Speaking, Public Address, Speech Correction, Speech Science, Phonetics, and, of course, Debate. The teachers were excellent. I learned how to emphasize a word, phrase, or thought by a gesture or measured pause; how to speak succinctly, packing a lot of information into the fewest possible sentences; how to vary the pitch, speed, and volume of my words so as to retain the attention of the audience; and how to incorporate humor, logic, and facts to make a point. Speaking is a science as well as an art!

The aforementioned prepared me well for debate competition under the supervision of the incomparable Dr. Virginia Craig. Craig, a spinster who retired at age seventy-six in 1952, the year I graduated, was a member of the first faculty at Missouri State Normal School Number Four, the predecessor of Missouri State University. She was of medium height, gaunt (almost emaciated), and brilliant; spoke in a high-pitched voice; and had an annoying habit of smacking her lips as she talked. As with Miss Jefferson, I would have doubted that she could effectively teach anyone how to speak if Mother, her student in the 1920s, had not told me about this brilliant, legendary teacher.

Dr. Craig was as intelligent as Mother had indicated, but she also was incredibly naive and often, unintentionally, said the funniest things imaginable. Here is one example: We traveled to debate tournaments by automobile, staying in motels along the way. In those days, inexpensive motels did not have telephones in each room, just one at the main desk—thus the need to convey messages from one room to another in person. We were having our evening meal at a café near our motel on one such trip, while I was trying to impress the pretty young waitress who was waiting on us. Meanwhile, Dr. Craig was explaining the plans for the next morning. In the presence of the waitress she innocently related, "We must get on the highway early tomorrow, so please be prompt. I asked the boy at the front desk to knock me up at five o'clock, and then, Mr. Strong, I will knock you up at five thirty." I was embarrassed, mortified beyond words, and the waitress could not suppress a giggle, try as she might. This gem, repeated by my debate colleagues to nearly every pretty girl I tried to impress on our debate trips, became part of the legends kindly referred to as "Dr. Craig stories."

College debate teams consisted of two members, not the four I had been accustomed to in high school, and there were two divisions, one for freshmen and sophomores, the other for juniors and seniors. Bob Redmond, a Carthage, Missouri, native, was the first speaker on both the affirmative and the negative sides; I was the anchor, or second speaker. It was at Baylor University that my recurring dream of being unprepared or late for something important, first experienced when I was in the fourth grade at Marshfield, became a reality. We reached the final rounds of the tournament and found, to our chagrin, that our next opponent was the host, Baylor University, with two outstanding debaters who were considered odds-on favorites to win the tournament. The home-court advantage was not just a sports phenomenon; it also applied to debate.

Al Teidland, one of our debaters, drove Bob and me to the building where we were scheduled to challenge Baylor. We stepped out of the car, and away Al drove, our briefcases and resource material securely in the trunk. Waving our arms, running after the car, and screaming as loud as we could brought no notice from the oblivious driver. We were about to face the most feared opponent in the tournament without our references, authorities from which to quote, outlines of our rebuttals to every conceivable argument, without even a pencil or piece of paper.

Fretting was not an option. We walked into the room where the debate was to be held with a smile, shook hands with our opponents, and asked if they could lend us a tablet and a couple of pencils. Being excellent debaters, but not necessarily the most sympathetic opponents, they consented to give us one pencil and a single sheet of paper. How considerate of them! We broke the pencil in two, sharpened both halves, tore the sheet of paper in half, and reconciled ourselves to the inevitable embarrassment.

In walked the three judges, who introduced themselves and sat down to judge an elimination debate between the skillful home team from a prestigious university with boxes full of references and authorities, and the other with debaters from a small school who each had half a pencil and half a sheet of paper. We were not about to forfeit—and a couple of circumstances gave us a chance. First, we won the coin toss and elected to argue the negative side of the issue, the side easier to argue without bushels of authorities, it being easier to attack and destroy (the negative's job) than to uphold a plan to fix a problem (the affirmative's job).

Perhaps we just were better than Baylor and deserved to win, perhaps the judges were impressed by the knowledge we carried in our heads and our ability to attack the weakness of Baylor's case extemporaneously, or perhaps they saw how unsportsmanlike our opponents had been and gave us a break. Whatever the reason, we won the debate by a vote of 3–0 and went on to defeat the University of Texas for the tournament championship. This, the most unusual college debate in memory, was the talk of the tournament. Maybe it was Baylor who gave birth to the suggestion that we had staged the whole affair for dramatic effect. Absurd? The story outlived the tournament and was cited in the 1950 *Ozarko,* our college yearbook, and again by college president Dr. Roy Ellis in *Shrine of the Ozarks.*

In my third and last year at SMS, my debate partner was Charles Strickland, studious, brilliant, with a charming voice and a clear, logical mind. I was anything but studious, but I knew how to identify, attack, belittle, and poke fun at the weak underbelly of an opponent's argument. A formidable pair, with contrasting and complementary styles, we compiled an impressive record, including victories at the University of Arkansas, where I received a certificate as the tournament's best debater. Charles and I had set a goal for ourselves at the first of the year to be the first team from SMS to be invited to the national finals at West Point, the equivalent of the NCAA Basketball Tournament, which determines the nation's best basketball team.

First, we needed to do well in Ames, Iowa, the last tournament of the regular season, to ensure an invitation to debate's "big dance." A few days before the event, however, Charles suffered what was called in those days a "nervous breakdown." He was out of the debate picture the rest of the year. When a star player on a basketball team is injured, someone takes his place, and so it also was in debate.

Yvonne Ray, who had transferred from an Oklahoma college that year, but with whom I had never debated, was named my colleague. Not good! Just as individual basketball players need competition to become a winning team, we needed months and several tournaments to refine our arguments and to identify the roles we would play. But we did unexpectedly well at Ames, received the coveted invitation, and traveled with Dr. Craig to compete for the national championship at West Point.

Each team in the tournament would debate eight times in the preliminary rounds, and the sixteen teams with the best win-loss records would be seeded and debate in the "one and done" elimination rounds. Yvonne and I had won five and lost three in the preliminaries and were seeded tenth in the elimination rounds. San Diego State, seeded seventh with six wins and two losses in the preliminaries, was our opponent—and victim. Next, in the quarterfinals, we squared off against the University of New Mexico, which, with seven wins and a single loss in the preliminaries, was seeded number two. We lost and were out. We had come close. If only we had been able to enter a few more tournaments together before being thrown into the lion's den, or if Charles had not been incapacitated, things might have been different.

Debate was an important part of campus life at SMS, as attested by the fact that a schoolwide assembly program was devoted to a debate between an Oklahoma college and us. Moreover, debaters, along with athletes and others, were honored at a special assembly. Although I had debated only three years, not four, as many before me had, the college president announced that I had won more debates than anyone in the history of the school.

School politics remained a passion as well, especially since the opportunities now were greater. There were 1,577 students at SMS my first semester, fewer than the enrollment at Senior High. The overwhelming majority of the freshman class was made up of my high school friends. I was well liked and without question the best-known freshman, a sure thing to be elected class president, a position I coveted. Then Murphy's Law (if something can go wrong, it will) struck. My brother's twenty-five-dollar Chrysler, which he left at the farm while he attended college, failed to start. I frantically ran the mile across the field to the nearest blacktop road, now called Division Street, and thumbed a ride to town. But I was too late. I had been nominated, but my name was withdrawn because I was absent.

I made sure Murphy's Law did not strike two years in a row and was elected president of the sophomore class. My third year, I had enough credits to be a senior, so I could not run for junior class president. I ran for senior class president, even though my former high school classmates would be unable to vote for me. Despite losing my main base of support, I was still able to squeak out a narrow victory over Jerry Nixon for another coveted position.

Strange as it may seem, considering my upbringing, my college experience also encompassed fraternity life. If Mother had lived, my joining a fraternity would have been out of the

Dressed for a debate.

question. Fraternities seemed to represent everything of which I disapproved—drinking, goofing off, showing off, and misbehaving. Since the eighth grade I had refused sodas and coffee because they contained caffeine, did not smoke or drink, and read a chapter of the Bible nearly every day. Besides, I was busy as the chief cook, housekeeper, and farmhand at home, in addition to owning a burning desire to excel in debate at school. I had neither the time nor the interest in joining a frat. Then the inevitable invitation to a rush party came from Kappa Alpha (KA). They understood that I was not interested in joining, but said to come anyway. There was no obligation, but I was sure to meet some interesting people, including campus leaders. It would be fun. Nature took its course. The first party led to others, and the "brothers" were friendly and persistent. So I joined, thinking that I did not have to make it a major part of campus life.

Lighting the Christmas candle my senior year.

Then came an election to an unwanted office, the only one in my life that I did not desire. Two fraternity brothers had campaigned earnestly to be president. Since the election was by secret ballot and formal nominations were not made, members could vote for any brother, without fear of being accused of betraying a friend vying for the office. The first ballot produced votes for eight brothers, several receiving a smattering of votes, even three for me. Neither of the two leading candidates received a majority, so there was another vote.

It occurred to me to withdraw my name, but I had received only three votes. There wasn't a chance that I, one of only two members who eschewed alcohol at frat parties, would be elected, and it would appear presumptuous, even arrogant, to announce that I did not want the most coveted office in the fraternity. It was one of the few times in my life when I had a chance to speak up and should have, but didn't. The second, third, fourth, and fifth ballots brought the leading candidates fewer votes and me more. It now appeared that I could be elected, but it was too late to say anything. If I did not want the office, I should have spoken up after the first ballot. I remained mute and was elected president on the seventh ballot. What a bummer! It was an office I filled with little enthusiasm.

One of my most memorable—and scariest—moments involved a small aircraft piloted by a fraternity brother. It was twenty-two feet, nine inches long, powered by a 65-horsepower engine and weighed 680 pounds empty. It could carry up to two people, if they, including their luggage and fuel, did not exceed 480 pounds. It could reach advertised speeds between 65 and 93 miles per hour and travel up to 230 miles on a tank of gas, depending on the weight of the load, wind resistance, and height. It was a Taylor Craft, an airplane of sorts, a survivor of World War II. It cost Bart Wagner, my fraternity brother, a mere $240.

Bart was proud of this war veteran, which he said could take off and land in minimum distances from unprepared landing strips. Planes of this type had typically been used for reconnaissance in much the same manner as an observation balloon, spotting enemy troop and supply concentrations and directing artillery fire on them. The seller had shown Bart how to operate it, using the two foot rudders and lever, which extended from the floor between the pilot's legs, but Bart had no other training to be a pilot, nor did he need any. Even a caveman could fly it without a single lesson from a professional instructor. At least that was Bart's story.

I flew with Bart in his pride and joy above Springfield and to some nearby towns. We followed the highways since Bart did not know how to navigate cross-country, and I was somewhat embarrassed to see cars on the roads below pass us. Apparently, our well-traveled transportation's top speed was little, if any, faster than its advertised minimum speed of 65 miles per hour.

Bart suggested a trip to Tulsa, Oklahoma. At 163 highway miles away (we would have to follow the highway because of Bart's limitations in navigation), the destination was well within range of our trusty T-Craft. The plan was to leave on Saturday, stay free at the KA frat house at Tulsa University Saturday night, and return on Sunday.

We showed up unannounced at the KA house Saturday evening and identified ourselves as fraternity brothers from the Gamma Beta Chapter at SMS. The first brother we met was friendly, as frat brothers are to each other, and said he would find the president for sleeping arrangements. Soon the president appeared and inquired, "Are you a fraternity man?" I explained that I was the president at Gamma Beta, and he asked again, "Are you a fraternity man?" Again I explained that I was the president at the SMS chapter in Springfield. He seemed puzzled, but polite, and gave us a place to stay. Before long another brother came to visit and, after some small talk, blurted out, "Are you a fraternity man?" I was starting to become annoyed at brothers who did not seem to believe that I was one of their own, but I replied by repeating who I was and where I was from.

On the flight back I remained perplexed by the question, repeated in exactly the same words by two different brothers, until it dawned on me that it was part of our fraternal training. When two brothers meet who do not know each other, they confirm the brotherhood by asking "Are you a fraternity man?" to which the second brother replies with the secret response only brothers know. The Tulsa brothers naturally were suspicious of a person who said he was a brother but did not know the secret response, especially since he claimed to be his chapter's president. Oh, well, they were kind enough to give us a room despite their doubts given the faux pas on my part.

With one successful long trip under our belts, Bart suggested flying to the KA chapter at the University of Missouri in Columbia. And something new would be added. This time we would fly cross-country since the roads from Springfield to Columbia were too meandering, making it difficult to follow them. His suggestion made sense to me. Climbing over the Ozark Mountains near the Lake of the Ozarks was a monumental task for our tiny plane, but we were clearing them with room to spare.

"How do you think the motor sounds?" he shouted over his shoulder to me, sitting directly behind him. "It sounds great," I replied. "I think so too," he said, adding, "I fixed it myself."

But the mountains proved more that it could handle, and it soon quit, suddenly with little more than a sputter. We looked down to see nothing but tree-covered hills and only one small pasture on a hillside about a half mile away. We were in deep trouble, and we both knew it. But Bart proved his mettle that day. He glided to the field, barely reaching it, cleared the fence, ran a hundred feet or so up the hillside, and came to a safe stop. Not a scratch was inflicted on human or machine. After determining that our hearts were still beating and our pants were still dry, we needed to find a way to get back home. I mentioned that my uncle Tom, who lived in Jefferson City, might pick us up if we called him. "What kind of a car does he own?" Bart asked.

I didn't think beggars should be particular, and personally, I would have been happy to thumb a ride on a passing ox cart, but I told him that it was the biggest, most expensive Chrysler made. "Perfect," Bart said. Soon I would learn what was in Bart's mind. We walked up the dirt road to a house that had a telephone and called Uncle Tom. When my uncle arrived, Bart unbolted the engine, lifted it out of the plane, and put it in the trunk of the Chrysler. I couldn't believe my eyes. I had trusted my life to an engine so small a person could lift it, and one that could fit in the trunk of a car?

Dad was not pleased when I arrived home and Uncle Tom told him what happened. Dad forbade me to fly in the plane again. That was an instruction completely unnecessary, for I was fed up with the T-Craft and the wild blue yonder.

When I saw Bart about a week later, he told me that he had fixed the motor again, had installed it in the plane, had stripped down to nothing but a swimsuit in order to keep the plane's weight at a minimum, and had asked nearby farmers to hold the plane's tail as long as they could while he raced the motor and urged the craft forward. Finally, the plane won the tug-of-war against the farmers, and the "little plane that could" rolled down the hill, flew over the fence and under the overhead electric lines strung about twenty feet above the fence, circled until it gained enough height to clear the mountains, and came home.

Bart thought he was destined to be a great pilot and joined the air force to prove it, only to flunk out of flight school. It may be that he did not have what it takes to be a pilot in Uncle Sam's air force, but that did not lessen my admiration for him. He had saved our lives by some savvy piloting, as good as World War II captain Eddie Rickenbacker could have done, as far as I was concerned. He was definitely a hero in my book.

Following graduation from SMS and preceding my entry into law school in the fall, I found myself involved in Oklahoma politics in the summer of 1952. Oklahoma politics was a unique and intriguing circus, as I learned that summer. The state was gerrymandered in such a way that two US congressional districts, the sixth and seventh, were combined to form a gigantic sixth district, which covered much of western Oklahoma. Two Democratic incumbents, Victor Wickersham (a friend of Yvonne Ray's family), from the old seventh district, and Toby Morris, from the old sixth, were pitted against each other. Republicans in Oklahoma didn't have a chance to win in those days, so the winner of the primary was destined for Washington. Yvonne, fresh from being my debate colleague at West Point, said Victor wanted her to help with his campaign. She told Wickersham that I would be an asset, so he consented to include me on the team. "If we hurry, we can help Victor get elected and have a lot of fun in the process; the primary election is just a little more than thirty days away," Yvonne insisted.

The two contestants in the election were both consummate politicians. The forty-six-year-old Wickersham, a high school graduate, had been elected Greer County's clerk at the tender age of twenty-one and had run for various offices at every opportunity until he was elected to the US Congress in 1941.

Morris, seven years older than Wickersham, dropped out of high school in 1917 to fight in World War I. After returning, he was elected court clerk and then studied law with his father. In 1937, he was elected district judge, but resigned in 1946 to be elected to the US Congress, serving two more terms before facing Wickersham in this epic showdown.

With two veteran congressmen running against each other, Yvonne's offer was tempting. Yvonne said we would have a car with loudspeakers on the top, the words *Victor Wickersham for Congress* in big letters on the side, and we would drive through the smaller towns in western Oklahoma to campaign for him. Even more important, we would each be paid a hundred dollars for the month.

I had always been a yellow-dog Republican, with little tolerance for people of the Democratic faith—but how could I pass up a hundred dollars and the chance to make speeches? It was a once-in-a-lifetime opportunity, too good to miss. We had a ball as we drove slowly down the streets of small towns shouting "Vote for Victor Wickersham!" over the loudspeaker, talking to groups of three to a dozen citizens at a town square, telling them why we would vote for Wickersham if we were old enough to vote, passing out cards, swapping stories with the townsfolk, just being friendly, and doing anything that would get a vote. We must have been a novelty—these two kids still wet behind the ears—because people kidded us and seemed to like us.

A few days before the election I had a special treat. I met Wickersham by chance in a town where we were campaigning. This was the only time I ever saw him. He was tall and looked intelligent. With no-rim glasses and black hair slicked back, he spoke in a friendly, low-key tone, as he shook hands and called almost everyone by name while working his way down the street. He was a professional, exuding confidence, nothing like what I expected. I was impressed and pleased to support him.

We also drove into a town where Toby Morris was telling a small crowd how his parents had named him "Toby" after their favorite mule, all the reasons they should vote for him, and all the things he would do for his district when he was elected. Toby, smaller than Victor and looking very much like the people in the crowd, was an impressive storyteller and speaker—a likable guy. It was a very close election, but Wickersham won. Yvonne theorized that we had done enough to tilt the election in Victor's favor. Apparently, Victor also was impressed with us, or at least Yvonne, because when he went to Washington, Yvonne went with him to serve on his staff.

After the campaign was over, I still had a month and a half to earn a dollar or two before law school began. Jack, now an engineer with the Ohio State Highway Department, provided a solution. I could live with him and another engineer while helping build a highway near Sandusky. The job involved shoveling cement, operating a jackhammer, carrying iron, running errands, and doing anything I was told. It was hot, heavy work, but I had experienced this before when thrashing wheat or doing other farmwork in one-hundred-degree heat.

When it was time to return home, I intended to hitchhike, just as I had done to get to Sandusky, but a coworker, a huge African American man with bulging muscles from years of shoveling concrete, offered to give me a ride as far as his hometown of St. Louis. Strange as it may seem in today's world, this was an offer I had to ponder. I had grown up in Springfield, a city that hosted a lynching of an African American in 1901, three more in 1906, and still was segregated in 1952. After the 1906 atrocity, many blacks fled in fear for their lives, leaving the small number remaining to experience segregation in the town's schools, churches, restaurants, and other public buildings. Well into the 1950s, only one motion picture theater, the Landers, considered second rate and showing older movies, accommodated blacks— and only in the top balcony.

Because of segregation and the racial makeup of Southwest Missouri, I never attended any school that included an Asian, Indian, Muslim, or African American—just a blanket of white folks who all looked pretty much like me. Yet I had always believed that while I was as good as anyone, I also was no better than anyone. I humbly accepted the gracious offer of a free ride.

The ride to St. Louis was relaxing and routine until an Illinois highway patrolman stopped our car and asked if I was okay. A smallish, white twenty-year-old kid riding in a rusty old car with a large black man raised the trooper's concern for my welfare. Black and white folks just were not seen together on the highway in daylight in segregated America unless something was awry, so thought the patrolman. Who would have guessed that fifty-six years later, black, brown, yellow, and white Americans would elect a black president?

5

Five Good Years

The year I applied for law school, no Law School Admission Test, better known as the LSAT, or undergraduate grade requirements existed. Any college graduate in 1952 could enroll at the tax-supported University of Missouri School of Law. But having the right to enroll did not mean the right to graduate.

The law school, located in Tate Hall, had three classrooms, one for freshmen, one for second-year students, and one for seniors. The professors came to the students' classroom instead of the students going to the professor's, as they had done at SMS. The classrooms themselves told an intimidating story. The first-year classroom had seats for a hundred students, the second-year classroom had seats for fifty, and the third-year room sat only thirty-five. Many might have been called to enter, but few would be chosen to finish. So it was with my class: thirty-three graduated out of more than a hundred who had entered.

Financial consideration added to the daunting challenge. When I worked for Mr. Rollings the summer after the seventh grade, I knew that money was hard to come by and even harder to keep. I saved it, bought cows, and sold the milk. I hoped cows would be my ticket to college and success. By the time we moved to Springfield in 1951, I owned five skinny, nondescript cows, castoffs from productive herds because they no longer could fill their quota. I bought them one at a time, as I could afford them, ınd unquestionably paid too much for each one. But I was too young and inexperienced to know their value or how to bargain for a better price. When Dad said he had sold the farm and that I should sell my cows, my seven-year business of selling milk came to an abrupt end. I paid too much when I bought the cows and received too little when I sold them, but I was forced to liquidate in a rush, so I had no bargaining power. In addition to my cows, I also took advantage of every opportunity to do farmwork for the neighbors. Twenty-five cents and then fifty cents an hour can add up to real money after several years if you don't spend it, and I spent very little.

During the summer between my first and second years of college, I was the sole employee working the night shift at Ellis' Filling Station, owned by Burt Ellis, an old, storytelling, pipe-smoking brother of the SMS president. The filling station was small, about two hundred square feet in size, junky and dirty, located in the less desirable part of town on the northeast corner of College and Main. During the day I milked my cows and often worked in the fields for our neighbors. I never needed much sleep, but that summer, when I worked both day and night, I got less than usual.

It was during the summer of 1950 that I received my first expensive, painful lesson in business. Dad did not work at night, so I had to provide my own transportation, a need I accomplished by purchasing a 1930s Dodge automobile at a cost of thirty-five dollars. As the summer drew to a close and I no longer needed a vehicle, I began looking for a buyer and found one in Hal, a guy who roamed the streets in the middle of the night with a couple of his buddies; he became my occasional conversation companion during the lonesome midnight hours at the station. When learning that my car was for sale, Hal bargained with me to buy it for fifty bucks, a sale that would provide me a nice profit on my investment. He paid me five dollars down, promised the remainder at the end of the month, and arranged to pick up the car my last day at work.

I had been taught that a person's word was his bond, and it was insulting to suggest that a bargain should be reduced to writing. So we sealed the deal with a handshake. It never occurred to me that someone would be so low as to risk his soul to eternal damnation by reneging on a promise. When I did not receive the remainder of the payment in the mail as promised, I knew the debt was in jeopardy. Then it dawned on me that I didn't even know Hal's last name, where he lived, or how to find him. A wasted two or three nights searching for him near the filling station made me realize that I had been had. I had received five dollars on an investment of thirty-five dollars because of my own lax business practice, a lesson in both economics and human behavior I had failed to learn.

At various times during school breaks after we moved to Springfield, I sold men's clothes at a store on the south side of St. Louis Street, a half block from the square. I knew nothing about fashion or what the desirable brands were, but I wasn't paid much, so the owners pretty much got what they paid for. The store later went out of business and was essentially forgotten by everyone. I can't even remember its name. Perhaps it hired too many salesmen like me who had no clue about what they were doing.

All the while, I had been saving with several goals in mind: to make something of myself and, yes, to make Mother, although gone, proud of me. To do this, I needed a law degree, and I was in a hurry to get it and to start making an impact on society. This was the reason I usually went without a car when nearly everyone around me had one, why I did not buy textbooks at SMS for some of the easier classes, why my social life suffered, and why I earned my college degree in three years instead of four.

When I entered law school I wanted to complete it without incurring a debt or missing a year to work. I had saved $2,000, mostly from selling milk, but in reality every effort contributed something to the pot. But there was no way that $2,000 would pay for three years of law school; yet it was a start.

I lived with David Hilton, an SMS debater, all three years in law school, and we cooked our own meals and cleaned our own apartment, sharing expenses to save money. As a result, I spent only $960 the first year and $930 the second year for tuition, books, room and board, and Christmas presents. Not having a car made dating a near impossibility, but it saved money in two ways: not having to support a car and not having many dates.

During the summers between my first and second and my second and third years, I worked for the Springfield law firm of Mann, Mann, Walter, and Powell, receiving a suitcase for my efforts the first summer and $25 per month the second. I did not work there for the money. I was looking ahead, getting my foot in the door with one of the best firms in town, and learning something about other firms that might one day be prospective employers.

My bank account was nearly empty at the start of the third year, yet my financial outlook was not as bleak as one would think. I had learned during my first year that two students from the senior class were often hired to teach two three-hour business-law courses to undergraduates in the university's business school. The pay was $1,500 for the year, more than enough to pay for the last year of law school. All I needed to do was be one of the two or three top students and impress upon the faculty that I would be a better teacher than my competition. It worked. I landed the position and graduated debt free with more than $400 in my pocket.

Meanwhile, I had learned that the study of law is not rocket science. It is not hard in the way that calculus, chemistry, medicine, or physics is hard. It does not take either the mind of a genius or any particular background. Law school is hard in a

different way. There is an overwhelming amount of work assigned, and a mind that can read rapidly, retain what it reads,
analyze problems, and employ good common sense and has
the ability to reason is essential. Those who have developed
good study habits and the ability to spend long hours concen-
trating on an assignment have a distinct advantage. Therein lay
my problem.

All through grade school, high school, and college, with the
exception of debate, I essentially did no homework. I made good
grades without ever learning to study, and this deficiency eventually took its toll. I tried setting a schedule of seven in the morning to ten in the evening seven days a week for schoolwork and
meals, except for weekends, when noon Saturday to noon Sunday was reserved for shopping, personal chores, writing brother
Jack, watching a football game, relaxing, or taking in a movie.
The time I spent on assignments would have been more than adequate had I known how to study.

I had been physically active all my life, and reading dull, un-
exciting cases or treatises put me to sleep. Even when I managed to stay awake, I often found that after a half hour or so,
I still was staring at the same page without comprehending a
single thing. The subjects were boring, and I was unable to stay
awake. And if I *was* awake, I was in a funk, floundering, getting
nowhere. In the first practice exam given by the "Fox" (Professor Pitman), my grade was an F followed by four minuses.
Trying to develop good study habits when I had started with
none was an uphill climb. Fortunately, I had a little time; our
grades depended on only one test, the one given at the end of
the course. In yearlong classes, a poor result on that one all-
important final exam could sink your boat. It took two years
for me to find the secret to mastering law school, but I finally
discovered it. In my senior year I taught two three-hour undergraduate courses, one on negotiable instruments and one on

wills and estates, wrote two *Law Review* articles, and participated in Regional Moot Court Competition in St. Louis, all of
this in addition to carrying a full class load.

Either preparing and teaching two new courses or excelling
in my studies was a full-time undertaking, but by adding moot
court and the writing of *Law Review* articles to the load, I
pushed the envelope. The odds were that either my grades would
plummet, or I would be a candidate for a mental breakdown.
The backbreaker was teaching. Planning to teach a new college course is time-consuming for the experienced teacher and
was doubly difficult for a novice. I did the best I could and
occasionally felt grateful to meet former students (one a former president of the University of Missouri Board of Cura-
tors) who said that I was tough, but my course taught him to
think, not memorize, and to reason a problem out. That was
the intent. Amazingly, even my grades improved that last frantic year. The icing on the cake was the "Judge Shepard Barclay
Prize," which I received for being "the Senior who has attained
the highest standing in scholarship and moral leadership."

I had started law school as a twenty-year-old kid, perhaps the
youngest in the class, not knowing how to adapt to the brutal requirements of the curriculum. But I persevered, finished strong,
and did well with a load that would have overwhelmed most students. In that last year I had learned how to make every minute
of many long hours count, to enjoy the challenge, and to excel
in the undertakings. It was a year that prepared me well for the
times to come when winning lawsuits depended on outworking
and outperforming my adversaries.

In the spring of my third year, I had been informed that Mr.
Matthew Herold, a partner in the prestigious twenty-five-man
(no women) New York City law firm of Mudge, Stearn, Baldwin,
and Todd, located at 40 Wall Street, in the same block as the New
York Stock Exchange, was making a trip through the Midwest,

interviewing one or two of the top students in several major universities. I was the only student he wanted to see at the University of Missouri.

I went to the interview not knowing the storied history of this ivory-tower firm, with roots that traced back to 1869. Nor did I care. The thing that caught my attention, after an interesting conversation with Mr. Herold, was his invitation to come to New York City for two days and three nights, all expenses paid. It was much too good an offer to refuse even if I had to spend part of the time in interviews. So I went and met the big shots—Rose, Guthrie, Alexander, and the others.

Just before I was ready to leave, Mr. Herold said he would give me a hundred dollars for my expenses in the city, much more than I had spent, and asked in what denominations I wanted the bills. When I first walked into the lobby of the firm, I was puzzled by a long, narrow room with a glass front, behind which old, stately-looking gentlemen, dressed in tuxedos, sat at attention, doing nothing. When Mr. Herold and I agreed on the appropriate breakdown of the sum, he pressed a buzzer, and in walked one of the men who had been sitting in the glass room. Mr. Herold said, "Please trade this one-hundred-dollar bill for five ones, five fives, five tens, and one twenty, and give them to Mr. Strong." Would you believe it? These little, old, tuxedo-clad men were errand boys.

Little did I know, as I discounted the possibility of practicing law in New York City, that the past history of the firm could not compete with what was soon to come. In 1964, Richard Nixon, later to become president of the United States, joined it at an annual salary of two hundred thousand dollars, and the firm was renamed Nixon, Mudge, Rose, Guthrie, and Alexander. Then, three years later, the firm absorbed John Mitchell's municipal-bond law firm and was renamed again to include Mitchell's name.

Nixon and Mitchell evolved into quite a team. Mitchell became Nixon's campaign manager in the latter's 1968 run for president. He then became the president's US attorney general and, later, our nation's only attorney general to be jailed for criminal conduct. The Watergate scandal not only sent Mitchell and his cohorts to prison, but also led to Nixon resigning the office of president. On rare occasions, I have speculated as to what might have happened if I, a yellow-dog Republican, had joined the firm, had impressed Nixon when he joined it seven years later, and had gone with him to Washington as a speechwriter or in some other position on his staff when he became president.

Instead of joining a law firm immediately following graduation, I chose to fulfill my military-service obligation, knowing that I would probably be drafted by January 1956. At that time, my army physical revealed that I was five feet, eight and a half inches tall and weighed 142 pounds, my present height and weight. With that, on July 20, 1955, just two days after I took the bar examination, I was in the army, stationed at Camp Chaffee, Arkansas.

Less than four months later, I married Wilma Ruth Owens, who grew up in a farm community just north of Norfolk, Arkansas. I had met Wilma through David Hilton, my law-school roommate, who arranged a blind date during Christmas break of my second year of law school. I was immediately taken by her. At five feet, three inches tall, petite as a model at about a hundred pounds, with gray-blue eyes, jet black hair, and a ready smile, Wilma was an eyeful. By then she lived in Springfield, where she was employed as a secretary in the law firm of Walker, Daniel, Clampett, and Rittershouse. They say that opposites attract, which may explain my attraction to Wilma. I was outgoing; she was reserved. I was aggressive; she was restrained. I was self-confident; she was somewhat insecure. I was competitive;

she was not. I needed attention and success; she couldn't care less. Wilma was just a sweet, pleasant, affable, strikingly attractive girl.

When I was home from law school on breaks or in the summer, my first phone call was to Wilma, and she, despite being pursued by other boys, usually was available. Things went well. No arguments, no criticism, no demands, no complaints, just a strong attraction, at least on my part. But there was no talk of an engagement or marriage, or even of dating exclusively. As a private, living in an army barracks, facing transfers to who knows where, I had no business thinking about committing to anyone, or asking anyone to commit to me.

Then, in basic training, amid the drills, marches, obstacle courses, rifle-range practices, KP duties, and "fill-time" activities, I was in the barracks following noon mess when the loudspeaker roared the command, "Private Strong to Company Headquarters on the double." What had I done? Or more precisely, what had they caught me doing? There were multiple acts of commission or omission that could have resulted in KP duty or worse. I reported to headquarters as instructed and was told that the company commander wanted to see me—not an encouraging sign. I waited nervously for a few minutes (in the army it is always hurry up and wait) before being told that the commander was ready.

I entered the office, saluted, and stood at attention. "At ease, soldier," said the captain. What happened next was completely inexplicable. He asked a series of simple questions such as who were the US senators from my state, who was the governor of Missouri, and who was my congressman. Was I going to end up in the stockade if I flunked this oral test on citizenship?

Apparently convinced that I was not an alien, the captain asked me to take a seat. He then explained that my records indicated that I had a law degree, had passed the bar, and had a high IQ. He said I was eligible to enter either the Judge Advocate General (JAG) program or the Counter Intelligence Corps (CIC) if I preferred either to the infantry. Was this the army's idea of a cruel joke? Any rational person would prefer a beating to the infantry.

I knew something about the Judge Advocate General option. I would be an officer, draw an officer's pay, and try cases in military courts. But I would have to serve three years. This ruled out JAG. I wanted to be a "real" lawyer, not a military lawyer, and I wanted to be one as soon as possible. I would not postpone making my mark as a trial lawyer one day longer than necessary, even if I had to stay in the infantry.

What is the CIC, I inquired, and how long must you serve? The captain explained that the CIC required me to enlist for three years and that I would be an officer with an officer's pay. There also was a two-year program, available for only a few more months. "But you would not be interested in it because you still would be noncommissioned and paid as a private." Why would anyone *not* want to be an officer? I suppose he thought.

"Tell me more about the two-year option," I requested, no longer fearing punishment for some wrongdoing. The captain seemed irked at being cross-examined by a private and curtly replied that I would attend a training school at Fort Holabird, Maryland, and then do whatever they told me to do. It wasn't much of an explanation, but that's all you could expect from the army. Actually, he had told me enough. If I joined the CIC, I could choose to serve two years and I would not have to be in the infantry. What more did I need to know? Thank God for large favors!

So, on October 2, 1955, I reported for duty at Fort Holabird, home of the US Army Intelligence school, located in Dundalk, a Baltimore, Maryland, suburb. Soldiers were trained there as undercover, clandestine 007 agents of sorts, and I got a taste of

it during my training—learning a little judo, being qualified on
.38- and .45-caliber revolvers, playing war games, finding my
way out of an unfamiliar forest, and learning how to interro-
gate prisoners and interview witnesses. The classes were interesting, and the conduct of the officer-teachers was professional,
like what one would expect in a college classroom. Even humor
was evident; two of the streets on the fort were named "Counter" and "Intelligence." What a difference from the crude, vulgar
treatment recruits received at basic training.

There was also reason to be optimistic about the future. After
graduation from the CIC, we would be issued a civilian car, wear
civilian clothes, and live as civilians. We would be addressed as
"Mr.," and although our pay was that of a private or whatever
our future rank would be, we would also be paid a per diem,
money to buy clothes, pay rent, and other expenses needed to
live in the civilian world. A frugal person could actually have a
little to spare at the end of the month. The Counter Intelligence
Corps was as good of a deal as Uncle Sam's military could offer.

The best students from the nation's top universities were in
my class of about twenty-five, including two former classmates:
Bruce Normile from law school and Bob Wallace, my high school
debate colleague. Bob had graduated from Harvard and Oxford
in England but was expelled from the CIC program when his
background investigation was completed. Every CIC agent had
to undergo "top-secret" clearance that evaluated moral character and loyalty to country and showed no criminal record. Uncle
Sam felt it could not trust Bob and booted him out. Perhaps he
had attended a meeting of some "pink" organization at Harvard
in that McCarthy era when everyone was considered a communist until proven otherwise.

Here, in as comfortable of an environment as the army could
offer, I began to contemplate life after my discharge. Several of
my classmates were married, and since I planned to live as a ci-

vilian after graduation, I began to think about that special girl back in Missouri. I was twenty-three years old, healthy, and confident, with a license to practice law and a career waiting for me less than two years away. The more I thought about it, the more it made perfect sense.

I was entitled to a pass on the weekend of November 5–6, 1955, a perfect time for a wedding. I had it planned. I would call Wilma and propose, she would accept, and we would be married. It was that simple. It never occurred to me that Wilma might be surprised at a proposal over the phone, or at any proposal for that matter, since I had never even asked her to go steady! Nor did it seem important to me that we wouldn't have a conventional wedding with friends and families present, a reception, a cake, and all the other things that are important to most brides.

On Saturday, October 15, I took a dollar to the fort's store and got change for the coin-operated telephone, nine minutes' worth, since I didn't want the conversation to be rushed. Wilma answered, and I told her of my plan. We would be married by Reverend Kenneth Rose at ten in the morning at the Lovely Lane Methodist Church in Baltimore, the mother church of American Methodism with roots dating back to 1784. Then we would go to Washington, DC, and spend our honeymoon night there, see DC on Sunday, and return to the base Sunday night. I told her I had found a room off base that she would like and it's where we would live. I had thought of everything.

There was a long silence at the other end of the line! Had we been disconnected, or had my time expired? After what seemed like an eternity, Wilma spoke. She had some questions, some concerns. This was pretty sudden. She would have to think about it. I was shocked. It had not occurred to me that she would have any reservations, that there was anything to think about. Suddenly, I broke into a sweat, realizing for the first time that this was not the most romantic way in the world to propose. She didn't give me an answer that day, but she did not say no, either. She said she would think about it and asked me to call her Wednesday night. She couldn't call me because I had no phone.

Sunday, Monday, Tuesday, and Wednesday passed like an eternity, and I was nervous when I made the promised call. I need not have worried. Wilma said yes. She had even talked to her boss, to get his thoughts about me. Everything was fine—the date, the place, the plans, the honeymoon, everything! No invitations were mailed, and no notice given except for an announcement, sans picture, in the *Springfield Leader and Press* on Sunday, October 23. No family or friends attended; it was too far, the notice was too short, and there was nothing for them to do except to see a ten-minute ceremony without songs, reception, or cake. Not even a single picture.

Two CIC classmates, Wayne Taylor and Manuel Valenzuela, were our witnesses. The marriage license, which had to be signed three days before the wedding, was purchased and ready for Wilma when she arrived on Tuesday. She was pleased with the one-room, third-story apartment I rented and the wedding ring I bought with my meager savings. We even received a wedding present, our one and only, a twelve-inch black-and-white TV, from brother Jack.

At half past eight on Saturday morning, November 5, 1955, Wilma, in her finest dark, conservative dress, and I, in my best suit, picked up our witnesses in my 1949 Nash Ambassador automobile, and the four of us headed for the church. We were relaxed and in high spirits; Manuel, a jokester who considered himself a ladies' man, told Wilma on the trip that it was not too late to back out. She could hook someone a lot better than me, maybe even someone like him if she played her cards right. He refused to take no as Wilma's final answer, so the discussion continued until we found ourselves at the church, where we were soon married and off to DC for our honeymoon.

Thus ended a most unconventional courtship, and thus began a solid, lifelong marriage. Of course, there were a few disagreements and misunderstandings along the way, but through it all love, loyalty, and respect prevailed. The traditional wedding vows that we took "to have and to hold from this day forward, for better or for worse, for richer, for poorer, in sickness and in health, to love and to cherish; from this day forward until death do us part" were fulfilled to the letter. I couldn't have chosen a better mate if I had lived as long as Methuselah and possessed the wisdom of Solomon. Wilma may have been on the short end of the deal, but, if so, she has always concealed it well.

Wilma and yours truly. The first picture after our wedding, taken in 1956.

Early in our marriage we relied on the aforementioned Nash, which I had purchased following basic training. With a 121-inch wheel base, it was huge. And with an aerodynamic body, it looked much like an upside-down bathtub. With black paint dulled by age and inattention, it was downright ugly. The auto did have one outstanding attribute, one that outweighed all of its deficiencies: it cost only four hundred dollars.

At Fort Holabird I did not want to go through the red tape that would allow me to bring the car on base, so I parked it on a nearby street and left it there for weeks at a time. Residents in the area apparently didn't appreciate having this unattractive monster in front of their houses, so after a few weeks someone attempted to encourage me to move it by using it as the target in an egg-throwing contest. One Saturday morning when I went to get the buggy for a trip to town, it was tattooed with eggs, now rotten, firmly stuck to it. It was an awful sight coupled with an awful odor. I didn't have either the facilities or the desire to wash it and figured that I could stand to drive it if the neighborhood could stand to see it. So I continued to park it in the place that, by now, I considered mine, and the neighborhood resigned itself to the spectacle. It received no further abuse, and eventually rain and other elements blended the remainder of the egg omelet into the color of the car so the desecration was hardly noticeable.

A problem relating to the conveyance's operation began to appear soon after I arrived in Baltimore. After it sat for a few days, it wouldn't start. I addressed the problem by parking on a downhill slope when possible, or by pushing it out into the city traffic, blocking other cars, and requiring their drivers to push my car until it started so they could proceed. The nonstarting Nash was a minor inconvenience most of the time, but occasionally it was a real embarrassment, especially when I wanted to impress my bride the first and only day of our honeymoon, by showing her the sights of Washington, DC. When we attempted to leave after visiting the Washington Monument, the rebellious heap would not start; Wilma and I are probably the only couple to have their car pushed around the Washington Monument on their honeymoon. My frustration continued throughout the day when it would not start at Arlington National Cemetery, at the Lincoln Monument, at the Tomb of the Unknown Soldier, or at any stop we made. If Wilma wondered what she was getting into with this guy she married, she never let it show.

I almost accepted this auto eccentricity as a permanent part of my life before deciding to tell Aunt Bess about it when we visited her in Cleveland in June 1956, on our way from Baltimore to my next assignment in Chicago. Aunt Bess speculated that the battery was old and weak, but I assured her I had bought a new battery when I purchased the car. Nevertheless, she wanted the battery tested. What she found begat a lot of jokes at my expense. I had purchased the cheapest and smallest battery manufactured for automobiles, too small for the Ambassador. She bought a new, properly sized battery, and the finicky machine never again had problems starting.

I graduated from the five-month challenging and exciting Counter Intelligence School on February 24, 1956, remained at the records facility in Baltimore until May 31, arrived in Chicago on June 2, and was stationed there at Fifth Army Headquarters until July 16. I was then transferred to Kansas City for my last year in the army.

By then something memorable, exciting, and new was on the horizon. Wilma was pregnant and expecting in late September. She experienced the usual trials and tribulations pregnant women have: morning sickness, cravings for pickles and ice cream, and mood swings. But the pregnancy was otherwise uneventful. In 1956 there was no way to predict the sex of the baby, so we waited with anticipation and excitement to learn if the blessed event would be a boy we would name Steven or a girl we would name Stephanie.

Getting Wilma to the hospital on time was a major concern. The Munson Army General Hospital at Fort Leavenworth, which afforded military members and their families free medical care, was across the state line in Kansas, forty miles away. Rush hour in Kansas City often reduced traffic to a snail's crawl. That posed a problem if the Nash wouldn't start or we were stuck in a line of cars on Main Street at just the wrong time. As it turned out, getting to the hospital was the least of our worries. When Wilma's labor began, the Nash did its job, and traffic seemed to part for us just as the Red Sea did for Moses. It was only after we reached the hospital that we were tested. Wilma, despite being two or three weeks past her predicted date of delivery, suffered through more than twenty-four hours of intense and painful labor with little relief.

At last, on October 11, 1956, the baby came, a girl, five pounds and twelve ounces, nineteen inches long, small but healthy in every way, voicing her own complaints, seemingly unmindful of the agony she had caused her mother or the anxiety she had caused her father. Stephanie Sue Strong took her place in our family, and all was right with the world.

All seemed well with my projected professional life. Being a CIC agent was not a full-time job in this era of peace, so I spent hours, perhaps more than I should, watching Kansas City's finest attorneys displaying their skills in the courtroom and visiting the city library, reading about modern, trend-setting trial lawyers. My favorite was Melvin Belli, the best-known personal-injury trial lawyer in the country. Belli was not without an ego, boasting that "there may be better lawyers than I, but so far I haven't come across any of them in court." He won more than six hundred million dollars in judgments in his lifetime and announced each victory by raising a Jolly Roger flag and firing a cannon from the roof of his office, which he claimed was once a brothel. To admirers, Belli was "King of Torts." To detractors, he was "Melvin Bellicose."

I wanted to meet this man and perhaps join his firm, even though he practiced in San Francisco, where I would be a fish out of water. I wrote him, and he responded, saying that he would be in Kansas City in a few weeks and would interview me. When the day for the interview came, I was dressed in my best suit and thought through all the things I should and shouldn't say to impress this lawyer for the rich and famous, as well as the poor and oppressed. The interview was anticlimactic. I was put off by Belli's arrogance and by the comments of one of his partners who told me in private that Belli was incorrigible and that no one in Belli's firm was ever more than his water boy. Perhaps the partner was correct; Belli was married six times and divorced five before his firm filed for bankruptcy in December 1995.

What about joining a Kansas City firm? I interviewed several but finally decided that even Kansas City was too big for me. I wanted to return to Springfield, where there were people like me, common folk who knew what a cow was, who could speak my language. I became homeward bound after July 12, 1957, when my army career came to an end. I received an honorable discharge and was transferred to the enlisted army reserve, eligible to be recalled to active duty until June 30, 1963.

6

Into the Maelstrom

I had made my decision to be a plaintiff's trial lawyer in Springfield, but there was little money in that part of the law at the time, and only one Springfield lawyer, "P", pretended to concentrate in that area. "P" was not held in high esteem by the lawyers in Mann, Mann, Walter, and Powell, where I had worked for two summers while in law school, and seemed unprepared when I saw him at a deposition or in the courtroom. I felt he could only teach me bad habits, so I never approached him for a job.

I liked all the lawyers in the six-person Mann firm and was flattered to be offered three hundred dollars a month, fifty dollars more than the going rate at the time. Bob Schroff had joined the firm while I was in the army, but the firm said I would come in with his pay and have seniority because of my work in the summers. The three-person Farrington and Curtis firm would match Mann's pay, and all of its attorneys were given "A" ratings by the prestigious legal directory, Martindale-Hubbell. I would choose between these two firms. But which one? In which firm would I have a better chance of becoming a plaintiff's trial lawyer? The Mann firm had three accomplished trial lawyers, Jack Powell, Wallace Walters, and Glenn Burkart. The Farrington and Curtis firm only one, E C Curtis (the only person I have ever known with only letters for a name), who was reputed to be a tough, demanding, accomplished defense lawyer. The "defense lawyer" part was not attractive, but the Mann-firm lawyers also were mostly on the defense side. E C could teach me a lot, and learning how insurance companies defended lawsuits would help me beat them when I represented injured clients against them. So the summer of 1957 found me as an employee of Farrington and Curtis.

With a family of three and a modest monthly income of three hundred dollars, we needed to be frugal. Our biggest expenditure was fifty dollars a month to lease a small, run-down house at 671 South Dollison Avenue (now John Q. Hammons Parkway), which had been abused for years. It had the essentials—indoor bathroom, electricity, and a telephone—and we still had our sometimes-functioning Nash. Here, in the very first month of my practice, I had met every financial goal I'd ever set for myself. I was living in the nicest house in which I had ever lived, was out of debt, and had a wife for a lifetime and a healthy baby daughter. I had the whole world in my hands. Not even Solomon in all his glory, with hundreds of wives and hundreds of concubines, had electricity, a telephone, and a Nash automobile. Now it was time to prove myself.

You have no enemies, you say?
Alas, my friend, the boast is poor;
He who has mingled in the fray
Of duty, that the brave endure,
Must have made foes! If you have none,
Small is the work that you have done.
You've hit no traitor on the hip,
You've dashed no cup from perjured lip,
You've never turned the wrong to right,
You've been a coward in the fight.[1]
I was determined to accept the challenge to dash the cup from

perjured lip, to change the wrong to right, to never be a coward. In short, I wanted to be the kind of lawyer that would have made Mother proud. I would have standards; I would also recognize that my client's case was the most important one in the world to me. I would recognize my importance in a trial. Later in my practice, when I was teaching at seminars, I would pose a riddle to the attorneys: what is not the judge, not a witness, never marked as an exhibit, and never admitted into evidence—yet is the most important component of any trial? After a silence, waiting for an answer that would never come, I would supply the answer: it is the lawyer. It is the lawyer's job to lift people up, not put them down; to be direct, not evasive; to clarify, not obfuscate; to be honest, not deceptive; to be sincere, not insincere. A lawyer should have the credibility of an affidavit.

Life is too short to take advantage of an injured client, so I would be fair when entering into a fee arrangement. In an appropriate case, I would work pro bono. Abraham Lincoln once was brought before his bar association for charging an "inadequate" fee when obtaining a guardianship for a disabled lady. In his defense, Lincoln said "the name of my firm is 'Lincoln and Herndon,' not 'Catch'em and Cheat'em.'" I would be like Lincoln in at least one respect: I would treat my clients fairly.

Life was different in 1957 when I began practice. Springfield, with 130 lawyers, only 3 of whom were women, and a population of 68,000 souls, was a small version of the present city, which has expanded to 165,000 residents and more than 850 attorneys. We all marvel at the changes that we have witnessed in our everyday lives over the past seven or eight decades, but few know that changes, just as drastic and revolutionary, have occurred in the practice of law. Let me take you back to what may seem to you to be the age of antiquity, the time I began my practice, the time when the practice of law bore little resemblance to that of the present day. When I entered the practice:

- A lawyer could be disbarred for the "unthinkable, degrading, despicable and unprofessional" act of advertising.

- Our firm, with five lawyers, was one of the larger ones in town, and everyone was supposed to be able to do everything from examining an abstract to writing a will to trying a lawsuit.

- Missouri followed the contributory negligence doctrine, which held that if an injured person was partly at fault for his own injuries, he received nothing. This oppressive doctrine could prohibit a pedestrian who received a permanent and devastating brain injury from recovering a single penny if he was hit by a drunk driver who had run a stoplight, just because the pedestrian was not in the crosswalk.

- The unconscionable doctrine of "remititur" (reducing the jury's verdict) was wielded as a sledgehammer by our trial and appellate courts in personal-injury cases. Thus, in 1964, when a jury returned a verdict of $270,000 to a 16-year-old boy rendered quadriplegic by the railroad's negligence, the Missouri Supreme Court said it was too much for a youngster with a life expectancy of 52.3 years, even though he would be paralyzed from the neck down for the rest of his life, and reduced his recovery to $220,000.[2] If the young man had suffered a single bedsore when he reached 35 years of age, his medical care for that one ailment alone would most likely have cost him more than the entire judgment the court had permitted him to recover.

- In the event a person was wrongfully killed by another in Missouri, the maximum recovery allowed to his or her dependents was $15,000. Thus, if a US president or an oil tycoon worth hundreds of millions of dollars had suffered the misfortune to be killed by the wrongful act of another in my state, the ridiculous and insulting sum of $15,000 was the most his dependents could have been awarded.

So, when I set out to be a "plaintiff's lawyer," it was impossible to obtain an adequate verdict for an injured client that would withstand appellate scrutiny or obtain justice for the family of a person wrongfully killed by another. Injured people almost never have money to pay a lawyer; they often cannot work because of their injuries and, as an additional insult, have monumental medical bills to pay. As a result, the lawyer must represent them on a contingent fee. It is the lawyer who must advance the expenses for the exhibits and the time of the doctors and other experts who testify and recover those expenses only if he or she wins the case. It is the contingent fee that gives the client "the key to the courthouse."

Why would any lawyer accept a case against Ford Motor Company in the 1960s, knowing that our Missouri courts would only allow a quadriplegic to recover a maximum of $220,000, a person stricken blind to recover no more than $125,000,[3] or a person sickened by a contaminated soft drink to receive no more than $250?[4] The law of averages said you would lose the case and be paid nothing for your sizable investment of time and money and be inadequately compensated even if you won. No wonder plaintiff's lawyers were reluctant to enter the field. They could be paid more doing something else.

Early in my career, the largest verdicts in some rural counties in Southwest Missouri had been in the range of $10,000 to $30,000. Perhaps this is why I was the only lawyer in my firm to try a plaintiff's personal-injury or wrongful-death case during the eighteen-plus years I was with Farrington, Curtis, and Strong. Fortunately, I had not become a plaintiff's lawyer to make money. I had grown up without it and was happy as a lark in the process. I became a plaintiff's lawyer because there were injustices that needed to be addressed.

Over a period of decades the above-mentioned inequities were eliminated, with the unfair doctrine of contributory negligence replaced by pure comparative fault in 1983,[5] and remititur being abolished in 1985.[6] I had entered the fray in the specialty's dark ages for the right reasons, but now many were flocking to the field just to make money.

During my eighteen years with Farrington, and Curtis (later Farrington, Curtis and Strong, and later Farrington, Curtis, Strong, Knauer, and Hart), there was almost no pretrial discovery (ways to learn what evidence your opponent would present or what witnesses he or she would call). Lawyers marched into the courtroom not knowing what arguments would be advanced, what exhibits would be offered, what witnesses would be presented, or what expert testimony would be elicited by their adversaries. It was trial by ambush, and it required an ability to anticipate the opponent's next move, a quick wit when faced with cross-examining a surprise witness, and a complete knowledge of the case. It was perfect training for the days to come when case preparation required dozens of depositions and endless discovery.

Just as everyone remembers his first love, a trial lawyer remembers his first trial. Mine came in February 1958, at age twenty-six, only seven months after joining Farrington and Curtis. Jack Powell, with the law firm of Mann, Mann, Walter, and Powell, the firm for whom I had worked in the summers while attending law school, came to E C Curtis with a request. Jack represented an insurance company that insured a trucking company. A company driver, John Bennett, had crashed head-on into an approaching vehicle, injuring its occupants, on a narrow bridge near Halltown. Each driver claimed the other was across the center line. As part of his defense strategy, Jack had filed a counterclaim for Bennett, claiming a chronic back sprain. Now, having failed to settle the claims of the injured car occupants, the trial was scheduled to begin on Monday, just three days away. Jack had a problem. It might be a conflict of interest for him to both defend Bennett, where he would represent the interest of the insurance company, and prosecute Bennett's claim for injury, where he would represent Bennett. Jack asked E C if I could enter my appearance for Bennett and sit at the counsel table with him. I wouldn't have to do anything of significance, mainly just be there. E C said fine. Wow! I was going to try my first case, even if it was a small one, and I would have a small role in it.

I was nervous and excited when I reported to the courtroom an hour before trial on Monday. Soon Jack and Milt Kirby, the opposing attorney, were there and began talking in hushed tones in the back of the courtroom. When federal judge Jasper Smith arrived, Milt said he and Jack were talking settlement and requested a little time to see if a trial could be avoided. Settlement! Why wasn't I involved? My client, Bennett, had a claim. Now I was really nervous. What if Jack and Milt reached a settlement and left me hanging with a case I was unprepared to try? That almost happened. Jack and Milt did settle, but Jack said he would stay and help me. Fortunately, the case was a simple one, and by the end of the day, we had picked a jury, made opening statements, and presented all of our evidence. The only excitement in the case came when Milt asked for an exhibit, which was on the floor at the far end of the courtroom. "I'll get it," said Bennett, before I could put my hand on his arm and whisper for him to sit down. The exhibit weighed at least fifty pounds, and we had told the jury that Bennett had a chronically bad back. What would it do to our credibility and his case if he lifted and carried a heavy exhibit several feet in full view of the jury? I am not sure if the jury heard Bennett's offer or noticed him rise halfway from his chair before I admonished him, but he did sit down. At last, the evidence was in, and the jury was told to return for final arguments the next day. Judge Smith gave each side twenty minutes to argue his case. Jack and I would divide our time. I would take the first ten minutes or so, Milt would argue for twenty minutes, and Jack would close.

There was little sleep for me that night. I wrote only a few key words on a sheet of paper, but refined my plea over and over in my mind, as I constructed what I believed was a compelling argument. The jury has to be unanimous in order to reach a verdict in federal court, and they did. They awarded John Bennett twenty-four hundred dollars for his sore back, a verdict three times its true value, said Judge Smith, who, nevertheless, did not reduce the award. I had won my first case. All of the dreams of my youth and the preparation to become a trial lawyer had paid off, I thought. Jack told E C that I had done a good job and paid him five hundred dollars for my services, two hundred more than my monthly income. Although I would try scores of cases, some lasting several weeks, the nerves, apprehension, excitement, inability to sleep, and thrill of combat, which I felt in the Bennett case, never completely left me. I just became more used to them and controlled them better. What I could not control were my recurring dreams of being unprepared, late for court, or incompetent in every conceivable way.

After Bennett, other cases would come by the dozens. One involved my only criminal trial. It occurred in a period when public defenders did not exist. Instead, judges appointed attorneys to represent those who could not afford to hire one. It was in this way that in the second year of my practice, I was called upon to represent a defendant with a long criminal record in a serious felony case. A codefendant was going to confess to his part in the robbery and say that my client, Chester, was his accomplice. I could not put Chester on the stand in his own defense because that would allow the prosecution to reveal his impressive criminal past. It seemed a forgone conclusion that Chester would be convicted. Perhaps that is why the judge had appointed a still wet-behind-the-ears attorney to represent him. Why waste the time of a more accomplished lawyer in an unwinnable case? Chester was bound for prison regardless of who represented him.

I began by pondering not only how I could cross-examine Chester's tormentor and alleged coconspirator, but also how I could humanize my client. He had no one to mourn for him, no one who cared. I wanted someone to be in the courtroom to at least show the jury that there was someone, one soul somewhere, who loved this lost human, who needed him and did not want him to go to prison. Chester had a divorced wife who hated his guts and a four-year-old son, Alfred. Well, if there was no one else, the son would have to do.

I met the boy, a cute little African American child whose African American father would be tried by an all-white jury in a still largely segregated county. I bought the boy a nice white suit, with short pants and white shoes. He was clean and shiny from head to toe from the moment the trial began and until it was over. It was little Alfred's job to sit quietly in the back of the courtroom during the trial so the jury would know that someone loved and needed Chester.

In those days, the jury had to walk through the courtroom behind the lawyers and clients in order to leave the room when a recess was announced. Alfred was an example of perfect deportment during the proceedings, but when a recess was called, he would run to our table and throw his arms around his father, in full view of the departing jury. He was cuteness personified, and the ladies on the jury were taken with him. The prosecutor asked the judge to instruct the boy to remain in his seat until the jury had left the room, and the judge did so, but at the next recess the child again ran to his father. The prosecutor protested and moved the court to order the child out of the room. What was the judge to do? Chester had a constitutional right to be in the room and hear the evidence against him, and there was no one else who could be with Alfred outside. The judge said he could not make Alfred stay in the hallway with no supervision, so the trial continued with Alfred inside, quiet as a mouse and perfectly behaved during the proceedings, but rushing to his father at each recess.

I had destroyed the prosecution's main witness on cross-examination, the admitted burglar who claimed Chester was his accomplice, and we might have won the case even without Alfred's help, but I could not take that chance. After the jury had returned a verdict of not guilty, the prosecutor angrily accused me of choreographing the scenario with the child. "Maybe I did and maybe I didn't. You guess. And so what if I did?" I responded.

I was an advocate, not a token lawyer to be steamrolled by the prosecution, and it was my duty as a trial lawyer to use all legitimate means to represent my client. Having Chester's future in my hands was an awesome responsibility, and I could leave no justifiable stone unturned in his defense. Not only was the evidence stacked against Chester, but prejudicial assumptions that had nothing to do with the evidence also aided the prosecution. Some believe if the state charges a defendant with a crime, he probably is guilty. Why would a prosecutor, elected to keep the community safe from criminals, prosecute an innocent person? Chester had an additional problem. This was 1959, when African American men and women could not eat in most of the city's restaurants or attend "white" churches or some movies and sporting events and were considered lazy, dishonest, and not as intelligent as Caucasians. Governor Orval Faubus, in my neighboring state of Arkansas, was considered a hero by many Springfieldians for resisting efforts to integrate

Little Rock schools. Blacks were different, supposedly inferior, and more prone to crime that whites. Prejudice against blacks was an unfortunate but real fact in my town.

It was my job as Chester's lawyer not only to expose the weakness of the prosecutor's evidence and the initial assumption that he would not have been charged unless he was guilty, particularly if he did not testify in his own defense, but to overcome the built-in prejudice against him because of his race. Chester was not being tried by a jury of his peers, but by one that did not consider him to be a peer. Most of the jury had never associated with African Americans and entered the jury box thinking that Chester embodied all the pernicious traits they believed were endemic to his race. I could not afford to allow him to appear as a lone, lonely, and unloved creature before this all-Caucasian jury. He was as much of a human being as any of them. I had to impress upon them that they were not judging some subhuman creature, but a person with the same needs, goals, and dreams as they. When I brought cute little Alfred, who adored his father, into the courtroom, I did not deceive the jury or misrepresent a fact. All I did was attempt to neutralize some hidden, perhaps unknown or unacknowledged prejudices. I could not have done less with a clear conscience.

An example of a civil "trial by ambush" took place in 1971. On November 18, 1970, George Easterly, a forty-three-year-old lathing foreman, had been helping build the Plaza Towers, a ten-story building located at the intersection of Sunshine Street and Glenstone Avenue in Springfield. The first eight floors of concrete superstructure were completed, and George was putting in wooden partitions on the fourth floor.

A material hoist was located on the south side of the building, which carried materials to the various subcontractors, including George's crew. Although workmen were not supposed to ride the hoist, on the morning of his injury, George noticed that one of the lathers was doing just that. He went to the hoist, placed his left hand on the hoist's tower to steady himself, and waited for the hoist to reach him so he could reprimand the passenger. As the hoist was nearing George, exposed rollers on the hoist-tower framework rolled over the fingers of his left hand, requiring amputation.

This proved to be a tough case to win because, in the first place, the law at that time required that I prove that Mayco, the hoist manufacturer, was negligent and that it failed to use the degree of care that a careful manufacturer would use when it produced the hoist. My theory was that there should have been a guard to prevent the roller from inflicting an injury such as George's, but how could this manufacturer be negligent when no hoists were made with guards for the rollers? Wasn't Mayco acting as "an ordinarily careful manufacturer" when it made its hoists in the same way its competitors did? The second major problem was Missouri's law that provided that George could not recover anything if he was partly at fault for his own injury. His negligence, however slight, in putting his hand on the hoist's frame and failing to see the roller as it approached would completely bar his recovery. Indeed, Mayco asserted that it had produced a state-of-the-art hoist, and George was the author of his own injury by not being a careful workman. It offered nothing to settle the case.

My evidence went in well, as I knew it would, having grilled all of my witnesses until they could withstand any cross-examination that might be thrown at them. Now came crunch time, Mayco's evidence, when I would be called on to destroy its experts. Under Missouri law at that time, I had no way to learn who those experts might be or the specifics of what they might say. But I was not without hope.

Experts tend to assume that their lies will never be discovered, particularly if the opposing lawyer has no advance knowledge of them. Self-confident, they appear on the stand as white knights to expose the shortcomings of a plaintiff's case. Bryant, one of

Mayco's experts, began his testimony by informing the jury of his impressive education and credentials, including the fact that he was listed in *Who's Who in America*. But there was something about a shift in his eyes and an almost unnoticeable fidget in his chair as he was talking that made me wonder if he was all he claimed to be. Upon returning to my office after court had recessed for the day, I checked my copy of *Who's Who*, only to find that he was not listed.

The next day the jury hung on his every word, impressed, as he finished his direct examination, explaining how Mayco was a conscientious manufacturer, meticulous in keeping up with the latest safety procedures, reading safety journals, making sure no competitor had any safety device it did not have, and how the rollers were open and obvious, impossible for a careful workman not to see. When he finished, it was my turn to cross-examine, and there was no doubt that my case hung in the balance. If I could not remove his facade of credibility, I might as well go home. I began my questioning slowly, pleasantly, calmly. It would not do for me to shove the *Who's Who* book in front of him and accuse him of lying. While it might prove the fact, I would be risking the possibility of a plausible explanation and, in any event, would look like a "typical lawyer" browbeating a witness. Furthermore, even if I were successful in showing that his name was not in the book, the issue might be addressed and over in less than a minute. I needed to make this a major chink in his testimony, his weak underbelly, the blow that would sink his ship. I had to show that the witness was a premeditated prevaricator while not looking like an overbearing lawyer in the process.

I politely handed him the book and explained that I, like he, had been selected to appear in the prestigious publication and, wanting to learn more about him, had unsuccessfully attempted to find his name. I asked for his help and waited patiently as he fumbled, looked embarrassed, and after what seemed like an eternity said he must have been inadvertently omitted from the latest volume.

"I thought there might be a simple explanation, but I can't find your name in this book, either," I said sympathetically, as I handed him the volume for the previous year. Again, more fumbling and fuming while the jury started to sit straighter and look at the witness with an ounce of suspicion. For the first time, the witness appeared a little unsettled and explained that he had not checked the publication for a couple of years, but I definitely could have found him if I had gone back three years. In an almost apologetic way, I produced the third volume. Again unable to find his name, he assured the jury that he had been selected to *Who's Who* and could not explain why he was not in the last three volumes.

The scenario was playing out just as I had hoped. The jury was starting to show its disenchantment with this expert who had gained their confidence and trust. Juries do not like to be lied to, as this witness was about to learn. Now I could produce the twenty volumes of *Who's Who* that I had checked out of the library and ask the witness to find his name in any of them, without fear of antagonizing the jury. Now I was their friend, their alter ego, acting as their spokesman in uncovering this purposeful deceit. The witness was caught and knew it. He started to look through one of the publications, but it was clear to everyone that it would be a useless exercise. He had never been selected to be in *Who's Who,* which he and everyone in the courtroom knew by now, so he admitted that he had just been trying to "pad his résumé."

I now had softened Bryant up, and the jury was waiting to see if there was anything else about him it should know. Just as I expected, Bryant was a fighter, a bright man with a string of college degrees, and he did not like being embarrassed. He needed to regroup, regain control, and rehabilitate himself, and I would "help" him in that endeavor by showing how thoroughly he had studied the manufacture and operation of hoists. "Mr. Bryant, I assume you inventoried how hoists in Springfield are made and used, not just in other places," I began. "Absolutely. I drove to several building sites in town yesterday and saw that none of them had guards for their rollers. The workmen using the hoists were using them properly, unlike George, well aware of the open and obvious danger of the rollers," he volunteered. So far, so good. Expert witnesses are inclined to talk too much, all too often telling more that they know. It is a congenital weakness of experts, and I was about to take advantage of it. "I suppose, then, you saw this hoist at St. John's Hospital," I continued, showing him a picture of the hoist taken from the street. "Yes, I did, and you will notice, even from this distance, that there is no guard on the roller," he replied. "And did you notice the workmen using the hoist?" I inquired innocently. "Of course," he said. "I watched them for several minutes as the hoist went up and down. Unlike your client, none of them were so inattentive as to put their hand on the frame while the hoist was moving." Bryant was feeling pretty good again, regaining his confidence, feeling that he was climbing out of the pit he had dug for himself with his *Who's Who* faux pas.

Again, it was time to pounce. The jury still had faith in me, thinking that I was not wasting their time for no purpose by letting Bryant repeat all the damaging testimony he had given on direct examination. Out came a second picture, this one a close-up of the hoist, showing a completely built bird's nest on top of the roller, obviously nestled there for a substantial period of time. The hoist could not have traveled up and down only two days before, as Bryant had just testified. He had lied again, unnecessarily, for no good reason. In a sense, Bryant's falsehoods were rather small and had nothing to do with the soundness of his opinions. It was an unassailable fact that Mayco's hoists were like all the others in the country and that George, in a sense, was at least partially responsible for his own misfortune. But Mayco had offered a witness who was willing to lie for the money Mayco paid him. Mayco called another expert, not much more impressive than Bryant, but that is another story, too long to include here. At the close of the evidence, the odds were that I would win a verdict. My opposing lawyer said he had never seen a case begin as a rose and turn to "shit" so fast.

Yours truly, early in my practice.

(Top) The "George Easterly" hoist. The roller that injured George is circled.

(Bottom) George Easterly, showing his position when he was injured.

In my final argument, I suggested that when a person gets sick after eating a bowl of stew, he doesn't have to guess whether it was the peas, carrots, beef, or potatoes that made him sick. He doesn't have to guess that some of the stew is good and eat that portion. The only way he can be sure not to become even sicker is by throwing out the entire bowl. In a like way, when witnesses tell premeditated, bald-faced lies, the jury need not ponder whether anything they said was worth digesting; the only way they can be sure not to be further deceived is by throwing out all of their testimony. The jury did just that.

Unlike the Easterly case, which garnered no publicity, I participated in two cases against labor unions arising out of strikes in 1969 and 1970 that made front-page headlines. I was not an-tiunion and believed in the right to strike. But neither management nor unions are above the law, and negotiations sometimes go awry when overzealous participants forget that strikes must be peaceful.

On a cold, dreary day in February 1969, Brian, an employee at the Royal McBee Typewriter Company in Springfield, attended a meeting of his union, the Allied Industrial Workers of America. The local president told the group that since the company had failed to meet their demands, a strike date had been set for February 22. The president's talk was about twenty minutes long, but the gist of it was this: "There are not two sides to this dispute. McBee is unwilling to pay us a fair wage, and we are not going to be treated like slaves." The president's voice swelled with anger at the insulting and condescending attitude of the company. He then challenged his members: "It is necessary that we are united, that we all walk out and stay out. McBee will try to break our strike by tempting enough of us to cross our picket lines to keep the plant open. If we stand up to them and they have a vacant, unproductive plant, they will knuckle under in a few days. It's going to take courage, but if we hang together, we can win." A vote was taken to strike or not to strike. The workers were fired up by the talk and ready to take on the tyrant. They would teach McBee a thing or two. Ballots were passed out, and the vote was unanimous—everyone, including Brian, voted to strike.

Then, as Brian drove home, his emotions began to cool. He pondered what he would say to his wife, Edith, and, more important, how he would make the next mortgage and car payment and support a wife and ten-year-old son without a paycheck. It was not a pleasant evening at Brian's house, even though everything the union leader had said was true. McBee must be convinced that it could not manipulate its employees like pieces or a chessboard. Bright and early on the morning of February 22, Brian was among the first to arrive at the picket line. He was there again on the next day and for a few days after that, but on March 1, his mortgage payment was due and he had no money. Other employees had crossed the line, and McBee had hired nonunion workers to take the place of strikers. It looked to Brian as if the strike might fail. At the very least, it would be a long strike, too long for him and his family to survive. With no prospect for employment, Brian crossed the picket line on March 3.

There was a bloodred-colored sign hung on the wall of union headquarters with the heading in large, capital letters: "REMEMBER OUR SCABS." Below the heading, also bloodred in color in smaller letters, were the names and department numbers of union members who had crossed the line to work. The twenty-ninth name on the list was "Brian (last name), Dept. 37." Brian was not well received by his former coworkers as he crossed the picket lines each workday. They threatened him and threw things at his car. Brian felt like a traitor, but his first responsibility was to his family.

Then came the evening of March 25. The strike had lasted more than a month, straining the composure of both sides. The union was determined to bring the company to the bargaining table, while the company limped along with former and new workers willing to ignore the strike. That fateful night, two of Brian's former acquaintances and coworkers at the plant, Earl and Dewayne, went to a bar for a drink to numb their pain. The strike was taking its toll on them, and their thoughts turned to the traitors who had crossed the lines. One of them, Brian, was their neighbor who had no more excuse for crossing the line than they. He could have found work elsewhere if he had tried, or borrowed money from a relative or asked his church for help. They would warn him of worse things that could happen if he didn't wise up. Earl and Dewayne developed a plan. They would drive by Brian's home at about eleven o'clock and shoot into his garage. Brian's family would be asleep. No one would be hurt, but he would get the point and stop crossing the line.

The street was vacant and the night dark, so there was little chance of being seen as Dewayne drove slowly past Brian's home. Earl shot into the garage, as planned. Then Dewayne gunned the car to get out of the neighborhood as quickly as possible. Perhaps it was the acceleration of the vehicle, as Earl claimed, or an intentional act to emphasize the point, but a second shot was fired, this time with near-fatal results. The bullet went through the wall of Brian's house and pierced the skull of Malcolm, Brian's ten-year-old son, who was sleeping in his bed. Malcolm lived, but the bullet, deeply imbedded in his brain, could not be removed.

It was not hard for the police to find who had fired the potentially fatal shots. Not knowing the disastrous consequences of their escapade, Earl and Dewayne had bragged to fellow picketers the next morning that they probably had scared Brian enough to keep him from coming to work.

Brian asked if I would sue Earl for Malcolm's injury. "That would do no good. You can't get blood out of a turnip," I confessed, "but I will investigate and see if anything can be done."

Earl poured out his story to me when I saw him at the Greene County jail. He was facing a felony charge and felt he had been a victim of union propaganda. The union leaders had become more and more desperate with each passing week. The picket line was not working, they said.

Members needed to be more physical; a good beating or bloody nose might help persuade some vacillating worker to stay at home. Maybe even a good, strong threat would be enough. Earl was doing just what the union wanted him to do, he contended. He had always been a good citizen and would not have conceived the idea or had the courage to carry out the evil deed without prompting. It was not an ironclad case by any means, but Earl's testimony was enough to justify a suit alleging that Earl was acting as an agent for the union when he fired the shot.

By the time our case went to trial in January 1970, the Royal McBee Typewriter Company had closed its Springfield plant, a victim of the strike. As a result, the local became defunct, and more than a hundred Springfieldians were out of work. The first week of the trial went well. Everyone on the jury knew about the strike and its aftermath from the newspapers and television. The strike was to blame for Springfield losing an industry and jobs and undoubtedly for Malcolm's devastating injury. They were receptive to my opening statement and witnesses, hungry for the time the case was over and they could render a verdict. When I arrived at the courthouse on Monday, the second week of trial, I had every reason to be confident and optimistic. I should have known better; Murphy's Law is universal and omnipotent. Before the jury was called into the courtroom, the trial judge met with the attorneys in his office. "I am going to declare a mistrial on my own motion," he said. "I am not going to give a reason, so don't ask. Just go home." A mistrial! With no reason? What was going on? I have never learned what was in the judge's mind, but there is no recourse when a judge orders a mistrial, so we had no choice but to regroup.

We wanted a retrial soon, but the union never wanted to see us again. Finally, when we obtained a setting for September 11, 1972, two and a half years later, our best witness, Earl, was no longer friendly. The first time he was motivated to help; he might get a lighter sentence if he could blame his troubles on the union. Now, with his three-year sentence for mayhem determined, he had nothing to gain by assisting us. He would be a reluctant witness at best. So the two parties—the union who did not want a trial before an antagonistic jury, and we who were without a cooperative witness—settled the case. It was an unsatisfactory result for both sides, a defeat for the union and a less than optimal recovery for a completely innocent child, sentenced to live with a bullet in his brain. There is a lesson to be learned from Malcolm's case, one the union missed: a worthwhile endeavor is worthwhile only if people play by the rules.

Audacity, innovation, and new legal theories are as important for the trial lawyer as is the ability to persuade the jury. Time and again I successfully asserted new theories of law that not only brought redress for my client, but advanced American jurisprudence as well. One example arose out of my second case against a union. On September 14, 1970, Teamsters Union Local 823 struck the Tri-State Transit Company in Joplin, Missouri. Sixteen days later, Bob Shuler, a member of 823, after consuming substantial quantities of liquor, shot a rifle at a Tri-State truck driven by John Galt, a "scab" driver who had crossed the picket line. The eighteen-wheeler was carrying twenty tons of dynamite, which the rifle bullet somehow detonated. The explosion caused a crater in the highway thirty-five feet deep, destroyed nearby buildings, broke windows fifteen miles away, disintegrated the truck to such an extent that only a few small fragments could be found, and left no trace of Galt's remains. The next morning a helicopter search found Shuler, whose car had been rendered inoperable by the explosion, and his union companion hiding out in the nearby woods.

John Merritt, an Oklahoma City attorney who had heard of my recent case for Malcolm, referred Nadine, Galt's recently married widow, to me. Merritt wondered if anything could be done. Shuler was in jail and certainly headed for an extended term in prison. Suing him would be a waste of time. I told Merritt I would look into the case. Perhaps we could sue the union on the theory that it, by word or action, had encouraged strikers to stop "scabs" from operating Tri-State's trucks. If things worked out, we would file a wrongful-death action for Nadine.

Every obstacle seemed against us from the start. Nadine knew little about her recently acquired husband and nothing at all about his relatives or friends. Consequently, tracing his past led us to one dead end after another. There was even doubt that "John Galt" was his real name. He had told Nadine that he once read a novel titled *Atlas Shrugged,* whose main character was named John Galt. The fictional Galt was his kind of hero, so he appropriated "John Galt" as his own name. Why he wanted or needed to conceal his past by assuming a new identity was a mystery to Nadine. There also was a disturbing rumor circulating at Tri-State, probably based on Galt's own admission or boast, that he had been married nine times but divorced only three times. Was Nadine even his legal widow? Then there was the union's assertion to the media that it had urged a peaceful strike and that the shooting was the result of a drunk's irresponsible action, which was contrary to union mandates. Even if we won, the statutory recovery for wrongful death in Missouri was still a maximum of fifty thousand dollars. Despite the obstacles, I told Merritt that I would see if anything could be done. Nadine needed a lawyer, and if I did not help her, who would?

The key to whether I had a viable case depended on whether Shuler was acting as a puppet for the union. If Shuler had just gotten liquored up and, on an impulse, grabbed a gun and shot at the Tri-State truck, I had no case. But the impulse scenario seemed unlikely. The crime seemed too well planned to be a random act of violence by a drunk. Shuler had taken a position on an overpass of Interstate 44, where he could steady his rifle on the railing and have an unobstructed view into the cab of an oncoming truck. A person staked out with a weapon on an overpass for very long would draw attention from passers-by, so Shuler needed someone to tell him when a "scab"-driven truck was leaving Tri-State. If Shuler had been waiting at a nearby phone and received such a call, he could calculate within minutes when the rig would be approaching the critical overpass. Still, it would be nearly impossible to identify a Tri-State rig as it approached head-on at night, so Shuler needed someone at the side of the highway to signal him—perhaps with a flashlight—when the truck was within range of Shuler's rifle. This must have been the assignment of the fellow union member, I thought. If I was right, there were three people directly involved—the man who phoned Shuler when the rig left Tri-State, the "flashlight" man, and Shuler—and probably more at 823 who had written the script for the cowardly, despicable act. All of this was speculation, of course, but if I was right, Shuler's intoxication served only to provide courage to carry out the malevolent act others had planned.

I visited Shuler at the local jail to see what he would be willing to tell me. I disclosed who I represented and said that I had learned he had always been an upright, hardworking citizen who had never been in trouble before. Surely, he would not have done such a dastardly act unless encouraged by the union. Shuler, meek, contrite, nervous, and evasive, seemed to have a conscience. When we began to discuss the union's role in the events of that fateful evening, he avoided eye contact, but admitted that the idea was not solely his. Now it was time to test my theory. "Bob," I said, "I know you don't want to admit what happened that night, so *I will tell you what happened.*" I watched Shuler closely as I recited my theory of the events of that nefarious evening. Eureka! He did not admit I was right, but neither did he deny it. More important, I could tell by the way he fidgeted in his chair and dropped his head that my hypotheses were right on target. I had a case!

Now, I needed to file suit as soon a possible, take the depositions of every 823 union member, and subpoena letters, memos, and records before evidence was destroyed and union members could not be found. Some honest members, perhaps friends of Shuler, when placed under oath, would not commit perjury in order to protect a union responsible for a man's death.

Even if I had a case, did it have any value? If Galt was a worthless drifter or an escaped felon with no saving qualities, perhaps Nadine was better off without him. We knew one thing no one could dispute: Galt was attempting to earn a living for Nadine and himself, even if it meant crossing a union picket line. Furthermore, the mere fact that he had read *Atlas Shrugged*, the 1168-page magnum opus of Ayn Rand, set him apart from most truck drivers. John Galt, the fictitious hero in the book who reconstructed a society that celebrated individual achievement, gave a 70-page speech in the original edition, proclaiming that "no rights can exist without the right to translate one's rights into reality—to think, to work and to keep the results." If our John Galt was so impressed by the fictional John Galt that he appropriated his name, surely he could not be all bad. What about the rumor that Galt had been married so many times and divorced so few? We could sort that out and learn at a later time about his life before he became "John Galt." Now, time was of the essence. We had to file Nadine's wrongful-death suit immediately.

Depositions and document discovery, which could be obtained only after filing suit, had to be procured before they became unavailable or destroyed. If they supported me, great. If they didn't, all I would lose would be my time and a few dollars.

The statutory limit of fifty thousand dollars for the wrongful death of any human seemed to be a paltry sum, particularly when horrific malfeasance had been committed. There should be redress commensurate to the wrong. In one of my nearly sleepless nights, an idea came to me. We would sue for Nadine under the wrongful-death act and win the fifty thousand dollars allowed by the statute. We also would file a second suit. When a person dies, he or she leaves an estate as well as a spouse. Creditors of the estate can sue the estate for debts owed, and the estate can sue debtors who are indebted to the estate. Galt had an estate: the clothes he was wearing, a pocketbook, some money, and perhaps even a watch. We would file suit in the name of Greene County's public administrator, Robert J. Smith, for Galt's estate, which the explosion had destroyed. We would claim Galt's personal property was worth one hundred dollars and also seek punitive damages because of the union's asserted wanton misconduct.[7]

Labor unions are represented by big-city lawyers with long records of success in court. Local 823 and the International Brotherhood of Teamsters, Local 823's parent, whom we named in our suit, were no exception. Two Washington, DC, firms—Morin, Dickstein, Shapiro & Gallagan, and Williams, Connolly & Califano—defended the case along with a Joplin attorney and two Springfield firms. This armada of opponents lost no time in filing a motion to toss my case out of court, and Judge Douglas Greene did just that, finding that my claim was an attempt to circumvent Missouri's Wrongful Death Act. I had expected as much and sought relief from the Missouri Supreme Court. Although my theory was novel, it was based on sound legal principals. In finding for us, the Supreme Court held:

The property damage action is not a ruse but a valid cause of action. In this case, a single set of facts gave rise to two separate and distinct causes of action, one for John Galt's wrongful death, which vests in those persons specified in the statute and which is not subject to his creditors, and another for the destruction of his personal property, which is for the benefit of his estate and is subject to his creditors.

The union's next line of defense, that punitive damages should not be allowed, was found to be equally without merit:

> Respondent also contends that allowance of punitive damages would circumvent the limitation on wrongful death recoveries, and be a double award....The circumvention theory does not stand up in light of our earlier finding that two separate and distinct causes of action exist....
>
> Finally, it is said we are threatened with a flood of litigation if we allow punitive damages in this case since every victim in a wrongful death action would be wearing clothing. We doubt any such result....In the vast majority of cases nothing close to the standard necessary to recover punitive damages will be met.[8]

We won! Hallelujah! The trial judge could no longer throw us out of court. Our legal theory had been blessed by the supreme court, and I was convinced that depositions of union members would confirm the union's complicity in the sordid affair. Our actual damages were limited to a maximum of fifty thousand dollars for Galt's wrongful death, but there were no arbitrary limits on his estate's claim for punitive damages. I had received phone calls threatening my life if I continued to prosecute the case, strong indications the union feared what I might discover. If it had nothing to hide, why was it paranoid? And if the Local 823 was taking orders from the International Brotherhood, the latter would also be quaking in its proverbial boots. When the unions resisted our attempts to take depositions, opposed our motions for records, and wanted to settle, I knew my suspicions had been well grounded. Both the local and the international were up to their ears in guilt. The case settled less than three months after the supreme court's ruling for what we believed was the largest punitive-damage recovery in Missouri's history.

Only twice in my career was I unable to obtain a recovery for my client, either by settlement or by jury verdict. The first such case was just seven years into my practice. My client was Sara, a short, middle-aged, plump widow who was looking for a house to rent. Because of her meager income, she was being shown a small, older one-bedroom house in a poorer part of town. During her inspection, Sara opened the door into a dark area and took a step inside. It was the stairway into the partial basement. Sara tumbled down the stairs. Fortunately, she suffered no broken bones, but the muscles in her back and neck were strained and sprained. She deserved representation, and I was the one who could provide it, I thought. We had some good arguments to make. The lady showing Sara the house should have warned her of the stairway, there should have been a landing so that the first step would not precipitate an injury, and the stairway light should have been turned on before Sara's visit. But the short trial of two days occurred in an era when contributory negligence was a complete defense. If Sara was even partly responsible for her own injury, she could recover nothing. In final argument the defense attorney argued that Sara should have watched where she was walking. If she was in a place strange to her and could not see the floor, she should not blithely have stepped into the unknown. He took a sheet of paper and tore off a corner no bigger than the eraser end of a pencil and told the jury that if Sara was even "this much at fault, compared to the entire page," she should lose. The jury agreed and turned Sara away.

In the forty-six years since I lost Sara's case, I have relived every aspect of it many times. I have rationalized that her injuries were not serious, and in all likelihood she made a full and complete recovery. But after all was said and done, there was no escape from the fact that I had lost her case. I had been unable to deal with the defenses and especially with the argument that Sara was partly at fault. No amount of rationalizing has helped to ease the pain of that defeat.

I enjoyed a change of pace in the spring of 1970, when Bill Thomas, Missouri State University's basketball coach, asked if I would represent Curtis Perry in his professional basketball contract negotiations. Perry was listed on the roster as a six-foot-seven, 220-pound forward, although, stretch as he might when he registered for the military draft, he could reach only six feet, five and 15/16 inches. He desperately wanted to be six feet, six inches, thus too tall for Uncle Sam's army. Still, Perry could leap out of the gym. He still holds the record as the leading rebounder in our school's history and currently its second leading scorer. Perry had been picked in the third round of the draft by the San Diego Rockets of the National Basketball Association (NBA) and the Virginia Squires of the American Basketball Association (ABA). Perry had no agent, and Thomas thought Perry did not need one, assuming I would represent him without charge. Perry, as the thirty-fifth pick overall and wooed by both the ABA and NBA, had a bargaining chip or two, according to Thomas. The recently founded ABA was seeking to attract talent in order to force a merger with its more established rival.[9] The trick would be to get the best possible deal by pitting the two teams against each other.

Our first visit was to the San Diego Rockets of the NBA. Arrangements were made for us to fly into the LAX Airport in Los Angeles, where we would meet Sam, a Rockets employee, and drive to San Diego and be interviewed by first-year coach Alex Hannum. We arrived on schedule, picked up our luggage, and looked around the gargantuan area to find the exit. At that moment, a man in a suit and tie approached and asked, "Are you

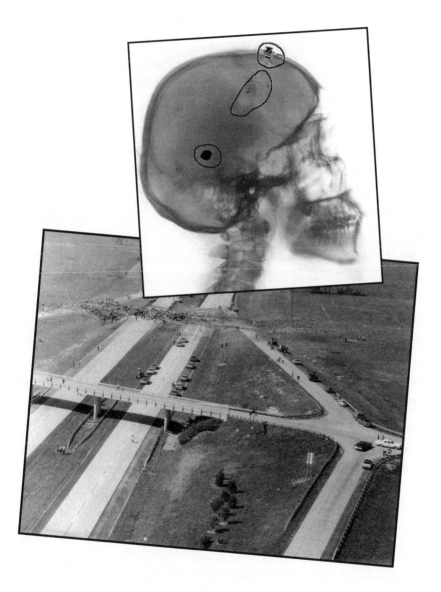

(Top) In 1969, a union member shot into the home of a "scab." The bullet pierced the house wall and lodged in the brain of a young boy, my client. We sued the union.

(Bottom) This is the scene of the crime that gave rise to the case of *State ex rel. Smith v. Greene.*

Mr. Strong and Mr. Perry?" I replied in the affirmative as we left to find his car. As we followed Sam, Curtis could not contain his curiosity. "Among these thousands of people, how did he know who we were?" he whispered to me. "Well, Curtis, look around. How many short, white guys do you see with a big, tall black guy? It didn't take a genius," I said.

On the flight, we had rehearsed our roles for our interview with Hannum. I would do the talking, and Curtis would be emotionless. "At some point, Hannum will talk money, and you must remember to show neither approval or disappointment. Above all, don't say a word," I lectured. Three times we played out the scenario of how we thought the discussion with Hannum might go. Finally, we were ready. When we were ushered into the impressive trophy-filled office, Hannum and two assistants were waiting for us. Hannum, at age forty-seven, was still an impressive figure at six-feet, seven inches and 210 pounds, the same size as when he played forward-center for twelve years in the NBA. Hannum began the conversation with the expected small talk, telling Curtis he had watched him play and was impressed. Then came some questions. "Can you palm a basketball?" Hannum inquired. "Sure can," came the response. The answer was true in a sense, but not true in another. Curtis had extremely long hands that could rap around the ball, but his thumb was so close to his wrist that he could not use it to grip the ball. "How tall are you?" was the next question. "About six-eight or six-nine," Curtis lied. "Stand up," commanded Hannum. Curtis and Hannum stood side by side, and it was obvious that Hannum was slightly taller; Curtis was nowhere near six-eight. "Now raise your hand straight up in the air next to mine." Curtis and Hannum, still side by side, raised their arms with their hands touching. The tip of Hannum's fingers could barely reach above Curtis's wrist. Curtis, with his long arms, could reach a full six inches higher than Hannum. Hannum seemed pleased.

"Take a seat and relax," the coach said. I knew what was coming next; it was contract time. This is when I would earn my nonexistent pay. We discussed whether the contract should be for one or three years and the advantages of each. Finally, Hannum said, "We will give you a three-year contract at [so many] dollars per year." Curtis grabbed a pen from his pocket and began calculating what his income would be for three years. So much for all the time we had spent on Curtis remaining emotionless! The cat was out of the bag. Hannum knew by Curtis's reaction that he had caught his fish. The contract was signed. We never interviewed with the Virginia Squires.

Back home, Curtis was a celebrity. "How much will you be paid?" a reporter asked. "More than a newspaper reporter, but not as much as the president" was Curtis's reply. Good for Curtis. He handled the question just right. Curtis played eight years in the NBA, averaging 9.5 points, 8.8 rebounds, and 1.9 assists per game. His career field-goal percentage was an impressive .455 and his free-throw percentage .770. He currently ranks ninety-sixth on the NBA's all-time leaders for rebounds per game. Curtis's jersey has long since been retired and hangs in the rafters of MSU's basketball arena. He has made us proud.

After representing Curtis, I was back in the legal arena, where I belonged. As a young lawyer, setting out to learn my trade, I contemplated how I would deal with this new and unfamiliar creature, the jury. I would have to relate to them, to appeal to their common sense and to their emotions. I needed to make them like me, to believe me, to trust me, to know that I was not mistreating a witness, to see that I respected the court and the American system of justice. I would not try to be funny or cute, or trick or otherwise deceive them, or talk down, or pretend to be smarter than them. I would be their friend, respect them, acknowledge that they were good, intelligent people, and help them in their effort to render the right verdict for the right reasons.

Curtis Perry signs his 1970 NBA contract. From left to right are yours truly, his attorney; Curtis; and Bill Thomas, his coach.

I learned to use common words, not speak in legalese, and that the manner in which a fact is presented is as important as the fact itself. I once tried a case against a lawyer from a large Kansas City firm. He was brilliant, knew it, and was able to discredit some of my witnesses on cross-examination. In doing so, however, he looked arrogant, belligerent, condescending, narcissistic, and insensitive. After losing the case he asked the jury foreman, "What did I do wrong?" The foreman said, "Mr. Duncan, you are an amazingly intelligent person, but you do not belong in the courtroom. You should stay in your office and write wills." It was an honest assessment made with a straightforward candor unusual even for an Ozarkian, and one that cut Duncan's ego to the bone—for a minute. Then he recovered. After all, he was a Harvard man, the best trial lawyer in a large, prestigious, big-city firm, and knew he could not be blamed for losing to a small-town hick attorney not qualified to shine his shoes. The loss was not his fault; like many losers before and after him, in his mind he just was the victim of a "stupid jury."

When I talked to jurors after my first few trials and heard others talk to them, I learned what turned them on and turned them off, what they liked in a lawyer and what they didn't. I remembered remarks such as, "Mr. Strong cares about his clients." "He likes them." "He is a nice man." "He worked hard." "He is kind." "He didn't talk down to us." "He is a gentle man." "We trusted him."

In the first half of my career, two or three weeks before a trial began, the court furnished us the names and addresses of prospective jurors who would be on our panel. Prior to computers, there was little public information about them. At the start of the trial, when the judge handed the lawyers the names and numbers of the panel, every lawyer would look at the sheet of names and then begin the inquisition. In the cold, forbidding, frightening, intimidating atmosphere of the courtroom, the lawyer's questions usually brought a chilly response, or none at all. Who would appreciate being asked personal questions by a complete stranger in front of other complete strangers?

I set out to find a solution. I drove by the houses of the panelists to see where they lived, how tidy their lawn was, what kind of car they drove, what bumper stickers were on their cars, what signs were in their windows. I was hunting for clues that would help me decide if I wanted them on my jury. By the time the trial started I had memorized their names and knew a lot about the forty or so panelists, and I spoke to them as I would to someone I had just met at dinner. I often knew where they worked, went to church, and of someone who lived near them. I could

say, "Mr. Smith, I believe you work at Kraft Foods, don't you?"
After an affirmative reply, I could add, "Aren't you in the same
department as Collin Adamson?" Other questions of an inoffen-
sive nature made Smith feel at ease. Smith and I had something
in common from our very first exchange. We now had a connection, and I could proceed to the important questions with Smith
more openly relating to the case at hand. I was not questioning
Smith; I was discussing the case with him.

Knowing the names of the jurors also had a positive effect after the trial started. If a juror was missing at the start of a day or
was late after a recess and the judge was scrambling through his
papers to find his or her name, I could volunteer, "Your Honor,
it is Mr. Wallace who is absent this morning. Perhaps one of his
cows had a calf." Or when handing an exhibit to a juror, I could
say, "Mrs. Gregg, would you please pass this to Mrs. Johnson,
next to you, after you have seen it?" After all the jurors had seen
the exhibit, I could take it from the last juror and say, "Thank
you, Mr. Stevenson."

It was my purpose in every trial to act as an extension of the
jury, to be their voice, to aid them in their search for the truth,
not be a performer they would watch as one would watch a movie or play. If I were to succeed in this effort, I must talk and act as
they did. I must even dress as they would on a Sunday morning
when they went to church.

Clothes may have had an impact in a wrongful-death case I
tried in rural Camden County in the days when its small, no-
frills courthouse did not even have air-conditioning. The defense lawyers came to court each day of the swelteringly hot
five-day trial in a clean suit and freshly starched shirt. But the
jury was composed of farmers who wore overalls and women
who wore plain dresses. The men probably did not own more
than one suit, if they owned any at all. They were country folks,
as was I, and I would not pretend to be anyone else. So I wore the

oldest, ugliest, most out-of-date suit I had bought on sale years before. Each hot, humid day I, as well as the other lawyers, would be sweating in our coats and ties. Nevertheless, on the second, third, fourth, and fifth days I returned in this same repulsive suit that was becoming smellier and smellier as the trial wore on. The jury and I got along famously. We not only spoke the same language but wore the same kind of clothes. Maybe their verdict, the largest in the county's history, was partly because I did not come to trial every day dressed like some big shot from the city.

As luck would have it, my most difficult encounter with a jury panel also involved an unbelievably difficult case. My client's husband had been electrocuted when he raised an aluminum ladder into an electric line. Anyone would know that the slightest miscalculation would bring the ladder into contact with the energized line and result in instant death. Why should any ladder manufacturer be required to produce an insulated ladder? Or anticipate that a worker would be so careless as to touch a high power line with a ladder? It was an unfortunate accident, but not the responsibility of the ladder maker to insure the safety of every inattentive user. At least that was the argument the defense would make when the trial began.

I knew my chances of winning were somewhere between zero and none. The defendant had offered no money to settle, and I entered the courtroom feeling as if a one-ton weight was on my shoulders. In came the jury panel, and I began the voir dire. In this case, one where I most needed a receptive jury, my efforts to establish a rapport ran into a stone wall. My questions undoubtedly were too direct, too blunt, too hurried. I was frustrated, failing to connect with the panel, and felt as if I were swimming through quicksand as I asked whether they could listen to my evidence with an open mind. A panel member named Quigley raised his hand, and when I recognized him he stood up and said in an accusatory voice that he thought I was trying to prejudice the jury with my questions. *The entire panel applauded!* It should have been no surprise that the jury did not like my case, but applauding Quigley's accusation had the impact of hitting me in the face with a sledgehammer. It is the only time in my life that I have ever heard of a jury expressing such antagonism before a single witness had testified.

I reacted to Quigley as best I could, saying, "Oh, my goodness, have I prejudiced Helen's case by being an incompetent lawyer? How could you possibly keep from punishing her for my malpractice?" The judge offered to give me a mistrial for what he considered to be jury misconduct, but there was no chance of a settlement, and I couldn't bear to go through the agony of preparing to try the unwinnable case twice.

In Missouri, after the interrogation of the panel is over, the lawyers for each side can strike three panel members, who then will be disqualified from sitting on the jury. I envisioned that Quigley would be the first to have a line through his name when I was given the list to make my strikes. But when it was handed to me, I realized the unthinkable: there were those on the panel who were greater threats than Quigley. I couldn't strike Quigley! He and several of those who had approved of his comments would be my jury.

Somehow, someway, Quigley and I made peace during the trial. He was an intelligent man who wanted to do the right thing, and my reaction to his accusation during voir dire was sincere. We both wanted the right verdict for the right reasons. When the verdict was read, everything had turned out fine. I had won a favorable, adequate verdict that Quigley had signed.

7

A Bad Case of Accident

This "trial by ambush" case began in September 1960 when David Holden, a friend of mine since high school, came to my office with the hope that I could persuade E C Curtis to represent him. David's client, Roberta Ward, had come to him because her husband, Marvin, had just been killed, and Penn Mutual Life Insurance Company had refused to pay its two policies that insured Marvin against *accidental* death.

The first question E C asked was an obvious one: why had Penn Mutual refused to pay? Roberta said Marvin had been riding on top of a friend's car when he fell off and died from injuries he suffered when he hit the pavement. The insurance company claimed that the death was not accidental within the meaning of the policy.

The law in Missouri was clear. If a reasonable person in Marvin's position should have foreseen that he might be injured if he rode on top of the car, his death was not an accident, and the insurance policy did not provide coverage. Conversely, if a reasonable person should not have foreseen being injured, his death was an accident, and Roberta had a meritorious claim. Everyone in my firm thought any sane person could expect to be injured if he rode on the top of a moving vehicle. They wanted nothing to do with the case, but I could waste my time with it if I wished. I wished!

I told David that E C was unavailable, but I would take a stab at the case if he did not object. I would at least investigate what happened. David had no better option, so he and I tackled the case together.

After talking to Roberta, it was plain that the key to the case was going to be the testimony of Harry and LeRoy, two of Marvin's friends and coworkers at Southwest Bell Telephone Company, who were with him when he was killed. Surely, they would cooperate, be friendly witnesses, and want to help their friend's widow recover from the insurance company. As it turned out, they were anything but cooperative. My attempts to talk to them were met with the admonition to "leave me alone." Evidently, Harry was afraid that there might be some criminal charge filed against him, so he retained a lawyer to represent him, and LeRoy decided to help his friend. Harry and LeRoy originally told the police that Marvin was not with them at the time of his death but had to confess that he was when independent witnesses placed them at the scene. They were looking out for themselves, and I would not have their cooperation.

Worse yet, not only were they refusing to help their friend's widow, but they were going to be witnesses for Penn Mutual. The company convinced them that they could help themselves by testifying that they had warned Marvin not to ride on the vehicle, but that he had done so anyway. They were convinced they had done everything right and Marvin had done everything wrong.

Harry and LeRoy did not talk to me voluntarily. So on January 5, 1961, I filed suit against the insurance company in order to have the right to subpoena them and take their depositions under oath. When I asked Glenn Burkart, the attorney for Penn Mutual, for an available time for the depositions, he said a subpoena would not be necessary, for he would produce them. This was more evidence that the two were in the pocket of the insurance company.

Harry and LeRoy were produced as promised and were obviously carefully rehearsed, for their testimonies were much too similar to be coincidental. This was their story: After they got off work shortly before five o'clock on September 21, 1960, Marvin, Harry, and LeRoy met at the Twilight Inn, a local drinking establishment. For the next four and a half hours they each downed about nine or ten steins of 5 percent beer. They then went to the Blue Ribbon Bar at the intersection of Commercial and Jefferson in Harry's 1958 Chevrolet station wagon. At the Blue Ribbon Bar, each had two "bowls" of beer and then ordered a fried chicken supper. At about midnight it was time to leave, since the next day was a workday. They decided to return to the Twilight Inn in Harry's station wagon so Marvin and LeRoy could get their cars and go home.

At Harry's station wagon, parked in the alley behind the Blue Ribbon Bar, Marvin stepped on the rear bumper and climbed on top of the vehicle. He laid facedown in a "spread-eagle" position with his face toward the front of the station wagon, pounded on the roof, and was cutting up. Both Harry and LeRoy told Marvin to get down. "You will kill yourself riding up there," they told him. LeRoy even grabbed Marvin's wrist and tried to pull him off the car, but Marvin was holding on tight to the top of the open-windowed driver's and passenger's doors, and they couldn't budge him. He told his buddies, "This is the only way I'm going to ride." When headed eastbound on Division Street, about eleven blocks from the Blue Ribbon, Marvin jumped, fell, slid, rolled, or was thrown from the vehicle and was killed from a massive skull fracture when he hit the pavement.

The trial began on March 20, 1961, almost six months to the day after Marvin's death. I studied for weeks how to present our case and have a chance to win, in spite of the hostile testimony of Harry and LeRoy. Our first witness was a taxi driver, the first person at the scene, who found Marvin's bloodied body a few minutes after midnight. He described the intersection:

Q. And then, as you get to Sherman Street, what does the road do?

A. It kind of smooths out there; there is a kind of level dip there.

Q. And then what does the road do?

A. It rises again; there is a kind of rise there in the road.

If Harry had been driving too fast, perhaps to give Marvin a thrill or because he was a little drunk, I reasoned he could have bounced Marvin off the car's roof, as he drove across the "level dip" and started up the "rise there in the road." And if Marvin trusted his friend not to drive too fast, then being dislodged from the roof was unforeseen and an accident. Our second witness was Richard, the police officer who photographed the blood found on the pavement just "thirteen feet, six inches from the south edge of the street, towards the middle" of Division Street. Our third and final witness was Dr. Harvey, the pathologist who described the wound to the back of Marvin's head, "a very extensive fracture, involving many of the bones of the base of the skull. . . . [S]everal of the lines extended from in back far to the front, even as far as the front of the skull."

All of our evidence consumed only twenty-one pages of the transcript, less than an hour of testimony. We proved the bare essential to make a prima facie case: that the two insurance policies were in effect and that Marvin had died a violent death. The ball was then in Glenn's court. He could present no evidence at all and argue to the jury that we had not proved an accident, or he could present evidence that Marvin's death was not accidental. We gambled that he would present evidence and were relieved when he called his first witness.

I feared that Marvin, Harry, and LeRoy were all drunk that night. People being investigated by the police usually underestimate the amount of liquor they have consumed, and I thought

it unlikely that Harry and LeRoy were accurate when they testified that they had consumed only nine or ten steins of beer at the
Twilight Inn and only two bowls at the Blue Ribbon. If the boys
were intoxicated, Glenn could contend that Marvin's judgment
was impaired when he decided to ride on top of a car driven by
someone as drunk as he was. If Marvin was sober, he would have
not been so foolish. Such an argument, if accepted by the jury,
would have sunk our ship.

But Harry and LeRoy would not want to confess to being
drunk, I thought. That would make them culpable, at lease partly to blame, for Marvin's death. And if they were not drunk, it
would be difficult for them to contend that Marvin was. This
was the theme I developed when I cross-examined Harry.

Q. Now as I understand it, your testimony is that you don't
know how much Marvin had to drink out at the Twilight or
the Blue Ribbon.

A. Quantity, no sir.

Q. He might have drunk less than you, might he not?

A. It is possible.

Q. And the drinking at those two places was over a period
of seven-and-a-half hours, was it not?

A. Yes, sir.

Q. And while at the Blue Ribbon, you all consumed a pretty
good chicken meal, didn't you?

A. Yes, sir.

Q. And as you all left the Blue Ribbon, all of you were perfectly able to walk and control yourselves physically, were you
not?

A. I would say yes, sir.

Q. And you were perfectly able to drive, were you not?

A. I would say that.

LeRoy was even more emphatic:

> Q. I will ask you whether or not any of you, in any respect, showed any influence of liquor?
> A. Not to my knowledge.
> Q. None of you?
> A. None of us.
> Q. And that includes Marvin, doesn't it?
> A. Yes, sir.

But the coup de grâce came from Glenn's own mouth. In rebuttal we were questioning Roberta about a phone conversation she had with Marvin about eleven o'clock on the night of his death. Glenn objected, wanting to avoid the emotional impact of Marvin's last conversation with his soon-to-be widow. At the bench conference that followed, Judge Douglas Greene asked how the phone call could be relevant. I said it would show that "nothing in his speech or conversation indicated that he was in any way influenced by alcohol." The conversation was relevant, I told the judge, because Glenn intended to argue that Marvin was intoxicated. Perhaps Glenn did not think before replying, or maybe he thought the just-before-death conversation would have such an emotional impact that it was worth giving up on the intoxication issue. In any case, he assured the judge, "I can't argue it; there is no evidence of it."

Glenn had persuaded the judge not to let Roberta relate the conversation, but I convinced him to permit me to ask one more question:

> Q. Was there any indication, from the manner in which your husband spoke or the substance, the words that he said during that conversation, that he was in any degree under the influence of alcohol?
> A. No.

Glenn's concession was more monumental than he, at first, realized. Alcohol was now effectively out of the case. I could argue anything I wanted to the jury, and Glenn could not respond. I took full advantage of the situation, arguing the sobriety of the boys and daring Glenn to challenge me if he disagreed. He was forced to remain mute, having given away an argument he might have won. On appeal, Glenn's sellout was even more significant, the appellate court stating, "And, in a colloquy near the close of the trial, defendant's counsel stated that he could not argue that (Marvin) was intoxicated, for 'there is no evidence of it.'"

But the case was not yet won. We needed to show that Marvin, thirty years old, six feet, one inch tall, and weighing 180 pounds, was strong enough not to be dislodged from the roof of the station wagon if it had been driven in a safe manner. Harry and LeRoy helped us prove it.

Harry testified that Marvin was "strong as a bull," that he was "as strong as any man out there" (referring to his job), that he could climb telephone poles with gaffs on his legs "like a cat," and that, while on the poles, he could "hang cross-arms" and pull up heavy materials that "would weigh as much as a hundred pounds or more." He related how he and Marvin had shoveled and moved by wheelbarrow three truckloads of gravel one morning and poured a cabin floor in the afternoon and how Marvin could hold a fifty-eight-pound bow in a cocked position when deer hunting (a heavier bow than Harry used) and had bagged two deer when hunting with Harry. LeRoy confirmed Marvin's strength: "[He was], I would say, an exceedingly strong individual."

It was important to show Marvin's strength and stamina because, while some people might expect to be thrown off a moving vehicle if they chose to ride on its roof, Marvin had no reason to expect such a fate if he had a safe driver. The matter was not overlooked by the appellate court, which noted: "It may be observed that many individuals (e.g., the members of this court) would foresee injury as a natural and probable result if they undertook to ride spread-eagled atop a moving motor vehicle. . . . Suffice it to say at this point that we are unable to escape the conclusion that we should not and may not hold, *as a matter of law,* that *Ward* reasonably should have anticipated and foreseen injury, as a natural and probable consequence of his conduct."

But we also needed to prove that Marvin had every reason to expect a safe ride from his friend Harry. In fact, Marvin had ridden on the outside of Harry's car before. My questioning followed:

> Q. Did you ever drive a station wagon when Marvin wasn't on the inside, with the exception of this night?
> A. Yes, sir.

Harry explained that when he and Marvin went deer hunting, he would drive the station wagon, and Marvin would stand "on the tail gate, with it down and hold on to the back handle of the top door. . . . We would usually do it the first thing early in the morning, just at daylight, in case we saw a deer from the area of our camping area to where we were going, why we were planning on stepping off of the vehicle and shooting the animal."

> Q. And how many times had he done that?
> A. I really don't know, several times.
> Q. Marvin had every reason to have confidence in the way you drove, didn't he?
> A. Yes, sir; I think so.
> Q. He had ridden with you before, hadn't he?
> A. Yes, sir.
> Q. He trusted your driving, didn't he?
> A. Yes sir, I would say.

Q. He had no reason whatever to think that you would do anything to endanger him, did he?

A. I wouldn't think so . . .

There was one final question I wanted to ask Harry, a question I knew would bring an objection that would be sustained. But just as you cannot successfully tell a young child to stand in the corner and not think about a pink elephant, a judge cannot successfully tell the jury to disregard an emotionally charged question.

Q. You say you were a good friend of Marvin?

A. Yes, sir; I was.

Q. Have you ever made a phone call or a visit to express your sympathy to his widow?

[Glenn's objection was sustained.]

Harry and Marvin were close friends, I told the jury, and riding on the outside of a car Harry was driving was neither new nor dangerous. Something must have happened on this particular trip, something different, something unexpected, something dangerous and unforeseeable. If Harry would give Marvin a safe ride in the wilderness where there were only rutted dirt trails, when hunting deer, why should Marvin expect to be bounced off of the car on the smooth pavement of Division Street where there was only a "level dip" and "a kind of rise"?

The physical evidence also proved indispensable. Glenn made some mistakes of which we took advantage, but calling Jess, an identification technician with the Springfield Police Department, was his biggest mistake of all. It may be that Glenn thought if he called a police detective, the jury would think the law was on his side. If so, anything he gained on direct examination, he lost many times over on cross. Jess had examined the roof of Harry's station wagon, and his findings helped seal Glenn's fate. On direct examination, Jess related: "Examination on the top of said station wagon, approximately two feet from the front, an oily spot was located; approximately three feet from the oily spot was found a bronze or brass colored mark on the roof. Approximately three feet further to the back, was found two crescent-shaped black marks on the paint surface, as if they had been made by a black rubber or plastic composition, or soles."

Jess's testimony was of little value to Glenn, since we admitted that Marvin was on the top of the vehicle, but if the testimony was put in context, it could help us a ton. It was my job, on cross-examination, to put it in context:

Q. Now Detective (Jess), in order that we may understand this more—I am not a very good artist—let's assume that I am drawing here the top of the 1958 Chevrolet station wagon. Now you say you found an oily circle about two feet back from the front—let's assume this is the front, and this is the rear (drawing on blackboard).

A. Two feet from the front, correct, sir.

Q. And in the center of the car, from the sides?

A. That's right. . . .

Q. It was your idea that this was made by Marvin's forehead, this oil mark, was it?

A. Yes, sir.

Q. Now detective, this oil mark, about how big around, what was its circumference?

A. Approximately five inches.

Q. In other words, about five inches as you go around the circumference, the outside of that circle?

A. Yes, sir.

Q. There was nothing about this oil mark that would indicate that Marvin's forehead had moved either forward, backward or sideways during that journey?

A. No, sir.

It was becoming clear to the jury that I was in the process of making an important point: if Marvin had not moved during the eleven blocks before reaching Sherman Street, Harry must have done something different there to dislodge him. Did Harry hit a curb? Was he driving too fast? Did he swerve suddenly? Had he forgotten there was someone on the roof?

It was time to discuss the brass-colored marks:

Q. Those marks compared in color and texture to the belt Marvin was wearing?

A. Yes, sir.

Q. And did you say they were about three feet back of this oil mark?

A. Correct, sir.

Q. Now, as to these marks, here (indicating on drawing)— about how long were they?

A. Approximately one and a quarter inch.

Q. About how wide was his belt?

A. About two inches and a quarter.

Q. There was nothing at all about the appearance of those marks that made you think that his belt had moved either forward, or backward, or to either side, was there?

A. No, sir.

So neither Marvin's forehead nor his belt had moved until something unforeseen had caused his body to leave the roof. What about his shoes?

Q. And then about three feet further back, you found these two black marks, I think you call them?

A. Yes, sir.

Q. And it was your determination that they were made from Marvin's shoes?

A. Yes, sir.

Q. All right. Now about these shoe marks. What do you say about how long they were? I mean about how thick were they from the front to the back of the car?

A. About one and three-quarter inch.

Q. Well, there was nothing about the appearance of these marks that would indicate to you that his shoes had moved either forward, or backward, or to the left, or to the right, while he was riding that car?

A. No, sir.

Things could not have gone any better, but I was not yet done. What about the smudge prints on the doors?

Q. Now, over here on the sides of the top, where the left and right front doors are, and in the windows of those doors, the top of the doors, there were many smudges from hand marks, were there not?

A. Yes, sir.

Q. All along both the left and right door?

A. Yes, sir . . .

Q. And isn't it your opinion that these smudges had been made from Marvin holding on to the door as he was riding along there on the top of that car?

A. Yes, sir.

Q. That is your opinion?

A. Yes, sir.

Marvin was doing his part, holding onto the doors so tightly that he left smudge marks in the short ride of only eleven blocks. It was time for one final question to explain the drawing

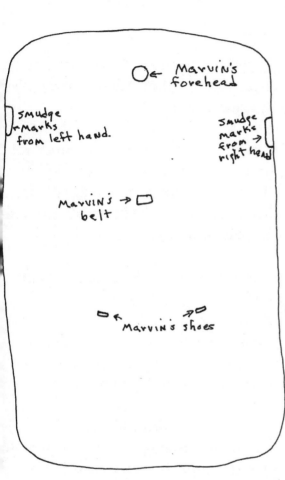

This is a re-creation of the drawing I made while Detective Jess was testifying.

I had made and summarize Jess's testimony about the evidence on the roof.

Q. My question is, detective, there is nothing at all about this oil mark here (indicating on the drawing), the belt mark here (indicating), or these two shoe marks back here (indicating), that would indicate that Marvin had not been able to stay stationary on the top of that car until the moment he was thrown off?

[Glenn's objection was overruled.]

A. There was no indication that the man had moved at any time.

Glenn had continually objected to the testimony of Jess, *his own witness*, during my cross-examination, but to no avail. Jess had done him in on a very crucial issue.

I was not yet through with the detective. Not only had he examined the roof of Harry's car, but he had also found "long scraped marks" on the soles of Marvin's shoes. Jess explained that when people walk, "twisting, circular marks" are made on the soles of our shoes, whereas the marks on Marvin's shoes included "long marks which went from the heel to the toe."

Q. And what does the fact that he had those marks on the soles of his shoes indicate to you?

[Glenn's objection was overruled.]

A. It indicated to me that the man landed on his feet, but was off-balance, throwing him backwards, causing him to fall on the back part of his neck, head slamming to the roadway.

Marvin had the coordination to land on his feet in a futile attempt to save his life right up to the end. He had not gone to sleep, or slid off, or let go of the door tops on purpose. He had done his part, holding on tightly and not moving on the car's roof, but Harry, his trusted friend, who now did not even have the decency to call his widow and express his sorrow, had let him down—in a big way.

We felt confident when Glenn rested his case. The jury was with us; we could see it in their eyes, in their body language when Glenn objected to a question they wanted answered, also in their reaction when Harry or LeRoy told the same story in almost the same words on direct examination, and in their pleasure when

I exposed their lies on cross-examination. When it was time for our rebuttal evidence, we decided not to take any chances that would result in a mistake. We decided to call just three short witnesses, each to make an unassailable point.

I knew from talking to Lavonna, a witness who saw Marvin's lifeless body in the street just a minute or so after the accident as she was driving to work, that Harry and LeRoy were parked with their lights off, headed south in an alley on the north side of Division, just a half block east of Marvin. No doubt they knew what they had done and were contemplating what to do, what their story would be, whether they could go home, thinking that no one would ever know what had happened. Perhaps this is when they agreed to tell the police that they and Marvin had parted company at the Blue Ribbon.

When I cross-examined Harry and LeRoy, I accused them of thinking up an alibi for their misdeed, as they sat in their darkened parked car in the alley. Predictably, they denied it all, even being parked in the alley. Lavonna could not know what they were thinking, but she did know that they were apparently trying to be invisible, as they took no steps to help their friend who was dead or dying in the street just a few yards away. Lavonna had no dog in the fight, no reason not to tell the truth, while Harry and LeRoy did. They lied, and the jury knew it. Glenn also knew it. He did not ask Lavonna a single question on cross-examination.

There was one more point I needed to clinch the case. I needed to prove that riding on top of a station wagon was not a dangerous act, but the only way I could think to do it was to have someone ride on top of a car. Who would do such a thing? I asked Royal, my nearest neighbor when I lived on the farm; he was Marvin's size and just a few years his junior. I explained to Royal what I wanted him to do, and, after some thought, he agreed. I obtained the use of a 1958 Chevrolet station wagon, which Royal mounted on top. I first drove at five miles per hour; Royal had no problem. As carefully as possible, the speed was increased to ten miles per hour, then twenty. Finally, we were ready for the test. At the trial, Royal testified that he had ridden on top of a station wagon identical to Harry's for one mile over a semi-blacktop road rougher than Division Street, up and down hills at about forty-five miles per hour, and around country square corners at about thirty miles per hour.

Q. Now, Royal, explain to the jury the best you can the sensations you felt on that trip.

A. As long as you held your head down, looking to one side or the other, or face down, there was very little wind resistance other than along your legs; when you held your face up into it, there was some wind resistance in your face.

Q. Tell the jury what, if anything, occurred when you put your weight on the top of that station wagon.

A. When you lay on top of the station wagon, it forms more or less of a cradle; you are bedded down more or less into the top. . . .

Q. Now, on that trip, did any part of your body that was in contact with the station wagon ever leave contact with the station wagon?

A. No, it didn't.

Q. Any part of your body ever bounce up away from the top of the station wagon?

A. No, it did not.

Q. As far as moving either forward or backward or to the right or to the left, tell what movements your body made in any of those directions during that ride.

A. There was no movement whatsoever.

Q. Your testimony here today is that your body didn't slip forward or backward or to either side.

A. No, sir, it did not.

Glenn made a lame attempt to cross-examine Royal, but to no avail. In a final gasp he asked how much "Mr. Strong has paid you for this testimony of yours." Nothing! Royal did it for free.

Our final witness was Roberta. She testified about Marvin's height, weight, and strength and produced a picture to prove his muscular development. She talked about what a hard worker he was, how he once held two full-time jobs to support his family, one for the telephone company from 8:00 a.m. to 4:30 p.m., five days a week, and the second as a taxi driver from 5:30 p.m. to about 2:00 a.m. seven days a week. She also testified that one time Marvin had ridden on top of a station wagon in her presence. It was in the city, on Glenstone Avenue.

Q. While he was on the top of that vehicle, tell the jury what bounces or noises of any kind that you heard.
A. None.
Q. Tell the jury what outcries, if any, you heard.
A. None.
Q. Did he fall off?
A. No.

Glenn knew better than to cross-examine Roberta, tall and attractive, sincere but sad, still grieving from the death only six months before of her tall, handsome, strong, and loyal husband. He knew the jury would punish him if he asked her a single question, so he did not try.

Now the evidence was in, and it was time to present my argument, an easy one to make. Harry should have given Marvin the ride he expected and the one he deserved. For some reason, due to inattention, or because he was a little peeved and wanted to give Marvin a little bounce, he had given his longtime friend a ride he did not expect. What had at first appeared to be an impossible case to win had turned out to be a slam dunk. It took the jury only a few minutes to return a unanimous verdict.

Penn Mutual appealed, but to no avail. The appellate opinion was handed down on December 20, 1961.[1]

When Glenn appealed our verdict, he received no comfort from the opinion of the appellate court: "(Harry) said that (Marvin) had ridden with him on other occasions, trusted (Harry's) driving, and had no reason whatever to think that (Harry) would do anything to endanger (Marvin)." The entire process from Marvin's death to the appeal decision had consumed fifteen months. Such speed would be impossible today and was probably a record then.

The case gained a lot of attention in the legal community, particularly because I had persuaded someone to ride on the top of a vehicle going up to forty-five miles an hour. No one would have thought to do such a thing. Some believed the experiment was innovative, audacious, and the sign of a budding twenty-eight-year-old trial lawyer with exceptional promise; others thought it was unprofessional and dangerous.

Of course, there was nothing unprofessional or dangerous about it. A lawyer's obligation is to find creative and innovative ways to persuade the jury that his case has merit. Royal's experiment cinched the case. It put in context Detective Jess's testimony and supported my argument that Marvin had no more trouble staying on the car's roof than Royal, until something unforeseeable occurred. Without Royal, there might have been a lingering doubt that a reasonable person in Marvin's position should have foreseen the possibility of injury when riding on the top of Harry's vehicle. With Royal, all doubt was removed.

Nor had I been unmindful of Royal's safety. Royal had been a friend since boyhood, and I would not have endangered his life just to win a lawsuit. The windows of the station wagon were open, and we were in constant communication during the experiment. At first, when I was driving five miles an hour, I asked Royal, "How is it up there, Royal?" "Not a problem," came the reply. With each small incremental increase in speed, I asked the same type of question and received the same type of reply. Royal was having fun, and he told me so. He did not move. He was not in danger of being dislodged or slipping off. He was comfortable, just as he testified. It is not dangerous to ride on top of a moving vehicle—but don't try it.

Over the next few years, lawyers referred several accidental death cases to me. They included a young man who was killed in a knife fight (the insurance company said he was the aggressor); one killed when bludgeoned to death in a hotel room, allegedly because he was making unwanted homosexual advances; one who was shot at three in the morning when the home owner claimed he was protecting his family from a break-in (a case that reached the Arkansas Supreme Court); one to recover for the deaths of six children who died in a house fire (a case of arson to collect the insurance, claimed the insurance company); one to recover for a man who died when his car crashed into the pillar of a bridge (a suicide according to the insurance company); and perhaps others I can no longer recall.

I never lost an accidental death case.

8

THE MALICIOUS TOW BAR

No "trial by ambush" case enhanced my legal reputation more than my 1967 encounter with the "malicious tow bar." Carl Koll-meyer, who became its eventual victim, was a typical teenage boy with typical teenage friends. School was out for the summer, and there was plenty of time to spend, or waste, depending on one's viewpoint. One of Carl's friends, Jim, had just purchased a used Ford Thunderbird automobile. Thunderbirds were highly prized by young males. If a teenage boy owned a new T-Bird, un-less he was a complete geek, he became the envy of every boy in school and could probably get a date with the prettiest and most popular girls.

Jim was not a geek, but neither was he a jock or particular-ly personable, smart, or good looking. A T-Bird, he believed, would help him with girls—and he needed all the help he could get. But his recent purchase was a half-dozen years old, didn't run, and was more than two hundred miles away in St. Louis. If Jim could transport it to Springfield, with a little time and work, it would be good as new. What girl could resist a ride in a glisten-ing bright-red Thunderbird?

Carl had the good fortune to be Jim's best friend, so he would be able to double-date with him and share the attraction of the coveted carriage. The two young men developed a plan to get the buggy to Springfield. They planned to borrow Jim's father's ten-year-old Chevrolet pickup and tow the T-Bird back to town. The thought of the T-Bird, and the trip itself, would be exciting; Carl had never been to St. Louis.

The boys planned the trip to the smallest detail. They bought a forty-dollar "Pilot"-brand tow bar, assembled all the wrenches they would need to hook the contraption to the vehicles, and put a camper shell on the back of the pickup. They even invited Herb, another friend, to go with them. After all the planning, they were ready.

On Wednesday, June 14, the three boys set off in the small, old truck. As with most teenagers, they had little money, which is why they had put the camper shell on the back of the Chevy. They planned to sleep in it on Wednesday and Thursday nights and tow the automobile back on Friday. Two nights in St. Louis! Who could think of anything more exciting?

After spending two days exploring St. Louis, they awoke late on Friday morning. The anticipation of getting the car to Springfield got the juices flowing, as they alighted from the camper shell and overcame any weariness from a late night on the town. They had promised their folks they would be home before dark, so they hurried to the used-car lot with the tow bar and the wrenches.

In 1967 no special safety precautions were required when a manufacturer shipped a tow bar to a customer. "Hookup" instructions were included in the shipping crate, and that was it. Jim, in particular, was mechanically inclined, so attaching the tow bar to the ball on the back of the pickup and the front bumper of the Thunderbird was a piece of cake. After every bolt was tightened and the rig was ready to roll, Jim jumped on the tow bar to be sure it was secure.

The boys started home on Highway 66, a two-lane concrete highway, which wound through the Ozark hills to Springfield and beyond. It was now afternoon, the initial excitement had worn off, and the effects of sleep deprivation were creeping up on both Herb and Carl. Carl decided he would crawl into the camper shell, take a nap, and let the other two occupy the cab. So off they went with Jim driving, Herb by his side, and Carl in the camper.

The undersized truck struggled to pull the T-Bird up some of the hills, but that did not present a safety hazard. Downhill was a different matter. The brakes on the car were not connected to the pickup, so they were inoperable. All the braking came from the pickup; thus, when going downhill, it was difficult to keep the towed chariot from weaving and jerking the little vehicle ahead. The Chevy's inadequate power and the lack of brakes on the T-Bird soon proved devastating to the destitute travelers.

It was hard to find a place to pass on Highway 66, with all the hills and curves, but that was not a problem most of the way because fifty-five or sixty miles per hour was top speed on level pavement. With no speed limit in Missouri at that time, everyone was passing the boys. That was the case until a line of traffic slowed like a funeral procession behind a sluggish car driven by a little old lady. The cars ahead of Jim passed, and finally it was his turn to go around her. He waited until the road ahead was straight and level.

When the opportunity came, Jim floored the Chevy, calling on every ounce of its power. Slowly, it gained speed, from thirty to fifty-five miles per hour, until it was alongside the lady. Just at that moment, at precisely the wrong time, Jim saw a car coming around the curve ahead. He didn't have time to complete his pass and needed to get back behind the lady without delay. He applied the brakes hard, and, in what seemed like a second, he was off the pavement, in the ditch on the left, his pickup on its right side.

It was a time before seat belts and air bags, so it was a miracle that Jim and Herb were able to crawl out of the driver's window with only minor scrapes and bruises. It was much different for Carl, who was thrown from the bed of the truck and lying motionless a few yards away. When Jim and Herb reached Carl, he was conscious but numb from the waist down and could not move his legs.

People stopped at the scene, and someone volunteered to go to the nearest house to call the police and an ambulance. Carl was not in pain as he waited for help to arrive, but he remained without feeling from the waist down. The ambulance came from Cuba, Missouri, a few miles north of the accident, and took Carl to the small local hospital there. After he was stabilized, Carl was transported to St. John's Hospital in Springfield. The diagnosis was grim: Carl remained paralyzed from the waist down, a paraplegic for life.

Evelyn, Carl's mother, a grieving, hardworking, intelligent, caring lady, who reminded me of my own mother, could not accept the news. In desperation, Evelyn sought the help of my lawyer friend David Holden, who in turn asked if I would represent Carl and his mother. My first action was to talk to the three boys. Carl, who was asleep in the enclosed camper shell, had no helpful information about the accident. Herb could tell about the speed of the cars involved, the attempt to pass, the oncoming auto, and the application of brakes. But the burning question in my mind was: why had Jim lost control of the Chevrolet when he applied the brakes? Herb had no clue, nor did Jim. Jim could only say that it was impossible to control the pickup after he applied the brakes.

This was potentially a big case for this thirty-five-year-old lawyer that required my confronting a major problem. Without a doubt, Jim was at least partially at fault. He shouldn't have tried to pass without more open road ahead, nor should he have kept his foot on the brakes after losing control. No doubt his liability insurance would have to pay Carl, but as might be expected, its

limits were inadequate to cover all the damages Carl would suffer for the rest of his life. If Carl was to receive full justice, I had
to find someone to sue in addition to Jim.

I needed to start from the beginning by getting the highway patrol report, by interviewing the lady being passed and
the other witnesses, and by inspecting the scene and vehicles.
What I found in Cuba started my brain spinning. I came back
to Springfield and asked Saul Nuccitelli, a mechanical engineer
friend, to inspect the vehicles. I had a theory, and if I was correct, I would need an unbiased, credible witness to identify the
physical evidence and be a witness at trial.

The Chevy, T-Bird, and tow bar were in the salvage yard with
the tow bar still attached to the T-Bird. The Chevy was a total
loss, and the tow bar was twisted and, as verified by witnesses,
had come unattached from the pickup when it overturned in
the ditch. The T-Bird had not overturned; nevertheless, there
was damage to its hood, a puncture hole near the top front, and
crushing damage across half the front. I told Saul I would prove
to him that this damage was made by the tow bar.

I had contacted Pilot after my first visit to Cuba and purchased a new tow bar from them identical to Jim's. The "accident" tow bar was too twisted to allow me to explain my theory
to Saul, so we took it off the T-Bird and put the new tow bar on.
Then I raised the tow bar and argued that it caused the damage
to the T-Bird's hood. "Look at the paint in the valleys of the tow
bar screw," I said. "It is the same color as the paint on the hood.
The tow bar had to come in contact with the car's hood to cause
that damage."

The left headlights on the T-Bird were broken, and the surrounding paint was disturbed. I showed Saul red paint on the
rear bumper of the pickup, which matched the color of the
Thunderbird, and called his attention to the fact that the attachment of the tow bar to the pickup was higher that its attach-

ment to the T-Bird. "So what? Why are you acting so excited?" was Saul's reaction. Saul was not following my thinking. "Don't you see what happened?" I exclaimed. The T-Bird weighed more than the pickup. When Jim applied his brakes, with the brakes of the T-Bird being inoperable and nothing to slow its momentum, it ran under the Chevy and picked its rear end up off the highway. The pickup had only its two front wheels on the pavement, and they could turn either left or right. How could Jim steer his vehicle when it was being pushed from behind and only his front wheels were on the pavement?

The T-Bird was prevented from going completely under the Chevy when the tow bar hit the hood of the Thunderbird. This is when the tow bar screw pierced the car's hood and paint from the hood was embedded in the tow bar's screw. Then, as the pickup was careening off the road to the left with its rear end still in the air, its rear bumper slammed into the car's left headlights, scraping off some of the car's paint in the process.

I paused, looked at Saul, and waited for his reaction, convinced that I had proved my case beyond a shadow of a doubt. But Saul was not convinced. He said the accident might have happened that way, or it might not. Well, I was convinced that the accident had happened that way, and I was the guy calling the shots. The tow bar, a cold, uncaring chunk of metal, was at least partly to blame. Why would any manufacturer sell a product that could cause serious injury or death with no admonition that a lighter vehicle should not pull a heavier one or that the tow bar's connection to the towed vehicle should be as high as its connection to the towing vehicle? As far as I was concerned, Pilot's negligence had ruined a young boy's life.

"Strict liability in tort" was not yet the law in Missouri, so I had to prove that Pilot did not behave as a prudent manufacturer should. Pilot *was* negligent, it seemed to me, when it failed to warn of the kind of danger that prevented Carl from ever being a father or leading a normal life. "Failure to warn" was the legal basis for my suit. Warnings were not considered necessary in 1967, so my theory, if successful, would break new ground and introduce new law in our state.

I had both a practical theory (how the accident occurred) and a legal theory (failure to warn), but they were just that—theories. My lawyer friends opined that I would have a difficult time selling an appellate court on the novel idea that a manufacturer had a duty to warn of what seemed an obvious danger, and lawyers and laypeople alike thought even less of my practical theory. The common reaction remained that it was the driver's fault, that the tow bar merely did what it was supposed to do, tow, and that the T-Bird couldn't possibly have lifted the pickup off the ground. A young man passing on 66 was taking his life in his own hands under the best of circumstances, they crowed.

My theory was either too difficult for me to explain or too hard for people to comprehend, or both. How could I make it clear that Pilot had some responsibility? If I could re-create the accident and prove that it occurred the way I claimed, then the doubters would have to agree with me. Consequently, I decided to re-create the accident. The Thunderbird was still at the salvage yard, its wheels would still roll, and a tow bar could still be attached to the front bumper. The pickup was a total loss, which required me to buy one just like it. It was not easy to find a ten-year-old pickup of the same make and model as Jim's, but I finally was successful. I already had an identical tow bar, so now I had the personal property necessary for the experiment: a pickup, the T-Bird, and a tow bar.

Next, I needed a place to conduct the test, which proved to be the easiest of the ingredients to find. There was a drag strip between Springfield and Ozark. It turned out to be the perfect place, isolated from the public eye, concrete like Highway 66, straight, and level. Saul agreed to supervise the experiment that we would capture on regular and slow-motion film.

But I still lacked the most important element of the test. I needed someone brave enough, or stupid enough, or both, to drive the rig down the drag strip at fifty-five miles per hour and apply the brakes to determine whether he would lose control and overturn. This would not be like my experiment in "A Bad Case of Accident," where I was driving the vehicle and knew there was no danger to Royal. This time there was a known danger. If the experiment played out as we expected, the truck would overturn and anyone inside could be hurt, or perhaps killed. This would have to be a business deal, and the driver would have to know what he was getting into. In fact, since I might be responsible if things went awry, he would have to re-lease me of any liability. I inquired around the local racetracks and rodeos and heard of someone known as "Crazy Max," who would do just about anything on a dare. He sounded like just the guy I was looking for.

Crazy Max came to my office. I told him about my case and explained my theory to him. The rest of the conversation went something like this:

"Well, Max, I must say that if you drive and things go as I expect, you will overturn."

"Yep, I think I will."

"Well, will you do it?"

"I'd have to have a seat belt."

Max knew about seat belts! No production-line car had them, but race cars did (not with a shoulder strap, just a belt). I learned later that Max raced cars on local dirt tracks.

"Yes, I will install a seat belt for you. How much will you charge?"

"How fast do you want me to go?"

I began to think Crazy Max might not be as crazy as I had hoped.

"Well, Max, how fast would you go?"

"I'd do a hun'rd."

"That won't be necessary," I said, quite relieved. "Fifty-five miles an hour would be perfect. What will you charge?"

"I'd have to have a hun'rd."

Max seemed to have a fixation on a "hun'rd." The deal was struck. One hundred dollars it was. I told Max if I was going to pay him a hundred bucks, he would have to release me from any liability if something went wrong. I held my breath as I waited for his reaction. To my amazement, there was no reaction at all. "No problem," he said, and the release was prepared and signed without further discussion or incident. We were ready for the test.

Saul, Crazy Max, two cameramen, and I gathered at the drag strip. We put bags of sand in the cab to duplicate the weight of Jim and Herb and in the bed of the pickup to duplicate the weight of the camper shell and Carl. The tow bar was fastened to the bumper of the T-Bird and the rear of the pickup at the same height of the original mounting. The speedometer on the pickup worked, so Max would know when to apply the brakes. To the extent humanly possible, we had replicated what had previously existed. Even the pavement of the drag strip was of the same texture as Highway 66. Crazy Max pulled his seat belt as tight as he could, and we were ready to roll.

Everything had to work perfectly. This was not an experiment that we could do twice. Hopefully, the underpowered Chevy could reach the speed of fifty-five miles per hour. Hopefully, Crazy Max would not "chicken out" at the last moment. Hopefully, the cameras would work and the cameramen would be able to track the vehicles and capture what was to take place on film. Needless to say, I felt relieved when the experiment achieved our highest expectations.

Since we still were in the days of trial by ambush, I did not have to inform Bob Langworthy, the superduper big-time defense lawyer from the big city whom Pilot had hired to defend the case, the results of our experiment. In like manner, of course, Bob did not have to tell me what evidence he had or what witnesses he would call.

Of necessity, I had sued two defendants, Jim and Pilot, Inc. I could not let Jim out of the case for fear the jury would punish me for releasing the person most at fault for Carl's injury. With both as parties, the jury would decide if each bore some of the responsibility for the tragedy.

In my opening statement to the jury, I asserted that Jim should not have attempted to pass without ample room, and Pilot should have warned of the danger of using its product. I told them of the damage to the tow bar, the flakes of paint on the rear bumper of the pickup, and the puncture hole in the hood of the T-Bird. I explained that the rear of the pickup was raised off the pavement, causing Jim to lose control. It took the negligence of both to cause the pickup to leave the pavement. If Jim had been a careful driver, or if Pilot had warned that its tow bar should not be used when a lighter vehicle was pulling a heavier vehicle, which had no working brakes and had a lower point of attachment than the towing vehicle, Carl would be walking today. I did not mention the reenactment.

Bill, a local defense lawyer who was hired by Jim's insurance company to represent him, made a weak opening statement, reemphasizing my argument that Pilot was at fault and excusing, as best he could, Jim's role in the catastrophe. Bill knew Jim would not get off scot-free and had offered the limits of his policy to get out of the case, which I had refused. Knowing that he could not save any of the insurance coverage and that the company would probably complain about his attorney's fee, Bill was just going through the motions. He had nothing to lose by being a lousy advocate.

Bob, on the other hand, had every reason to give Pilot the best defense possible. Not only was Bob justifiably proud of his reputation as the best defense lawyer in Kansas City and the surrounding area, but Pilot might hire him to defend other cases if he won this case. Bob was a big man, more than six feet tall, handsome, with a deep bass voice. He had what lawyers call "jury appeal," a sharp mind, quick wit, a pleasant and relaxed demeanor, and a commanding presence in the courtroom. He always appeared to be in perfect control. I thought my opening statement about the physical evidence and my claim that the tow bar had lifted the rear of the Chevy off the ground might catch him off guard. If it did, it didn't show. In fact, he had a surprise for me.

Bob told the jury in his opening statement[1] that "Strong did find the evidence he claimed, and it *was* from the accident, but that is the only thing about Strong's theory that is correct." He argued that when Jim left the pavement and his pickup overturned and was sliding on its side, the T-Bird caught up to the pickup and crashed into its rear end, causing the damage to the tow bar, the rear of the pickup, and the hood of the car. The damage was caused *after the vehicles left the pavement and the pickup overturned, not before.* Then came Bob's ace in the hole:

We have retained the most prominent physicist in the nation to analyze the forces in this accident. He is a professor at the Massachusetts Institute of Technology, and he has created a formula that considers all the elements of the collision: the weights and speeds of the vehicles, the resistance of the concrete highway, the weights and placement of the boys, the effect of the braking, the thrust of the T-Bird, and the connections of the tow bar to the vehicles. Everything that went into causing this accident was considered by this professor in his formula. What Strong told you happened couldn't happen. It is a physical and scientific impossibility. I repeat, it is a physical and scientific impossibility for the T-Bird to have lifted the rear of the pickup off the ground.

Bob was a worthy opponent, a powerful speaker, someone who had done his homework and obviously had impressed the jury. Fortunately, he didn't know about my reenactment and stepped into my trap.

I set the stage for Saul's testimony by calling the highway patrol investigators, the witnesses at the scene, as well as Jim and Herb. Photographs of the scene, vehicles, and tow bar were in evidence. The jury understood *what* had happened, and now it was time to tell them why. I placed Saul on the witness stand, where he explained the test he had supervised. The pickup was a duplicate in make and model, even to the horsepower of the engine. The car was the same one that was in the accident. Bags of sand duplicated the weight of the occupants and the camper shell. The experiment was conducted on a concrete drag strip, which mirrored the same surface as Highway 66.

Q. Then what did you do?

A. I instructed the driver to apply his brakes when he reached fifty-five miles per hour and keep them on.

Q. How can you be sure the driver was going fifty-five miles an hour when he applied his brakes?

A. I verified his speed by using a stopwatch, calculating how far he traveled in a specified number of seconds.

Q. Mr. Nuccitelli, please tell the jury what happened in the test.

A. The pickup overturned in exactly the same manner as the vehicle in the accident. Even the tire marks were within three feet of the same length as the accident marks.

Q. And what about the rear end of the pickup? Was it lifted off the pavement?

A. Yes, it was, and it caused the same damage to the Thunderbird as was caused in the accident. The tow bar came off the ball on the rear of the pickup when the pickup turned over and twisted the experiment tow bar almost exactly the same way the accident tow bar was twisted. The rear bumper of the pickup hit the headlights of the car as it did when Carl was injured. It would be impossible to duplicate an accident more closely.

Q. Mr. Nuccitelli, was there any way humanly possible for Mr. (Crazy Max) to keep control of his car with only the front two wheels on the ground?

A. It would have been impossible for anyone to have controlled the pickup under the conditions that existed at the time of the accident.

Q. Mr. Nuccitelli, do we have to take your word for this?

A. No, of course not. We captured everything on film with both a regular and a slow-motion camera.

Bob appeared unconcerned during all of Saul's testimony until Saul mentioned that he had captured everything on film, apparently believing that he could attack Saul's credibility and the accuracy of his test on cross-examination. But cross-examining a film is something different. If the film showed what Saul claimed it did, if it did replicate the accident as he had testified, Bob might be facing a mountain too tall to climb. How silly would he look to the jury, after assuring them that "what Strong told you happened couldn't happen. It is a physical and scientific impossibility"? And what good was the MIT professor going to be now, with all his physics and formulas and calculations? Bob's entire defense might be down the toilet.

"Your Honor, we offer in evidence exhibit 74, the movie we took of this reenactment," I said. Bob was up in a flash, trying to look unconcerned but failing in the attempt. "Your Honor," he said, "we have not seen this exhibit. It is very likely objectionable. Could the jury be excused while we view it?"

(Top) The Thunderbird with the new Pilot tow bar attached.

(Bottom) Red paint from the Thunderbird was found on the handle and in the valleys of the tow bar.

(Top) Paint found on the pickup's bumper came from the Thunderbird.

(Bottom) A frame from the film of Crazy Max's experiment.

The jury was excused, and the equipment was set up to view the film. By now, word had spread through the courthouse that "Strong is up to his old tricks again. Let's go and see." The courtroom was packed—standing room only. The slow-motion film was shown, and everyone gasped. Bob fell back in his chair and roared "God damn" so loud that people in the hall, peering through the glass in the courtroom door, heard his exclamation. Bob made a lame attempt to object. The film was inflammatory, he said. It was repetitious of Saul's oral testimony and unnecessary. It appealed to the jury's emotions. All of his arguments were to no avail. The judge ruled that the jury could see "exhibit 74."

The trial was all but over. Bob asked for a recess so he could call Pilot and relay what had occurred. He came back with an offer to settle the case, an offer I promptly and indignantly refused. I told the judge that the jury should not be kept waiting while Bob was wasting the judge's time, the jury's time, and my time with inadequate offers. Bob pleaded for the chance to make one more call, and it was granted. The case settled.

The jury did not get to see the film. And I did not get to cross-examine the vaunted MIT professor or remind the jury in final argument how Bob had boasted in opening statement that what I said happened couldn't have happened. But the most important goal was met: justice had been served, and my client was pleased. As a bonus, I had defeated Missouri's best-known defense lawyer in the process.

About a month after the trial, Bill Barclay, the friend who had given me Crazy Max's name, came to my office. He told me that he had recently seen Max perform at a typical small-town country rodeo held at a softball field. About halfway through the rodeo, when the events weren't very exciting and the crowd was getting a little restless, Max came out to the infield on his motorcycle. Max and a couple of other men then spent about ten minutes assembling a wooden ramp, about thirty feet long at ground level on one end and approximately five feet high at the other.

People began to speculate. In all likelihood, Max was going to ride his motorcycle up the ramp and jump over something. But what? More important, the ramp was pointing toward the crowd in the stands, not away from it. The dunces who were assembling the ramp obviously didn't have a clue what they were doing. But before the audience could agree on who would tell the assemblers that the ramp was pointing the wrong way, there was Max on his motorcycle, racing, heading straight for the ramp— and the crowd. In an instant, Max was up the ramp and flying through the air. The crowd ducked, hoping that Max and his steed would go over them, or below them, or to one side or the other. Instead, Max and his cycle hit the hog-wire fence, which protected attendees at ball games from foul balls, about fifteen feet above ground level, and then both fell harmlessly to the ground. The crowd was scared to death, but unhurt, and Max was the hit of the rodeo.

Well, the tale was entertaining and sounded like something Crazy Max would do, but Bill had not yet reached the punch line. Crazy Max was paid twenty-five dollars for the stunt, not the hundred he had charged me! He had overcharged me, *cheated me,* out of seventy-five dollars. Maybe Crazy Max wasn't so crazy after all. He knew a pansy when he found one.

9

A Supportive Family

The "malicious tow bar" and a host of other cases brought an end to the first of an almost five-decade career. Throughout those years I was not tempted by the afflictions that have sidelined so many: a weakness for liquor, drugs, or gambling; extramarital affairs; bitter divorces; the inclination to take advantage of a client; or the need to belong to numerous organizations and be seen at every local social event. I was fortunate to have few diversions and to benefit from an extra something not every lawyer can claim: a rock-solid family supporting me at every turn. First and foremost was Wilma, a stay-at-home mother who devoted her life to her brood. Then came three children, each one of whom taught me more than I could ever teach them.

Our firstborn, Stephanie, had a trait from birth that dominated all others. It was a passion and love for all kinds of animals —big and small, tame and wild. She coveted wild animals, daydreamed of finding a baby raccoon or fox and making it a pet. She played with her first dog, Taffy, as if she were a little sister, dressing her up, making her sit on a chair at the table, trying to teach her tricks, carrying on a conversation with her, and dragging her places she didn't want to go. As she grew older, she read books on dogs, owned them, and labored to train them.

Stephanie has told us that she can never recall a time when she did not want a horse. We thought she was cute as she played horse on her hands and knees, bucking, whinnying, and pawing the floor, but Stephanie said that she was not just pretending; in her mind, she actually was a horse. When she was old enough to read books, she read all the books—fact and fiction—she could find about horses. She rode ponies at local fairs and tame horses that followed each other on a winding path at Fantastic Caverns. She talked about them incessantly and begged me to get her one. "Our backyard is too small for a horse, but if you still want one when you are twelve, old enough to care for one, I will buy one for your birthday," I promised when Sue (as I call her) was eight or nine. It was a promise I thought I would never have to keep. I believed she would outgrow her passion. She did not. In the summer when Stephanie was eleven, I bought her a horse, Cocoa; then I decided to buy myself a horse so I could ride with her; then I bought a farm for our horses and then cattle to put on the farm. But it was worth every cent. Nothing could have created a closer bond with my daughter than rounding up cattle or exploring the national forest on our horses. Stephanie never outgrew her love of animals. Every sick, abandoned cat or dog we saw by the side of the road received her personal attention.

Stephanie obtained a law degree from the University of Missouri, practiced for seven years, and now lives with her husband on a farm where she pampers and coddles Arabian and half-Arabian horses and a host of other creatures. Compassion is a virtue, and Stephanie has demonstrated that it is impossible to have too much of it.

A year after arriving in Springfield and less that two years after Stephanie was born, our second child, John (Jack), arrived in August 1958. Three weeks after his birth, Jack appeared listless and his lips turned blue. A panic call resulted in a frantic trip to the hospital, where a pediatrician listened to a heart that was racing at a rate too fast to count, then ordered a massive dose of digitalis to slow the misbehaving organ. Racing-heart episodes were Jack's frequent companion through grade school and high school. Even at Greenwood, with only about thirty junior and senior boys, Jack had neither the size, the strength, nor the coordination to make the basketball team—and there was always a threat that his heart would suddenly decide to start its rampage. He feared that he might become an outcast who had to stay home and not be part of school activities. Being a weakling was no fun.

During Jack's junior year in high school, he made a fateful decision, one that would affect his life forever. Damn the heart problem; he would exercise! After school he regularly visited the YMCA, lifted weights, and ran a mile. By the time he was a senior, the new track coach, John Charles, saw Jack do a twelve-minute run in gym class and told him that he was going to field a track team in the spring and wanted Jack on it. Jack was amazed and flattered that there was someone who saw potential in him and was determined not to disappoint this newfound mentor. Jack was selected captain of the track team that year, another boost to his self-esteem. He was neither quick nor fast, but he had a long, graceful, smooth, seemingly effortless stride that covered a lot of ground with minimum exertion. Plus, he had extraordinary stamina, despite his uncooperative heart, that made him a contender in his specialties, the one- and two-mile races. I watched Jack at track meets with the pride most fathers feel in a son who is giving all he can give. I remember him at the Greenfield, Missouri, meet, where he ran the mile in under five minutes—and then went to the sidelines and threw up from having expended every ounce of energy he possessed. He had been working out for less than a year and had become competitive, despite a secret affliction about which neither his coach nor his teammates knew. Jack learned what it meant to try, and that if he tried, he could do almost anything. He might not be *the* best, but he would be *his* best.

Being in top physical condition helped make the racing-heart syndrome less frequent and less severe when it came, but the affliction could appear suddenly, changing from a normal rhythm to a machine-gun pace, and then, just as quickly, return to normal after several seconds or a few minutes. Amazingly, Jack never permitted the episodes to alter his conduct. As a teenager when he was running track, or later in life when climbing a mountain, scuba diving, or teaching classes at Missouri State University after receiving his PhD from Union Presbyterian Seminary, Jack persevered, even when under siege by an attack. I have often wondered if the mental toughness, a hallmark of Jack's personality, had compelled him not to yield to this congenital affliction, or if it was the affliction that helped mold his iron will.[1] I learned from Jack that sheer determination can overcome almost any obstacle.

Our third offspring, David, arrived in April 1970, when Jack was twelve and Stephanie fourteen. By this time I was feeling the stress of my work and badly needed the diversion and entertainment that came with watching David grow. As a preschooler, David was a natural mimic and assumed the identity of characters in the television shows he watched. On *Sesame Street*, a child's television show, David relegated the part of Oscar the Grouch, a disagreeable character who lived in a trash can, to Jack—Jack's room being the trash can. Thus, when Jack told David, "Good night, David," David replied, "Good night, Oscar," or "Good night, yucky Jack."

But it was *Joe Mannix*, a show about a Caucasian private detective and his African American secretary, Peggy, that made the longest and strongest impression on David. David became the detective. When an acquaintance saw us at a restaurant and asked David, "What is your name, young man?" David did not hesitate: "I'm Joe Mannix, and this is my secretary, Peg," referring to his mother. He was Joe Mannix at home. He was Joe Mannix

(Top) Stephanie as a high school senior.

(Middle) Jack, age twenty, in a fifteen-kilometer race.

(Bottom) David as a high school senior.

at church. He was Joe Mannix everywhere. And every day our own Joe Mannix produced a new episode with more surprises, humor, and entertainment than any we could see on television. There were times, however, when David pushed his luck too far, as when he would order Peggy (Wilma) to do something she did not have the time or inclination to do. Wilma's rebellion produced a comic scene for everyone but David, who could not understand why she ignored his commands. Peggy never refused an order from Mannix on the television show.

Later, when David entered Greenwood, the school he attended from kindergarten through high school, he made contributions beyond mere entertainment. It was there that he developed a relaxed, charming, winning personality, his trademark throughout life. It was there where he became the resident counselor for the traumas of his schoolmates. One would come to our house, weeping, to tell David of her woes arising out of her parents' contentious divorce. Another, the class outcast, needed someone who would accept him as a friend and found that person in David. As a friend and confidant, David, in his calm, empathetic, caring way, provided an understanding and comfort no psychologist could have equaled. His classmates' concerns were his concerns. Their problems were his problems. David cared!

After Stephanie and Jack departed for college, Wilma suffered occasional bouts of depression. It was then that David became her comfort, companion, and most reliable friend. A mother has no favorite child, they say, and that is usually true. But mothers do have special relationships, and it was David and his mother, more than any two people I have known, who shared that rare, unique, beautiful relationship that words cannot explain or describe. It was a day of mixed emotions, sadness that enveloped us, yet a sense of confidence and pride, as our last child was leaving the nest to study architecture at Washington University in St. Louis.

No man is an island. All of us need support. Mine came from a devoted wife, a compassionate daughter, a son determined to overcome all odds, and another with empathy for those who needed comfort.

10

Breaking Away

The best part about Farrington, Curtis, and Strong was that the senior partners never attempted to dictate how I prepared and tried lawsuits. I could do it my way, as long as I did not ask for anything from the firm. With this latitude, I handled cases as no one else in my part of the world did. I developed a unique and personal relationship with every client, partly because it was the right thing to do, but also because no case can be successfully tried without their trust and confidence. A copy of every letter I wrote, whether to opposing counsel or to others, as well as a copy of every paper, brief, or document that either my opponent or I filed in court, was sent to my clients. Every client's phone call was returned as promptly as possible, and questions were answered in a calm, unhurried, and relaxed way. I became both an advocate and a friend, but I never made promises that I couldn't keep and never allowed clients to influence me to engage in unethical or unprofessional conduct. The cases invariably ended with satisfied clients, the best public relations representatives anyone could have. I was developing a winning formula, winning scores of cases, impressing jurors who would come to me when they later had a problem, gaining disciples from clients who referred me to their families and friends, while earning the respect of the legal community in the process.

Farrington, Curtis, and Strong treated me fairly, but it did not understand my vision of how a plaintiff's practice should be conducted. We still had too few secretaries, three for six lawyers, and my work, regardless of deadlines, still took second place to that of more senior attorneys. I wanted a staff that could network with other firms to obtain information the defense would not disclose in discovery. I wanted to hire a paralegal to free my time for other matters. With the right team, I could be unbeatable, I thought. The firm never heard of a "paralegal" and thought that I wanted a layman to do a lawyer's work. The firm would never dilute its work product by letting a supposedly underqualified layman perform a professional's job. There would be no paralegal at Farrington, Curtis, and Strong, nor could some of my other needs be met.

The inevitable break came in 1975. I told the firm that beginning on January 1, 1976, Matt Placzek and I would leave to form a plaintiff's firm. The leap was a huge one, and the thought that now I alone was responsible for the success of the new firm was frightening. While I owned two farms and a house, I had little cash to meet a payroll, buy office furniture and a law library, and pay office rent. Matt wanted to be an employee with a guaranteed income, not a partner, at least at the beginning, and I would have a secretary and soon a paralegal to add to the overhead.

With law firms specializing in restricted areas of the law in today's world, it may be hard to understand the new ground I hoped to plow. I intended a firm exclusively devoted to representing deserving clients: the injured and the survivors of those wrongfully killed. Our clients would be people grievously wronged, in desperate need of justice. We would speak for them with sincerity and compassion. The jury would see that we cared for them and believed in them and the cause we were advancing. If the jury liked us and our clients, if we could show the defects in the testimony of our opponent's experts and the error of our opponent's arguments, then the jury would see that we were on the right side of justice and treat us fairly. Unsafe products would receive our special attention; we hoped to make the world a better, safer place by what we did. Our goals were lofty, but now I was in the real world, not some dream fantasy. It was time to sink or swim.

I did not have long to wait. My first trial was in March, only three months after the new firm was launched. We termed the case the "Tunas Massacre" because of the destruction resulting from this horrible rear-end collision near Tunas, Missouri, between a large truck and a "camper" pickup. We represented all the occupants of the pickup: the five injured and the survivors of the three killed. We chose not to consolidate any of the cases, but to try them one at a time, with the one with the most potential (a death case) first. After obtaining the largest verdict in the history of the county, the remaining seven cases were settled, and the new firm thereafter would never look back. We were a success from the start.

Now, with money in the bank, I could begin to implement my dream of what a plaintiff's firm should be. My number-one priority was to hire a paralegal, a person who could keep our files organized, interview witnesses and prepare them to testify, take photographs, and do anything that he or she could do to help me, since I could not do everything at once. There were no schools that taught someone how to be a paralegal, books to tell a lawyer how to train one, or firms I could visit who had them. I would be on my own, without a guide, hoping I could train the right person to perform select chores as well as I could do them. But who was the "right" person?

Wilma and I were good friends of Dick Priest and his wife, Dickie, a college graduate, an intelligent woman, and an unemployed mother of a teenage daughter. She might be available for a new challenge. She became the first of many paralegals for the firm. As time passed, we would have as many as eight, in addition to a couple of nurses to help with the medical aspects of our cases.

With Matt and I as the attorneys and with Dickie to help, that same year the jury awarded us the exact amount we requested. Then, early in 1977, came a trial I dreaded, one I knew would come sometime and could not be avoided, but why did it have to come so soon? It was the case of Mary and her two children for the wrongful death of Paul, her husband and the father of their children, against a Monett, Missouri, cooperative. It was a good case, but not a perfect one. Contributory negligence was still the law of Missouri, so if Paul was even slightly at fault for the collision that caused his death, Mary and the kids were entitled to nothing. Furthermore, E C Curtis, my former partner, mentor, and the area's best defense lawyer, had been retained by the defendant's insurance company to oppose me. I knew E C was unhappy, to say the least, because I had left his firm and would go the extra mile to present the best defense possible.

I did not miscalculate. I had been with E C in several trials while at Farrington, Curtis, and Strong, and although he was always good, he was never as good as when he defended this case against me. One of his strategies was to use his version of the "good cop, bad cop" routine against me. Bill Hart, E C's partner, objected, it seemed, to anything I said, to any question I asked, and to every answer of my witnesses. All the while, E C was just trying to be friends with the rural Barry County jury. While E C had extra motivation to perform well, I had even more. I was determined not just to win an adequate award for my client, but to show E C that I could be a success on my own.

It has long been a time-honored tradition in damage suits for the plaintiff's evidence to be in a particular sequence: first present evidence of the defendant's wrongful conduct, and then present evidence of your client's damages, which flowed from that conduct. It is a matter of cause and effect, so it seems only logical to prove first the misconduct that caused the injury or death and then reveal the dire consequences that flowed from that misconduct.

In many of my cases, however, particularly when the injuries were horrific, or the deceased was an exemplary parent or spouse, or the liability was a little shaky, I did just the opposite. I wanted the jury to understand as soon as possible that the case was about real people and their plight, not just an analysis of whether the plaintiff was barred from recovery because of his contributory negligence or whether the defendant had violated some rule of the road, or building code, or safety standard. I wanted to soften them up, so to speak, so they would not view the evidence on liability with such a critical eye. If the evidence on liability is in and the jury is leaning against you, it may not be sympathetic to your evidence of damages, no matter how devastating it may be.

Every good speaker knows the rule of primacy and recency: you are inclined to be most impressed with what you hear first (the rule of primacy) and remember best what you hear last (the rule of recency). In the case for Mary and the children, I wanted to invoke the rule of primacy—to implant in the jury's mind at the very outset of the case what an unfathomable loss Mary and the children had suffered when Paul was killed. Thus, the first three days of my trial were spent showing what an exemplary husband, caring father, and loyal employee Paul had been. He had been a deacon in his church, a playmate to his kids, a coach of their athletic teams, and active in Monett community service. The last act of this exemplary man on the morning when his life was snuffed out was to give Mary a good-bye kiss as he left for work, just as he had done every day of their marriage. It is hard to attack a dead man, so E C was careful when cross-examining

Mary, the children, friends and family members, Paul's pastor, his supervisor and coworkers, parents of kids on teams he coached, and Monett's mayor.

On the morning of the fourth day of trial, before the jury was called into the courtroom, Judge William Pinnell summoned the lawyers into his office. Pinnell, typically in good spirits, displayed a great sense of humor and presided over trials in a congenial, relaxed way. This morning was different. There was no "Good morning," no jokes or small talk. It was evident that the judge had something on his mind, something solemn, grave, something causing him overwhelming anxiety, as he called the lawyers into his office. "Sit down, gentlemen," he ordered in a low monotone. The room was so quiet you could hear a pin drop as the lawyers waited for what seemed to be an eternity. Finally, the words tumbled out, one after another, to my horror. "Gentlemen, I am going to declare a mistrial. I will call the jury in, thank them for their service, and tell them to go home." I was dumbstruck! "Oh, Judge, please don't do that," I pleaded. "We have worked for weeks and imposed on all the witnesses to be here and testify. Mary and the kids need closure after Paul's death. Rescheduling the case months from now, keeping haunting memories alive, and having to testify a second time will devastate them. What possibly could have happened to justify a mistrial?"

"Well," said the judge, "I have been listening to the evidence about this saintly man for the past three days, and I have decided that he is no longer dead—*He is Risen.*" Then the judge roared with laughter. He had pulled off the ultimate practical joke a judge could play on a lawyer. Paul was still dead. He had not really "risen," so the trial continued.

The evidence about how the driver of the cooperative's truck was negligent and why Paul was free of fault went as well as we could hope. In those days when "contributory negligence" was the law, when the slightest degree of fault on the part of Paul would doom our case, there was no margin for error. But we had held our own during the liability part of the case and were optimistic when it came time for the jury arguments.

In Missouri, the plaintiff (the party with the burden of proof) has the right to open and close the jury summations. In long cases with complicated issues, each side may be granted as much as two hours, while in more simple cases, such as the one for Mary and the children, an hour is typical. Whatever time is allowed, the plaintiff must use at least one-half of it in the opening argument. Just as in the case of presenting evidence, there is a customary and logical way for the plaintiff to make the final argument. In Mary's case, in the opening argument, her lawyer typically would tell the jury why the collision was solely the fault of the cooperative's driver, why Paul was guiltless, and why Paul's death had resulted in a substantial loss to Mary and the kids. The defense then would have one hour to tell why the cooperative was not at fault and Paul was partly to blame and say that Mary's lawyer was seeking an unrealistic amount for damages. Finally, in rebuttal Mary's attorney would take the remainder of the time, perhaps ten or fifteen minutes, to respond to the points made by the defense.

I again had a different approach, one I used in Mary's case. I divided my time equally between opening and closing: thirty minutes in my first argument and thirty minutes in my last one, with E C's one-hour argument sandwiched in between. In my opening, I thanked the jury for its attention, emphasized the importance of their role in the American system of justice, explained the written instructions the judge had given them, and argued how much Mary and the children were entitled to receive. I said not one word about who was at fault for the collision!

Now it was E C's turn. He chided me for ignoring who was at fault, the crucial issue in the case, and claimed that Paul bore at least some responsibility for his own demise. Under the law, if Paul was responsible in any degree for the collision, his dependents could recover nothing, he argued. Paul was partly to blame, and while the jury might think the law harsh, they had taken a solemn oath to uphold it. Under the facts and the law, E C's client was entitled to a favorable verdict regardless of the plight of Mary and the kids. Finally, E C attacked my claim for money. I wanted a pot of gold, blood money, an outrageous sum, he claimed. His client should prevail, but even if I was entitled to a verdict, my request was absurd.

I would have the last word, the final say to punch holes in E C's argument. In stark contrast to my calm, tutorial, professor-like analysis of the law and evidence in my opening argument, now I was angry and indignant, and my voice swelled with feeling and passion, as I ridiculed E C's attempt to place part of the blame for the calamity on a dead man who could not speak for himself. E C's distorted logic in drawing inferences from the evidence, and his impudence, insolence, impertinence, and audacity to malign a dead man were beneath what I had expected from an opposing counsel. I had to fight to control my emotions, to hold back tears. My claim for a monetary award may have been "blood money" in E C's eyes, but to Mary it was the children's only hope for a college education and for a decent life for her, and it would have to provide for them for the rest of their lives. They could not come back in ten or thirty years and explain that the jury had failed to foresee the effects of inflation or a need that had arisen. How cold and heartless could E C, or anyone with an ounce of humanity, be? Would the jury demean the memory of this wonderful husband and father by giving Mary and the kids an inadequate verdict?

I had applied the laws of both "primacy" and "recency" in my arguments. The loss to Mary and the children would be foremost in the jury's minds as they started to deliberate, and my argument on the critical issue of liability, why the blame lay with the truck driver and not Paul, the one that would determine whether we would win or lose, would still be ringing in the jury's ears as they left the jury box. I had the last word. E C could not contest anything I had said. All he could do was rue the fact that the case was over and bite his tongue in frustration.

This strategy, arguing liability only in the second and last of my arguments, worked for me in case after case. Yet, for some unfathomable reason, I was never able to convince the lawyers who attended one of the more than one hundred seminars I taught that it was meritorious. Somehow, they were not brave enough, or gamblers enough, to accept a new approach. "That's just not the way it's done in my jurisdiction" was a common reaction. "Of course that's not the way it's done in your jurisdiction. Except for me, it's not the way it's done in my jurisdiction, either. But if all a lawyer does is what has always been done, why would you need me to teach this seminar?" I replied.

The verdict for Mary and the kids exceeded the liability insurance coverage of the cooperative. E C said he would not appeal if I would accept the insurance coverage and not try to make the cooperative pay the excess. Mary said "settle," and the case was over.

11

LOVE, MARRIAGE, AND FRAUD

Our law practice continued to grow in the next decade but no case then proved more significant than the one covered in this chapter. Its origins began on September 4, 1981, when our receptionist told me that two rather somber and depressed-looking ladies were in the lobby. They had no appointment, preferred not to tell the receptionist their names or what they wanted, but they seemed desperate to talk to me. The ladies were well dressed, the younger in her forties and the other perhaps fifteen to twenty years older. After accepting my invitation to take a seat, the older lady, Lela, began talking and talking. Her story was bizarre, unbelievable, like something out of a fiction book. It went something like this:

This is my niece, Doris. She was married to Hugh (last name excluded) on October 24, 1958. She was seventeen years of age, had no money and little education, and has spent the past twenty-three years as a dutiful housewife and mother of three children. Although Hugh is uneducated, he developed into a savvy entrepreneur. He owns a bank and several farms—he is worth millions. But he is an abusive and unfaithful husband. He would force Doris to sign papers without reading them, flaunt his extramarital affairs, and physically assault and mentally abuse Doris, all without explaining his frequent absences from home. In a volatile outburst a few days ago, Hugh said something that made

161

Doris ask me to go with her to their lockbox at the bank. What we found was shocking.

The papers in the lockbox indicated that Hugh and Doris were divorced three years ago, on September 8, 1978, in Barry County, Missouri, where neither of them had ever lived. Hugh obviously did not want anyone to know of the divorce, which must be why he obtained it in a distant county where no one would take note of the proceeding. He never told Doris, and they continued to live as they had before, with Doris cooking his meals, doing his laundry, sharing his bed, and caring for their children. The divorce decree in the lockbox said Doris was to receive one thousand dollars per month, nothing more. Actually, Hugh had given Doris one thousand dollars per month, before and after the purported divorce, to pay for groceries, clothing for the family, and other household expenses, so the thousand dollars was for the family, not Doris. What could we do about all this? Doris didn't mind being divorced from the scumbag, but she wanted her fair share of their assets.

During the discussion, Doris sat as if in a stupor. She said nothing, nor did she react to anything that was said. If the aunt was telling the truth, why did Doris not at least affirm the accuracy of her story? Why was she not outraged? Was she a pawn in some far-out scheme the aunt had conceived? Was she on drugs? How could she sign divorce papers and not know it? How could she live with a man for three years without knowing that she was not married to him? It all was too preposterous to be true.

After the ladies left, we decided it would be easy to discredit Lela's story by checking the abstract offices in the counties where Hugh supposedly owned farms. What we found there led to a further investigation. Hugh owned 30 acres where the family residence was located; 1,382 acres with a brick house and farm buildings in Cedar County; 520 acres with a house and barns in Christian County; 280 acres with two houses, sheds, and barns in Webster County; the Mike Johnson Chevrolet building in Wright County; and almost 90 percent of the stock in the Southern Missouri Bank, a small bank in Mansfield. The aunt's account of Hugh's assets was even understated. And if Hugh owned these assets, what else did he own that the aunt did not know about? We needed to look further.

Since Lela was telling the truth about Hugh's wealth, perhaps she also was on target concerning the clandestine divorce. A search of the Barry County records disclosed that a divorce indeed had been granted as alleged. Doris had signed papers, which entered her appearance, agreed to the divorce and property settlement, and permitted the trial to be in Barry County. But time had long passed to contest the divorce, ask for a rehearing, or appeal. Furthermore, as Lela had said, Doris was glad to be divorced, though humiliated that she had been sleeping with and keeping house for a man to whom she had not been married for the past three years.

Doris and Lela had told their story to three lawyers before they came, tense and unannounced, to my office, but were turned away by each one. "It is too late to appeal from the decree of divorce." "You signed all of the divorce papers, so you signed your rights away." "Never sign something you have not read." "I can't believe you didn't know about the divorce; why did you wait three years to complain?" "There is nothing I can do." These were the reactions of the previous attorneys. Perhaps this was why Doris appeared in a stupor that first meeting. She was beaten, despondent, and without hope, her pleas having been repulsed by the lawyers she had seen. The rejections also explained why Lela poured out her story to me in such a machine-gun fashion, almost without inhaling. If she took a breath, I might interrupt and tell her to go home, as had the other lawyers. Doris's problem was not even in my field of expertise, but she had been badly mistreated and apparently no one else was interested in helping her. There should be redress for Hugh's inhuman treatment, and I was determined to find it.

We decided to sue for fraud in tricking Doris into signing the divorce and property-settlement papers and in cheating Doris out of half of the marital property. If we could obtain her share of the assets, we would let the divorce stand. If not, we would set the divorce aside, ask for a division of the marital property, and get a divorce later. Since the property settlement had been approved in Barry County, our suit to set it aside also had to be there. Hugh was served with suit papers at his bank in Mansfield.

We took Hugh's deposition, as soon as the law allowed us to, in order to get his version of the divorce. He testified that the marriage had been in name only, one with neither love nor sex, for several years. And it was Doris, not he, who asked for the divorce. "Fine, tell me what you want, and you can have it," he claimed he told her. She wanted the divorce to be kept secret from the three children until they were out of the home and in college; therefore, it would have to be a secret from everyone. She asked Hugh if this was possible, and he thought it was. If both of them consented, they could file the papers in a distant county where no one knew them, where the local newspaper would not write a story about it, and where people reading the notice of divorces would not recognize their names.

What else did Doris want? She just wanted out and enough to live on, a thousand dollars a month, Hugh testified. The divorce was Doris's idea; the decree gave her everything she wanted, and it was fair. Doris had even discussed the matter with her brother, who was a judge in Arkansas.

This was Hugh's story, and he was sticking to it. We knew that Hugh's word, even under oath, wasn't worth much. He had sworn to tell the truth when he had testified in a deposition in another case against him just seven days before our lawsuit was filed:

Q. How long have you been married to Doris (last name)?

A. Oh, probably twenty-two years, I would say.

Q. And during the period of twenty-two years, you're not well enough acquainted with her signature to say whether or not that is her signature; is that right?

A. That's right.

Q. Are you still married to Doris (last name)?

A. Yes.

Q. Never been divorced?

A. No.

Hugh and Doris had also continued to file joint income tax returns after the divorce. The perjured testimony and income tax returns were a damning sentence on Hugh's credibility, but it would have made sense if Hugh had claimed he was lying to comply with his wife's request to keep the divorce a secret at any cost. "Greater love hath no man than this, that a man commit perjury for his wife," he could have claimed. At least this far-fetched explanation would have been consistent with Hugh's claim that the divorce was not obtained by fraud and that the settlement was all that Doris wanted. If the judge had bought this implausible defense, Hugh might have won and kept all of the plunder accumulated during the marriage. Hugh had a second option. He could agree to let the court set aside the divorce, including the property settlement, and redistribute the marital assets. In this event, no more than half of the marital property would go to Doris.

Knowing Hugh as I grew to know him, I am sure he never entertained the second option for a moment. Under no circumstances would he consider letting Doris have a substantial portion of their assets, which he had earned through hard physical labor in the early part of their marriage and through shrewd business dealings in the more recent past, while all the time viewing Doris as a cold, lazy, dull-witted wife.

The first option also apparently had little appeal to him. If the judge didn't believe his tale about the divorce being Doris's idea, again, he could lose up to half of all the wealth he had accumulated. This just would not do. Hugh had a better idea, one that he later expressed to one of his daughters, a plan that would ensure him of all the marital assets. It was based on the assumption that it would take at least a year to get the case to trial if Doris had the best lawyer in the world and two or three more years for a court of appeals to affirm a judgment. He would hire lawyers who would delay the proceedings at every stage, so it might even be six or seven years before there was a final disposition. By the time the case was over, all of "his" property would be secreted. He would have all the assets, and Doris would have a piece of paper saying she had won the case.

Hugh set out with a passion to implement his scheme, but the best-laid plans of mice and men sometimes go awry, and Hugh's was destined to be a comedy of errors. Perhaps he would have succeeded if the lawyer opposing him had been as lazy and incompetent as he had expected, or if the judge had not been astute and assertive, but neither was to be the case. Hugh would ultimately realize what many before him, as smart, devious, and unprincipled as he, had learned: the odds are stacked against you if you think you can outsmart the American system of justice.

From the beginning, we sought to keep Hugh from secreting his wealth, from seemingly transferring it while actually retaining control of it. Hugh, on the other hand, had countless tricks up his sleeve to apparently dispose of his property. Who could win this battle of wits and stamina was an ongoing contest for the next twenty months.

Fourteen days after Lela and Doris were in my office, we filed suit and simultaneously sought a restraining order to prevent Hugh from disposing of any of his assets. Hugh was served with the papers on September 30, and on that day, based on our verified application, the court issued its temporary restraining order "enjoining the Defendant from transferring, encumbering, concealing, and in any way disposing of any property belonging to Hugh (last name), . . . real or personal except in the usual course of business or for the necessities of life." We had won round one.

Hugh, however, was not one to be easily discouraged. He certainly would not take orders from us or from some country judge who might be influenced by us. Hugh needed a new judge; in fact, a series of new judges would be even better. They would not only delay the proceedings while Hugh was disposing of his property, but also present new faces who, not knowing what had gone on before, might be susceptible to Hugh's arguments. So Hugh began moving to disqualify each judge assigned to the case, claiming bias. Three judges quickly came and went, only too happy to be removed from a case that was at the very first glance a monster that would consume an inordinate amount of time and effort. The fourth, Judge Jack Powell, formerly an attorney with Mann, Mann, Walter, and Powell, assigned by the Missouri Supreme Court, was not so easily dissuaded.

Judge Powell, less than five feet tall and weighing no more than eighty pounds, with a badly deformed body from a childhood illness, looked so physically fragile that he might collapse at any moment. But inside that frail body existed a keen mind, an iron will, and an unusual devotion to his job that had made him succeed against all odds, first as a trial lawyer and thereafter as a judge. Hugh, badly misjudging this new judicial assignment, decided on a strategy to deal with him. He would wear him down physically and mentally to the point where he would be happy to sustain Hugh's motion for disqualification.

Because the suit was pending in Barry County, either party could demand that all motions be heard there. Of course, this would be an inconvenience to everyone; Hugh, Doris, the judge, and all the lawyers were in Springfield, and Cassville, the county seat of Barry County, was nearly two hours' driving time away.

When Judge Powell was first assigned, he suggested, to accommodate everyone, that motions, argued almost weekly, be heard in Springfield. Hugh, using some perverted reasoning, decided it was to his advantage to inconvenience everyone and demanded that we travel to Cassville for every motion. He occasionally agreed to a hearing in Springfield, but when the parties, attorneys, and the judge were ready to begin, he demanded that we all go to Cassville. Everyone resented the absurdity, audacity, inconsideration, and vindictiveness of Hugh's game. I suggested that we carpool on the trips, but Hugh would have none of it. Thus, Hugh, his lawyers, the judge, and we occupied four different cars to and from Cassville. It was too ridiculous to be funny. You could almost see smoke coming out of Judge Powell's ears, as he passed us or we passed him, going to or coming from the courthouse. If there was a perfect way to alienate a judge from the very beginning, Hugh had found it. Hugh gave the judge several chances to get out of the case, but Judge Powell was even more determined now to proceed. All of Hugh's repeated motions to disqualify were overruled.

Hugh's plan to defeat Doris's suit seemed to go a dozen different directions at the same time. If I attempted to relate the case as it unfolded, every reader would be as confused as the attorneys who were players in the drama. I will try, therefore, to take one topic at a time and carry it from the start of the case to the end.

We must have caught Hugh off guard when we deposed him shortly after our suit was filed. That deposition, 335 pages long and lasting parts of two days, let us know at the beginning of the case what kind of person we were dealing with, but it also allowed Hugh to evaluate us. Hugh decided that never again would he submit to being questioned under oath by us. Judge Powell ordered Hugh to appear several times for further depositions, but to no avail. Hugh was used to giving orders, not taking them. Once, when he was ordered to appear, he claimed a broken toe kept him from coming. Another time he checked himself into a hospital the day before a scheduled deposition, claiming a heart attack, then checked himself out two days later. On still another occasion, we learned that he had gone to the horse races in Hot Springs, Arkansas.

Hugh wanted to tell his story and, more than once, asked the judge for permission to do so, but only if he were not cross-examined. At the trial, Hugh's attorneys told the judge that Hugh would answer their questions on direct examination, but would take the Fifth Amendment when we attempted to cross-examine him. We anticipated such a move and advised Judge Powell of the US Supreme Court decision in *Brown v. United States,* which held that a trial court had the power to imprison for criminal contempt a person who attempted such a tactic.[1] Judge Powell read the case and then told Hugh's lawyer that "I will put your client in the calaboose if he tries such a thing in my court." Hugh knew the court was as good as his word and decided to remain a free man.

Hugh was bent on stopping our every attempt to learn about his assets, which included our deposition of Jody, a mean-appearing woman who looked as if she could bite a nail in two. She was Hugh's girlfriend and a Southern Missouri Bank employee. After being sworn, the questioning began:

Q. Would you state your name, please?

A. JoAnna (last name).

Q. Where do you live?

A. I refuse to answer on the grounds that my answer might tend to incriminate me. And I intend to avail myself of all my rights under the Fifth Amendment of the United States Constitution.

The answer was written out for her to read, which she did for every question except the one asking her name, although most

could not possibly have incriminated her. Here are some examples of Jody's claiming the Fifth Amendment:

Q. Did you ever live on Ingram Mill Road?
Q. What was your telephone number at the Ingram Mill
residence?
Q. Ma'am, how old are you?
Q. Are you married?
Q. Where are you presently employed?
Q. Do you know where Hugh (last name excluded) has lived
in the past sixty days?
Q. Have you ever been to Hugh's (last name excluded)
Stockton, Missouri, property?
Q. Did you ever have any conversation with Doris (last
name excluded) about her marriage to Hugh (last name ex-
cluded)?
Q. Ma'am, do you know anything about the record-keeping
procedure at Southern Missouri Bank?

Finally, after twenty-three pages of questions, each of which
brought the same answer, Hugh's lawyer told her that she didn't
need to respond further, and they left the building.

On eleven different occasions, the court sustained our motions to require Hugh to produce his airplane, to allow us to
inspect his farms and car dealership, to examine his bank records, and to obtain his financial statements, but Hugh would
not comply. The trial judge's frustration was noted in his opinion at the end of the case, when speaking of our efforts to visit
the farms: "The court and the parties were in a difficult position
in this cause to determine the financial worth and value of the
assets of the marital estate. . . . The problem is an evaluation of
these properties for the reason that Mr. (last name) would not
permit persons to go on the properties to make appraisals, even

though ordered by the court to do so; . . . and in all ways possible tried to prevent anyone from ascertaining what properties he owned or what those properties were worth."

There were pluses and minuses to Hugh's attempts to stonewall our efforts to obtain information. On the plus side, from his standpoint, it took more time and effort for us to learn what he owned—but learn we did. On the minus side, his attempts to conceal information from us drew more interest from federal prosecutors, who began to attend all of our court hearings. This made Hugh very nervous. He neither needed nor wanted their attention.

Hugh developed a unique "defense" to our case. He had impregnated Bennie Nell, a young girl, in 1954 and married her "in order to give the child a name." When the baby died shortly after birth, Bennie Nell divorced Hugh, who had never lived with her, and sought a life of her own, remarrying in 1957. What if Bennie Nell's divorce was invalid? Hugh reasoned that, in that event, he was still married to her, and his marriage to Doris was invalid. Without a legal marriage to Doris, his property was not marital property, and so Doris was out of luck—according to Hugh.

Hugh checked the records in the Arkansas court where the divorce was granted, and, lo and behold, a page of the records, which would have contained the judge's order dissolving the marriage, soon vanished. What a wonderful coincidence! Hugh contacted Bennie Nell, still married to her new husband and now the mother of two children, and made a proposal she could not refuse. If Bennie Nell would come to Missouri and accept the divorce papers Hugh had filed against her, he would pay her $20,000 in cash as a "property settlement." Bennie Nell didn't mind being divorced twice from this creep, and the money sealed the deal. She came, and the divorce was granted. How the second divorce somehow helped to prove that the first one was ineffective, I still cannot understand.

Hugh's lawyers acted as if they had struck gold when they filed their motion and made their argument to Judge Powell, but the judge was not impressed. Nor was the court of appeals, when the issue was presented to them: "The divorce obtained by (Hugh) from Bennie Nell (last name) in 1982 was a sham. The 1958 marriage of (Hugh) and Doris was valid. The sham divorce in Webster County is an illustration of the extent to which (Hugh) has gone in money and effort to preclude Doris from having any rights to any marital property of any significance."

All Hugh had accomplished was to assert that he was a bigamist, waste $20,000, let his children know that he was willing to make them bastards by claiming that he and their mother were never married, and look dishonest and silly in front of both the trial judge and the appellate court.

Had Hugh stolen the missing page of the Arkansas records? Who cares?

Hugh wasted no time in an attempt to intimidate this upstart attorney, Tom Strong, who had the temerity to challenge him. Hugh's first salvo was to bring a lawsuit on behalf of his bank. In it, he alleged that I had hired process servers, who had "descended" on the Southern Missouri Bank, brought it into contempt in the community, and disrupted its business when they delivered Doris's petition to him. It sought actual and punitive damages from me in the sum of $10 million. Hugh would make me sorry that I had chosen to tangle with him, or so he thought. He should have known that I was just as determined to make him sorry that he had chosen to tangle with me.

I pursued the case with a laser commitment, and Hugh resisted in his usual ludicrous way. By the time the case was over, the judge was so frustrated by Hugh's contempt for all of its orders that he ordered him to pay me an attorney's fee of $163,000 for time I had spent dealing with his attempts to pervert justice, saying, "The history of this case is just almost unbelievable." Naturally, Hugh would not pay me a penny, let alone $163,000. So how was I to collect it? Well, Hugh owned a bank, something he could not move or hide. I obtained a court order to auction off Hugh's bank stock on the steps of the Barry County Courthouse. I was not interested in owning a bank, but what better way would there be to show Hugh who he was dealing with and, at the same time, be paid the fee the court had assessed against him? How humiliating was it going to be for Hugh to divvy up the money to avoid losing the bank?

The day of the sale came, and Hugh was not among the assembled people. Not to worry, he would have someone bidding for him. At the appointed time, I announced to the small crowd, "The court has ordered Hugh (last name) to pay me $163,000, so I will bid $163,000 for his bank stock. If I buy it for that sum, it will not cost me a penny; I will just mark Hugh's debt paid. I do not want to own a bank, so if anyone of you will bid $1 more and no one bids against you, you will own a bank." The auction began and I placed my bid. Then there was silence. "Going, going, gone!" Now that I owned 90 percent of the stock in the bank that had sued me for $10 million, I dismissed the suit. Jokes began to float around town: "How does Strong defend a lawsuit? He just buys the party suing him."

But Hugh had lost more than his bank. Federal authorities were very interested in it and how it was being run. There was a short-grass landing strip on Hugh's Cedar County farm, which Hugh could have used to bring in illegal drugs with his single-engine plane. Then he could launder the loot he got for the drugs through the bank, the feds suspected. Now that I owned the bank, they would have full, unfettered access to it—with dire consequences for Hugh.

As you might expect, Hugh's war against me was not fought on one front. Soon after the suit papers were served, Hugh called to tell me what he would do to me if I persisted in the suit. When

I explained that I could not talk to him because he had counsel, his threats continued. I hung up. I reported the calls to Hugh's attorneys to advise Hugh that I would record all future calls in order to prosecute him criminally if his conversations were actionable.

Hugh continued to call, usually at two or three o'clock in the morning. There was no way I could avoid the calls. In those days, phones could not be unplugged, and there was no way to turn them off. If someone called, the phone rang until it was answered or the caller hung up. When Hugh thought that I was recording his calls (I wasn't), he selected his words more carefully. While his prattle might not be a direct threat, his message was clear. For instance, one of his calls went something like this: "Hi, Tom, this is your good friend Hugh. Tom, I see your son every day at three thirty, when he gets out of school. It is so dangerous for children nowadays. Kids can be hit by cars or kidnapped. You can't be too careful." The call was frightening; my son, David, did walk to and from school each day. On another occasion, I was in Jefferson City to argue a case in the supreme court. At four thirty in the morning, my hotel room phone rang. It was Hugh. He said, "I just want you to understand that I always know where you are and what you are doing."

"Sticks and stones can break my bones, but words can never harm me," so the saying goes. But I feared that Hugh was capable of transferring his words into action. It is no wonder I was suspicious when a woman called me just before Christmas 1982, about a month after the trial, and asked if I would be in my office at ten o'clock the next morning. I replied in the affirmative, without thinking, before asking the caller to identify herself. "I can't tell you who I am," she said, "but I have a Christmas present for you, and I will deliver it to your office at ten o'clock tomorrow." "What is the present, who is giving it to me, and who are you?" I asked again. The lady chuckled and said she couldn't divulge the name of the donor, but assured me that I would like the present.

The next day, at nine o'clock, I told the lawyers and staff of the call before asking them to leave and come back after noon. If Hugh wanted to harm me, there was no way to avoid him forever, but there was no need to subject the entire office to a desperate and perhaps deranged man. Ten o'clock came and passed with no lady. As I thought about it, it played out just as Hugh had hoped it would; he had frightened a lot of people, but he couldn't be identified as the culprit and had done nothing that would land him in jail.

Shortly after lunch, the lady called again. "I'm sorry I missed you this morning, but I will bring your present tomorrow. What time will be convenient?" As before, she would not give her name or identify the donor. She would only say that it was a wonderful present and that I would be thrilled with it. Not wanting to endanger lawyers and employees, I asked her to choose a different location, which she did: "There is a service station, the first one on the west side of Highway 13, just north of Kearney Street. I will see you there at eleven tomorrow."

Meet at a service station? What did Hugh have up his sleeve? At least there would be witnesses to whatever transpired, so I said, "See you there." I arrived at the appointed place fifteen minutes early to see if anything looked threatening. Eleven o'clock came and went. I decided I had been alarmed twice for no reason, but just as I was about to leave, a lady, driving a pickup truck and pulling a trailer, drove up and stopped in front of my car, blocking my exit. "Your present is in the trailer," she said. "Come and look." It was a registered Arabian horse, a Christmas present from Lantz Welch, a Kansas City lawyer friend of mine. Hugh had nothing to do with it. The joke was on me.

The end of the case did not bring an end to Hugh's calls. A year or two after the case was over, I received a call from a phone

Yours truly riding Ivanhoe, the present from Lantz Welch.

company in Canada. "Are you a friend of Hugh (last name)?" they inquired. "Definitely not." The person on the phone appeared not to believe me and persisted, "Then why did he make three thousand dollars' worth of long-distance calls to you, on a phone bill that he did not pay? If you know him, please help us find him so we can collect what he owes us." I explained that the calls to me were not friendly and that Uncle Sam wanted to locate Hugh even more than they did. "If you find him, please call me back." The calls from Canada were the last threats I received from Hugh. He now had the feds to fear and to elude.

From the beginning, the contest was whether we could anticipate and foil Hugh's attempts to conceal his assets. Simultaneously with filing the lawsuit, we filed a *lis pendens* (a notice of the pending litigation), in every county where the farms were located, to keep Hugh from selling or mortgaging them, thus stymieing his attempt to borrow $950,000 using one of them as security.

But a *lis pendens* was just a small hurdle for Hugh to jump. He would use his teenage son, Phillip, to make his real estate unavailable to Doris. Money corrupts, they say, and the possibility of it was enough for Phillip to become his father's ally. Hugh leased all of the real estate, the farms, the Mike Johnson Chevrolet building, and even the thirty acres where Doris and the daughters lived, to Phillip, a college dropout, who did not know of the *lis pendens* when Hugh involved him in his nefarious plan. What rent, I wondered, was Hugh going to charge his penniless son for the property? It was when I inquired in court about the rent that the charade began to unravel:

Q. And how much rent are you paying on (these properties)? You said it was supposed to be a business like venture.
A. Oh, I can't recall right off the top of my head.
Q. Was it paid bi-monthly or by the year?
A. I believe all of them were annual sums.
Q. Can you give us even an approximation of what you're paying every year?
A. I believe it's in the several thousand dollar range. I'm not quite sure.
Q. Have you paid any on it?
A. Not yet.

Phillip had leased the Mike Johnson Chevrolet building and thousands of acres without knowing how much rent he would have to pay or when he would have to pay it! Unbelievable! But Phillip did know what he was going to do with the properties: buy farm equipment and cattle to make a lot of money. He even knew what he would do with the Mike Johnson Chevrolet building, as revealed in my questioning:

Q. And tell us how the Mike Johnson Chevrolet building was going to fit in with your cattle plans.

A. Namely, the place where I could hold equipment . . . something along the lines of a bailer, good-sized tractor, and maybe some type of truck. And other than that, it would just be, you know—I haven't sat down yet and formally drew up any plans.

Phillip would use the truck to haul the farm equipment from one farm to another, he said, thus saving money. How was he going to haul a tractor or hay bailer on a truck? Phillip had not thought about that, but figured that he would buy a trailer to carry them. But the Cedar County farm, the largest one, was more than a hundred miles away.

Q. And then how are you going to get the hay wagon those hundred miles? Had you thought that far?

A. Well, no, once you get down to it, I wasn't really envisioning hauling all of the equipment from Mansfield up to Stockton and bringing it back the next week. Now, you keep asking me all these questions about what I envisioned on doing. I guess I just haven't had the time to sit down and do all of this, you know.

Not only had Phillip leased thousands of acres without knowing how much rent he would have to pay, but he had not the foggiest idea of how to proceed. Most of all, he had given no thought to how he was going to buy hundreds of head of cattle and the equipment necessary to operate the farms, with no money.

Q. Do you have any income, I mean, the first thing that you do in a cattle operation is spend money to buy cattle. You don't have an income, do you?

A. There's no income.

Q. All right. How was it that you were going to have the money to pay for the help and buy or rent the tractor and bailer and the truck?

A. I wasn't really sure, yet. . . . I haven't sat down and really made any definite plans. The only definite plans that I do have is that I'm going to do this when I can pay the rent on the leases.

Poor Phillip—just out of high school with no experience operating a farm or money to make lease payments or buy cattle or farm equipment—had been used as a pathetic pawn by his father to sequester his real estate from Doris. Any judge, let alone Judge Powell, would have been outraged by Hugh's eagerness to include his only son in a ploy that had only one possible disastrous outcome.

Hugh's imagination in hiding assets actually took multiple forms. He installed Phillip as president of a corporation that "owned" some of his wealth. He made his revocable trust irrevocable, but retained the right to amend it. He retrieved all of his financial statements from banks where they had been filed and fired his lawyers when they attempted to comply with court orders. His willingness to involve his own son and to encourage him to be a part of his illicit intrigues offended me more than anything else.

Hugh needed time to conceal his assets so that Doris could never retrieve them. But Hugh needed attorneys to help him in his plot, and therein lay a problem. He was too much to handle for some of them who constantly had to apologize for his failure to comply with court orders. After all, Hugh's Springfield lawyers would have to appear before Judge Powell in other cases and, if for no other reason, needed to maintain their credibility. So lawyers came and went: two dozen of them more or less before the case was over because Hugh was displeased with their performance, or they were displeased with his behavior. Hugh didn't seem to mind seeing his attorneys come and go. When there were no more Springfield lawyers who would consent to represent him, he invaded Kansas City for a handful.

New counsel had one legitimate argument that aided Hugh's delaying tactics. Each one could justifiably tell the judge that he was new in the case and needed time to get up to speed. But by the fall of 1982, Judge Powell had heard this song before and was not about to listen to it again. He had set the case for trial on November 8, 1982, and intended to try it then. On October 15, three weeks before the trial was to begin, all of Hugh's Springfield lawyers were granted permission to withdraw because Hugh had refused to comply with court orders. Judge Powell told the new Kansas City attorneys that the trial would proceed as scheduled, and they had better be ready. Any inconvenience to them was totally the fault of their client. This latest motion for a continuance, as with the previous ones, was overruled.

The Kansas City lawyers were determined to give Judge Powell one more chance to change his mind. They let him know that they were deadly serious, and if he could not see the justice of their claim, they would seek relief later from the appellate court. So what was originally intended to be the first day of trial instead was spent hearing eight witnesses testify, filling 342 pages of record, on Hugh's renewed motion for a continuance.

Reviewing the testimony of Dr. Earl, Hugh's local family physician, will give a flavor of the entire proceedings. Dr. Earl, who had practiced medicine in Springfield for thirty years and had been Hugh's doctor for more than ten, was Hugh's ace in the hole. In his direct examination, he told the court that he had recently seen Hugh, who was complaining of chest pains and of being under a great deal of stress. Dr. Earl had admitted Hugh to St. John's Hospital, where he was seen by a specialist before being released two days later. The doctor claimed that Hugh could suffer permanent heart damage if he was subjected to cross-examination at trial and said, "My medical plan is to keep him on medication for about a month and then try to get him off of it and see if he couldn't handle the stress better."

Just one more month was all that Hugh needed! What harm could it possibly do to grant a man with a heart condition thirty days, give or take, to regain his health? But the soundness of Dr. Earl's diagnosis began to wither under cross-examination. First, Dr. Earl could not assure the court that after thirty days, Hugh would be able to testify: "I think it would be dangerous at this time. Now, I can't state that it won't be dangerous later on." So, contrary to Hugh's lawyers asking for *just* thirty days, any reasonable person could see the same scenario playing out again and again, ad infinitum. The doctor's request sounded too much like one of Hugh's schemes.

The hospital records of Hugh's confinement in the hospital also did not substantiate the doctor's conclusions. All of the tests, including an EKG and an angiogram, were negative, and his blood pressure readings were within normal limits, ranging from a low of 100/70 to a high of 126/98, except for two which were 145/80 and 136/85. Interestingly, Dr. Earl saw no need to prescribe medicine to control Hugh's blood pressure.

The major weakness of Dr. Earl's testimony was that Dr. William, the cardiologist in charge of Hugh's care in the hospital, disagreed with Dr. Earl's conclusion that Hugh had heart problems. Good doctor Earl must have thought that we would not read the hospital records. But we did and confronted Dr. Earl with them:

Q. And also under the heading of discharge diagnosis, it says: "Patient's arteries were normal and he is to be discharged, reassured he does not have arteriosclerotic heart disease. To be discharged to resume his normal activities." Does it say that, sir?

A. Well, my glasses give me trouble, too. Yes, it looks like it.

Dr. William's conclusion that Hugh could resume his normal activities and Dr. Earl's testimony that Hugh had a serious heart problem might, at first, seem like nothing more than two doctors reaching different conclusions from the same medical evidence. I needed something to demonstrate, beyond a shadow of a doubt, that the doctor did not believe his own testimony that Hugh had a heart condition.

As Dr. Earl was testifying on direct examination about Hugh's dire ailments, I pictured in my mind Hugh flying his airplane, a gravely dangerous thing to do if he had a heart condition. I wondered, what doctor would have given Hugh's Federal Aviation Administration medical examinations? Could it be Dr. Earl himself? If so, the good doctor's testimony would look ridiculous to the point of absurdity if he claimed that Hugh was fit to fly a plane but unfit to testify. It was worth a try.

> Q. Doctor, in addition to being his doctor when he was admitted here in October of this year, have you given him his exams so he can obtain a license to fly an airplane?
> A. Yes.

Pay dirt! In fact, the doctor had given Hugh all of his flight exams since 1966, and Hugh had passed each of them with "flying" colors.

> Q. When was your last examination?
> A. In 1979 he was okayed on a flight check, also in 1981.
> Q. What month of 1981?
> A. September.

A person who is healthy enough to be responsible for his own life and those of his passengers as a pilot is healthy enough to

estify, we contended, and the judge agreed. Dr. Earl and the re-
naining seven witnesses Hugh's lawyers called in an effort to ob-
ain a continuance did nothing more than waste a day of Judge
Powell's time. "Justice delayed is justice denied," so said William
Gladstone, and so thought Judge Powell. There would be no de-
ial of justice in Doris's case.

In less than a year after Hugh had been served with suit pa-
ers, after numerous hearings and ignored court orders, after
awyers who represented Hugh came and went in rapid succes-
ion, after he had refused to produce his airplane, after he had
nswered written interrogatories under oath that he had no
assport although he was later discovered to have vacationed in
Australia where one would have been required, and after repeat-
d attempts to delay the inevitable, the day of reckoning had ar-
ived. The trial commenced, and the wheels of justice ground on
o their predictable conclusion, much to Hugh's chagrin.

In the usual case, after a trial court has entered a judgment,
verything remains status quo until an appellate court has af-
irmed or reversed the trial court. There was nothing usual about
Hugh, however, so when Judge Powell awarded the farms to Do-
is, Hugh attempted to convey them to other parties, thus requiring an after-trial hearing and a ruling by Judge Powell: "The
Court is aware that actions have occurred since the entry of said
udgment and Decree which may cloud title to certain portions
of said real estate. Therefore, in addition to the award to Do-
is (last name) of the items of property described in Appendix
B' and other relief granted in this Judgment, the Court enters a
money judgment in favor of Doris (last name) and against Hugh
. (last name), in the amount of $1,348,000.00."

At the beginning of the case, Hugh had several options of
defense, any one of which would have been better than his at-
empts to intimidate and bulldoze his way to victory. If he had
played by the rules, it is conceivable that the property settlement

in the 1978 divorce would have been upheld, and Doris would have gained nothing by her claim, but under no circumstance would he have lost more than half of what he considered to be his property and what Doris thought to be marital property. Hugh had refused to play by the rules and had paid the price.

By alienating judge after judge, going out of his way to show his contempt for the courts, refusing to divulge what property he owned or allow appraisers to view the property we had dis covered, faking a second divorce from Bennie Nell in a hare brained attempt to claim that marital assets were not marital assets, lying when there was no possible benefit to lying as with his sworn statement that he had no passport, and looking silly by attempting to have us removed as Doris's attorneys, he had sealed his doom.

It did not take a brilliant lawyer to win Doris's case, just a dog gedly persistent one, one who would not rest or allow Hugh to rest, one who would not be intimidated by his less than subtle threats, and one who would make sure that the various judge along the way knew how this lower than life worm of a man was thumbing his nose at the courts. "Energy and persistence con quer all things," said Benjamin Franklin, and he was right. We could have lost the case a hundred times if we had not always been on the offensive, but it was the most important case in the world to Doris, so it also was the most important case in the world to us while we represented her.

Because Judge Powell could not be sure what Hugh owned, he awarded *everything* except Hugh's car and single-engine airplane to Doris. So Hugh ended up losing his bank, the Mike Johnson Chevrolet building, his farms, and his residence and was saddled with debts that exceeded his assets. The judgment was uncon scionable, thought Hugh and his attorneys, so they appealed.

After plowing through the sixteen volumes of the transcript on appeal (containing the testimony of the eleven hearings be ore the trial, the weeklong nonjury trial, and the three hearings fter the trial), as well as the motions and pleading file, which xceeded five hundred pages, the court of appeals came to the ame conclusion as Judge Powell:

It is difficult to imagine a case or set of facts which disclose such a clear overreach on the part of one party as to another. . . . In order to avoid fraud between husband and wife, agreements between husband and wife as to settlement of property rights should be fair, just and equitable. These conditions did not exist. . . . Fraud on the part of (Hugh) permeates the entire record. Possessed of a remarkable talent to make money, (Hugh's) conduct proves him to be a master villain, a man whose deceitful actions with respect to Doris are matched, in odium, only by his repeated and outrageous acts of contempt in defying proper orders of Judge Powell and his predecessor judges.

The case may have taken its toll on Judge Powell, for he died in early death on October 15, 1984, just over a year after he was inished with Hugh's case and long before the appellate court vould affirm his rulings. Hugh's strategy to wear out the diminitive and fragile judge may have worked, but Judge Powell had tuck it out, done his duty, and refused to be intimidated by the ascal. To paraphrase the words of the Good Book, Hugh reaped what he had sowed.

The "love, marriage, and fraud case" also involved federal legslation related to money laundering. What if Hugh had made a ot of money trafficking drugs and used it to buy a car agency in Mansfield or a farm in Webster County? Cash for the purchase vould raise many questions, because it would be uncommon for someone to have hundreds of thousands of dollars in curreny on hand. But if you owned a bank and deposited the "dirty"

money in your bank, you could then write a certified check fo
the investment you wished to make. It was just this type of sce
nario that persuaded Congress to pass a law to prevent launder
ing money (turning dirty money into clean) by requiring ban|
cashiers to report cash transactions and deposits of more thai
ten thousand dollars to the Federal Crimes Enforcement Net
work as "suspicious activity."

When Shull, a bank auditor with the FDIC (Federal Depos
it Insurance Corporation), was making his routine audit at th
Southern Missouri Bank, he found evidence that seventy-fou
certificates of deposits (CDs) in excess of ten thousand dollars
had been issued, perhaps with Hugh, the owner of the bank, a
the payee. When he attempted to question Jody, Hugh's girl
friend and the bank's cashier, and Hugh about the transactions
he received no cooperation. He then reported that the bank may
have violated the statute against laundering money to the FBI
and a grand jury was called to investigate the matter.

On April 15, 1982, right in the middle of our fight with Hugh
the grand jury issued a subpoena requiring the bank's cashie
(Jody) to produce bank records that would explain the certif
icates of deposit in question. Surprise, surprise! When the re
cords were produced, they contained all the bank's records *excep*
the records and CDs covered by the subpoena. The FBI then be
gan its investigation, and Hugh began feeling the heat—on tw
fronts, our civil case and the feds' criminal investigation.

Hugh stuck it out in Springfield until our trial and the after
trial hearings and orders were concluded on June 30, 1983. Ther
he and Jody vamoosed to Grand Cayman, which had no extradi
tion agreement with the United States. There they were safe unti
they could work out their problems. Perhaps Hugh would wir
our case in the appellate court, have his property (now Doris's
returned to him, and not be criminally charged with a crime
Hope runs eternal, they say.

But any hope Hugh may have had to avoid criminal charges was short-lived. On December 15, 1983, the FBI issued identical indictments against Hugh and Jody, alleging that they had ordered the destruction of between 150 and 200 boxes of documents and records of the Southern Missouri Bank; that they had threatened Jacklyn, a bank employee, telling her to "forget anything she might know" about what happened to the records; and that Hugh had threatened Doris's life if she divulged any information that would aid the FBI. The records were gone, so the government could not prove that Hugh had laundered money, but it could prove that he and Jody had obstructed justice by destroying evidence and intimidating witnesses. When Hugh heard of the indictment, he knew that he must stay in Grand Cayman until the heat was off, or at least be able to return there on short notice. He and Jody did venture to Puerto Rico and Canada, where Hugh had made his threatening phone calls to me, but he quickly returned to the safety of Grand Cayman when the FBI discovered his whereabouts in Canada.

In June 1985, Don, the FBI's special agent responsible for the criminal investigation, died, and Hugh devised a new plan. Hugh, the selfish coward that he was, would send Jody back to Missouri and demand an immediate trial. Without its key witness, Jody might be acquitted or be convicted of an offense without jail time. So, within ten days of Don's death, Jody returned to Springfield and demanded an immediate trial, to act as a human guinea pig for her spineless lover.

After Jody was in Missouri, it occurred to Hugh that he could be deposed (his testimony taken) in Grand Cayman— something he must avoid at all cost. Not only could his testimony incriminate Jody, a small matter, but it could also incriminate him. Hugh found an answer. If he and Jody were married, he could not be required to testify against her in her case, and even more important, she could not be forced to testify in his case if he decided to return. But how could they marry, with her now in Missouri and him in Grand Cayman? The telephone provided the answer. As unromantic as I am, not even I could visualize being married on the telephone.

Jody got her speedy trial, was convicted of obstructing justice by destroying the bank records the grand jury had subpoenaed, received a three-year suspended sentence, was ordered to perform two hundred hours of community service, and was placed on probation. Not too bad! Maybe Hugh could return and fare as well or, with his wit and wisdom, even better. So, in October 1986, Hugh returned to Missouri, because of the "encouragement of my family members," especially Jody and his ill seventy-nine-year-old mother.

Hugh's trial was much like Jody's, with some added features. Doris testified that Hugh had threatened that she would never see her grandchildren and that she would be dead in thirty days if she aided the FBI in its investigation. Hugh, who had no interest in testifying in Jody's case, would be his own best witness, he thought. His testimony, consuming 114 pages of the trial transcript, was devoted mostly to denying the testimony of the bank employees who had testified for the government. They all had lied, he insisted. And, of course, Doris had lied.

Then came his plea for compassion. Everything he once had owned was gone. What follows are the key questions from his attorney:

Q. Your (bank) stock was sold on the courthouse steps?

A. By Tom Strong, the attorney—my ex-wife's attorney.

Q. Was it by Tom Strong or by Judge Powell of the Greene County Circuit Court?

A. I have no idea. It was over Tom Strong's attorney fees awarded him in the divorce for so-many-hundred-thousand dollars plus 45 percent of all the profit in the bank.

Q. And did you lose title to your ranch, too?

A. I lost title to every piece of property I had. . . . I lost everything, yes sir.

Later, the subject was revived:

Q. Now, you claim that you lost everything when you left: is that correct?

A. I lost all my property, my bank, and all my assets.

Q. That was a result of court orders, was it not?

A. It was a result of my ex-wife's attorneys and the judge.

Neither Hugh's testimony that everyone was lying except him nor his financial plight convinced the jury to set him free. They found him guilty of "obstructing justice by tampering with witnesses and destroying subpoenaed records," and federal judge Russell Clark sentenced him to one year in federal prison.

In a sense, Hugh's strategy had paid off. If he had not destroyed the bank records and they had disclosed that he had laundered drug money, both he and Jody might not have fared nearly so well at the hands of American justice. In another sense, he had lost everything, including his wife, his daughters, his earthly goods, and, in the end, even Jody.

The world stands out on either side
No wider than the heart is wide;
Above the world is stretched the sky,
No higher than the soul is high.
The heart can push the sea and land
Farther away on either hand;
The soul can split the sky in two,
And let the face of God shine through.
But East and West will pinch the heart

That can not keep them pushed apart;
And he whose soul is flat—the sky
Will cave in on him by and by.[2]

The sky had, indeed, caved in on Hugh. Judge Clark sustained his motion to appeal as a pauper; he did not even have enough money to pay his attorney for the appeal. I am not sure the thought is original with me, but I have often said that "life is too short to try to cheat someone." It is a lesson Hugh should have learned, but never did.

There are very few Hughs in the world. Thank God for that!

12

Growing Pains

After a year and a half in our new venture, it was apparent that we needed more lawyers and more space. In 1978, I had built a new building on two levels (one underground) at 2060 East Sunshine that would accommodate five lawyers and an adequate support staff. We then added a new lawyer, John Wooddell, the following year.

As time passed, the firm had several names: "Strong and Placzek," "Strong, Placzek, and Wooddell," "Strong and Associates," and finally "The Strong Law Firm." New lawyers were added from time to time to replace those who had left or to handle an ever-increasing case load. By 1983, we had outgrown our office on Sunshine Street, and so I set out to build a larger one at 901 East Battlefield.

Attorney John Hulston soon called and said he was interested in buying the Sunshine Street building. Thus began one of the simplest transfers of ownership imaginable. I told John how much I had paid for the lot and my construction cost. "You are a friend. If I sell it to you, I don't want to make a penny's profit," I said. John did not ask for evidence of my investment. My word was all he needed, and the price was fair, he surmised. John said he would put a down payment in escrow and asked about drafting the agreement. I told him there was no reason for escrow, and his word was as valuable to me as anything we could reduce

191

to writing. I would give him a deed, and he would pay me when the building on Battlefield was completed and we had moved in. "Fine," said John, and the deal was struck. There was no bargaining, no posturing, no real estate agent, no writing of any kind, not even a letter confirming the sale. It all happened in one ten-minute phone call.

Over the next eighteen months I kept John updated on the progress of the construction of the new office, and on January 1, 1985, I located into our new office on Battlefield while John moved into my old one on Sunshine. I gave John a deed, and he gave me a check. Two pieces of paper was all it took.

The new building was large, 16,300 square feet on two levels (one underground), in order to allow room for as many lawyers as I could ever have in my firm. More lawyers were on the way. The 1986 graduating class of the University of Arkansas School of Law produced three who would have the greatest impact on our firm: Steve Garner, who had graduated with the highest grade point average in the history of the law school; Clif Smart, who had graduated with the second-highest grade point average in the school's history; and Steven Harrell, who was fifth in his class.

Over the years the firm accepted every type of personal-injury or wrongful-death case imaginable but refused all criminal defense and divorce cases. Our goal was to promote safety on the highways, in the air, on the job, in the places we visit or do business, and, in particular, in the products we use.

One example will illustrate how we prosecuted defective-product cases. On March 2, 1977, Kathy was involved in a collision at the intersection of Industrial Park Road and Highway 65 in Harrison, Arkansas. Kathy was driving west on Industrial Park when she was struck by a southbound pickup driven by Ronald on Highway 65. Kathy, alone in her car, suffered a devastating head injury, which erased any memory she otherwise might have had of the collision. There would have been no way to prove that she had the green light except for the state-ment of the driver of the car following her, who said the light just changed from green to yellow as Kathy entered the intersec-tion. Ronald, southbound, said the light was simultaneously red and green for him, while another southbound driver said Ron-ald had the green light. It was difficult to explain Ronald's claim that the light was showing two colors at the same time and im-possible to accept the contention of the two witnesses that the light was green for their respective directions of travel. Someone must be lying. Yet both witnesses, with no dog in the fight and no reason to make an unfounded assertion, were adamant con-cerning the color of the lights.

As we investigated the crash, we heard rumors that there was something wrong with the lights. People who went through the intersection daily told of instances when traffic from both di-rections was simultaneously entering the intersection. They be-lieved the lights did not always function properly. Complaints had even been made to the city, but when city officials observed the lights for several hours at a time on different days, they per-formed just as they should. There was nothing wrong with the lights, they concluded. Well, someone or something was respon-sible for Kathy's catastrophic injury. We would sue.

One possible defendant was Ronald, on the theory that he had run the red light, despite the impartial witness who said Ron-ald had the green light. A more serious impediment was Ron-ald's woefully insufficient insurance coverage, inadequate to pay even a fraction of Kathy's anticipated enormous lifelong medi-cal bills, let alone compensate for her disability. Ronald would be one defendant, but we must have another one with deep pockets. What about suing the city on the theory that its traffic lights had functioned improperly? We dismissed this idea out of hand—Arkansas law granted immunity to its cities from claims like ours. This left Crouse-Hinds, the manufacturer of the light; Ve-Ped, the distributor; and Trafco, the installer (collectively Crouse).

Crouse had something the others did not: the ability to pay any judgment we might obtain.

We needed to prove that the traffic lights malfunctioned, but how? They were operated by a controller, a metal box containing electrical relays and circuits that govern the color of the traffic lights. If the controller sent the wrong signal, the lights could show green simultaneously in all four directions, we reasoned.

We must buy the controller, so we approached the city with an offer it couldn't refuse. Our message: There are people who claim that the traffic controller at the Industrial Park Road\-Highway 65 intersection sometimes malfunctions. A recent accident there has destroyed any chance a young lady once had for a normal life. We want to buy the city a new controller with every possible safety device, so there will never be another accident at the intersection because of a flawed controller. We will pay every cent of the purchase price and installation cost. All we want in return is the old controller to test and make sure it is never used again. Believe it or not, the city hesitated.

> City: Think of the bad publicity if you are able to show that we installed an unsafe controller.
>
> Me: If you are concerned about publicity, think of the publicity if there is another accident at the intersection and the public learns that you had a chance to trade a dangerous controller for a safe one.
>
> City: How do we know you won't sue us?
>
> Me: If you are really concerned about that, we will give you a release. Furthermore, we couldn't sue you if we wanted to. The law prevents it. Just ask your attorney.

A few days later, at considerable expense, we owned the controller at the Industrial Park Road\-Highway 65 intersection, and Harrison owned a new state-of-the-art controller. Now we

vould see if our gamble paid off. Missouri University of Science
ınd Technology had a fine electrical engineering department,
o I contacted Dr. Earl Richards, a professor there, explained
he situation to him, and asked if he would help us. His assign-
nent was twofold: first, determine if the controller could mal-
˙unction, and second, tell us if there was some feature that could
ıave been incorporated in the design to make it safe. Dr. Rich-
ırds was a true professional. First, he made a scale model of the
ntersection, complete with tiny traffic lights. Then he connect-
:d the controller to the model and watched the lights operate on
he model. Now he could see exactly what a person standing at
he intersection in Harrison could have seen.

Dr. Richards watched the lights on the model operate for a few
ıours, but observed no flaw. Then he hired students to watch it
˙or twenty-hours at a time; still no glitch. Things were not look-
ng good. It was evident that if there was a defect, it was going to
ǝe hard to find. At that point, some experts might have given the
nodel and controller back to us and told us that there was noth-
ng wrong with the system, but Dr. Richards was not an ordinary
:xpert. He devised a mechanism that would lock in an irregu-
arity, if one occurred. Then he turned on the system and let it
˙un day after day, week after week, just as it had run at the Har-
˙ison intersection. Two weeks passed, and Dr. Richards called
with bad news: the controller was working perfectly. "We have
ıothing to lose by letting it run, so keep at it," I said. "Please call
ne every week so I will know that you still have the model under
;urveillance." Every week Dr. Richards called, and every week it
was the same news: the controller was working fine. I grew to
dread the calls. It looked as if Kathy was out of luck. Yet, somehow, I had a premonition that the witnesses were right, that the
lights were green both directions. How frustrating it was going
to be if we could not prove it.

After three months the call finally came. *Bingo* was the first
word I heard from the unidentified caller. But I knew who was

calling and the significance of that single word. "The light i
showing green in all four directions. We have locked in the flaw
and have taken pictures of the green lights. We've got them." Dr
Richards was as excited as I was. "Now we have proved half o
what we need to prove," I said after the initial thrill had passed
"Next, we need to know if any manufacturer of traffic control-
lers produces a fail-safe device. If they do, we are in hog heav
en. If they don't, is it possible to design one?" "I will be back to
you in a few days," Dr. Richards said. "I am confident someone
makes a safe controller. If they don't, I can design one myself
There is no excuse in today's world for not having a fail-safe de
vice on a controller."

True to his word, Dr. Richards called a week or so later. "Not
only do other manufacturers make a safe controller, *so doe.*
Crouse! In Crouse's case, they sell a 'conflict monitor' at a cost
of ninety dollars, which can be added to the controller to correct the imperfection." Crouse knew of the deficiency and did
not have the decency to spend ninety dollars to make it safe! I
was incensed, on my soapbox, preaching to Dr. Richards: "Unbelievable! Typical of too many manufacturers, Crouse's morals
are green, the color of money. It had been willing to place the
public at risk and, in our case, destroy a wonderful life in order
to sell a controller a little cheaper than its competition. I have
seen the same scenario play out too many times. Gas tanks that
can explode, unprotected gears, you name it. This is my calling—to drag manufacturers who feel no guilt, no compassion
into court and expose their degenerate souls. Crouse will pay for
this horrible injustice at the expense of an innocent girl." "Calm
down, Tom. Take a breath," said the good doctor. "The best is yet
to come. I have designed a conflict monitor that would cost fifty
dollars to manufacture, probably what it cost Crouse to produce
its monitor." I started to interrupt with another rant but was
stopped in midsentence. "Hold your horses, Tom, I'm still not

through. Guess what! I could have made the Crouse controller fail-safe by adding four simple additional electric relays you can buy at most hardware stores for a few dollars. Crouse just didn't give a damn about safety."

I couldn't sleep much until I had drafted and filed my petition naming Crouse and Ronald as defendants. Crouse's defenses were just what I expected from a manufacturer with no conscience: The State of Arkansas did not specify a controller with a conflict monitor when it requested bids (the "so we underbid our competition with an inferior product" defense). If the controller malfunctioned, it was because of improper maintenance (the "it's someone else's fault" defense). The flaw resulted from a lightning strike (the "act of God" defense). Our traffic controller meets industry standards and is better than our competitors (the "our inferior product is better than our competitor's inferior product" defense). They were ridiculous defenses, but Crouse would produce expert after expert to prove them, to stress that they had complied with every industry standard, to challenge our claim for future medical expenses, to contest every point we made.

I expected that about one hundred witnesses would testify and fourteen hundred exhibits would be introduced in the anticipated five- or six-week trial. We would have some damage evidence every day, usually the first thing in the morning, to remind the jury that the case was about a person with no future, not an academic debate among experts. Defense lawyers spent thousands of hours preparing to defend a case they knew they could not win. But they were being paid for the time they spent, so they didn't mind. Predictably, as the trial approached, settlement negotiations got serious. "Tom, you are demanding more to settle than any Arkansas jury has ever awarded an injured plaintiff," they pleaded. "How can I recommend that my client pay so much?" I responded, "Don't tell me your troubles. Ask

the president of Crouse to leave his ivory-tower office in Syra-
cuse for a day, get on the company jet, and come to Arkansas and
meet Kathy. Let him see what his company's insatiable appetite
for a few dollars' profit has done to her. Let me ask him what he
thinks a fair settlement would be if his daughter were in Kathy's
place. Then let him look me in the eye and say I am asking too
much. Tell him, if we go to trial, I would like to see him in the
courtroom. I would love to put him on the stand and ask him a
few questions about why he allowed his company to manufacture this piece of junk." No surprise—the case settled.

Automobile fan blades, tires, seat belts, seat backs, gas tanks,
farm augers, railroad equipment, fishing boats, air rifles, earth
bores, brush hogs, corn pickers, hay bailers, insulated extension
lift buckets (cherry pickers), and fork lifts were among the many
products we exposed as unsafe. I, as well as other attorneys,
brought changes in the way products were made. Soft drink
bottles now are plastic, not glass. Pellet guns now have safeties
that do not permit guns to fire "half cocked." Cars have safer gas
tanks, seat belts, and air bags. Many items, from farm equipment
to electric lamps, are safer because of what I and other trial attorneys have done.

How did I play my part in the campaign for safer products?
Once having accepted a case, only victory was an acceptable result. If I needed to assume a position under a car that had fallen
on my client, or buy the remains of an airplane, or erect electric
poles and a billboard skeleton, or build a model of a track drill
to help prove an issue, that is what I did. I produced a variety
of exhibits. Twenty-five hundred years ago, Confucius noted, "I
hear and I forget. I see and I remember," valuable nuggets of information for a trial lawyer. With the intelligent use of exhibits,
explained by a witness, the jury would both hear and see. I told
lawyers who attended my seminars that they learned everything
they needed to know to be a good lawyer in kindergarten. It was

alled "show and tell." My opponents made fun of my numerus exhibits. They called them "Tom's dog-and-pony show," but won and they lost, so who was the better lawyer?

My ability and that of my colleagues to influence safer products was partially due to a change in Missouri law, which abandoned "trial by ambush" and made it possible to learn not only he identity of the opposition's witnesses but also the exhibits hat would be introduced at trial. Now I would need different kills to succeed. This meant spending days, if necessary, to learn very conceivable fact about each witness before he or she testified. Many lawyers, who had enjoyed the thrill of questioning surprise witnesses, did not have the patience to investigate the background, read the literature, and discover the testimony adverse experts had given in other cases. And those who had that bility often were "bookworms," ineffective in the courtroom. Thus, there were few lawyers who had excelled in the old system who could now excel in the new. I was one of the few.

Let me give you two examples of how advance knowledge of an expert's identity can allow you to bring that person to his knees. First, consider Dr. Terry, a medical rehabilitation MD, retained by my opponent in a case where I represented Joe, a quadriplegic. Terry was well educated and astute, had a nice mannerism on the witness stand, and always testified that it would take less money to care for the injured plaintiff than plaintiff's doctor had said.

When Terry was listed as a witness in Joe's case, I set out to earn about him. I found a video of him speaking to a convention of State Farm Insurance officers about how "we, in the insurance industry," can *reduce jury verdicts* relating to future medical expenses. A perusal of the records of the Colorado secretary of state disclosed articles of incorporation of a business Terry had formed, stating that one of its purposes was to provide expert testimony that would *hold down expected verdicts*.

Terry had testified in his deposition that Joe, a twenty-two-year-old quadriplegic, had a life expectancy of ten to twelve years; thus, he asserted that it was improper for us to claim medical expenses on the assumption that Joe had a normal life expectancy. Terry underestimated me. I had found an article that Terry had published in a medical journal years previously. He had written that "with good medical care," a quadriplegic would have a near-normal life span. I had a ball questioning Terry at trial. If Joe had only a ten- to twelve-year life expectancy, perhaps it was because Terry's proposed medical care for Joe was not the "good" care he had suggested in his article. I suggested that if Joe could receive the good care our doctor had proposed, he could live a near-normal life expectancy just like the patients mentioned in Terry's article. Terry stammered as he unsuccessfully attempted to justify his dire prediction of Joe's future, looking more ridiculous in the process.

Then came the questions about his speech to State Farm. What was Terry's motive in identifying himself as a member of the insurance industry? Was he trying to get more business as an expert witness by claiming that he was one of them and could help them reduce jury verdicts? And what about the corporation he had formed for the purpose of keeping Joe and others like him from receiving a just verdict? Was he trying to persuade the jury that Joe did not need good medical care in order to earn the money the defendant was paying him to testify? Hadn't Terry taken the Hippocratic Oath to "never do harm" to anyone?

Terry left the witness stand a beaten man. A defense lawyer who was going to use Terry in a future case, which I had filed and he was defending, heard my cross-examination and said that I had been merciless in my cross-examination and had destroyed Terry to the point that the jury felt sorry for him. Not so! I had treated him with all the respect he deserved and more. Terry had destroyed himself, had shown himself to be a charlatan and a fraud, and in the process had tainted the entire case for the defendant that hired him. At the end of the case, the jury awarded Joe the largest verdict in an injury case that had ever been awarded in the history of Missouri up to that time.

The second case involved an expert in mechanical engineering. He became involved when I represented Debbie, whose stopped Ford Aerostar was rear-ended by a fifty-three-thousand-pound gravel truck traveling about forty-five miles an hour. There was much controversy about what happened inside the vehicle as a result of the collision, our claim being that Debbie's seat collapsed, allowing her to slide up the back of the seat and hit her head against the back of the immovable rear seat, crushing her spine and rendering her a paraplegic. Ford should have manufactured a stronger seat, one that would not collapse in such a collision, we alleged. So we sued Ford, the truck driver, and the truck owner. Since the truck driver and owner had little insurance and no significant assets, our target was Ford.

Ford's view of who was responsible for Debbie's injury differed significantly from ours. It asserted that no seat, unless made of concrete or its equivalent, could withstand the impact of a fifty-three-thousand-pound truck going forty-five miles an hour. Much like a baseball player softens the sting of a hard hit ball by not holding his hand stiff when catching it, the seat had been purposefully designed to "yield, bend, but not break." If the seat had not yielded, Debbie's neck would have snapped back violently, causing a worse injury, a broken neck and quadriplegia or even death, it claimed. It would make no offer to settle, in what it labeled a frivolous lawsuit.

The trial was long, lasting one day shy of six weeks, two weeks of which consisted of Ford's fourteen witnesses, all of whom claimed to have special knowledge or expertise on one or more of the issues. Each Ford witness was suave and highly trained, but each left the stand a beaten man or woman. In the final analysis, Ford would have fared better if it had presented no evidence, relying on the weakness of our testimony, but like most megacorporations, aloof and full of itself, it could not resist explaining how it had done everything right, complying with every existing safety standard, and how Debbie and the trucking company had done everything wrong.

Ford's main expert, Dr. Priya, was a biomechanical engineer employed by Ford in its department of safety and research. His testimony consumed 304 pages of the appellate transcript, including 160 pages of my cross-examination, much too long to be summarized here. One segment of his testimony serves as an example of what can happen to a witness who is highly educated, undeniably intelligent, and tried and true in the courtroom when he finally is exposed for the fraud he is.

Among many other topics, Priya testified that Debbie was not wearing her seat belt, despite her testimony and that of her passengers, and that a seat belt would have prevented her from ramping (sliding up the seat back into the rear seat when the seat back collapsed or "yielded"). The weakness of this part of Priya's testimony came from his own hand, an article he had coauthored when a graduate student at Wayne State University—an article that neither Priya nor Ford's attorney could possibly imagine that I had found. In the article, Priya described rear-end crash tests he and his costudents had performed with belted and unbelted cadavers. His tests proved that in rear-end collisions, the cadaver slid right out from under its seat belt into the backseat, the belt being no restraint, the exact opposite of his present testimony.

I had shown the error of Priya's testimony on issue after issue and now was ready to address his conclusion that a seat belt would have kept Debbie from sliding into the backseat. His article that he had written as a student when he had every reason to be fair and objective would be the key to attacking his credibility.

First, Priya admitted, in fact elaborated on with pride, how he had conducted tests using four hundred cadavers in rear-end collisions while a student and had written an article on his findings. Then, when I produced the article and his conclusion that seat belts do not prevent ramping, Priya began to backtrack: "When you say that there are two persons on this who are my bosses. Like Albert King, he was my adviser and Larry Patrick was another adviser. And they are also part of the writers of this paper. It is not just I. So you should not be misleading people about what I said." Great! I thought. Just what I wanted, a witness contesting an issue he could not win. He had signed the article, had not found fault with it, and certainly should have done so if the findings in the article were fallacious. But Priya persisted: "That's what people believed in 1975. . . . And the people who believed that were Albert King and Patrick. I had no reason to disbelieve them at that point in time."

But it was not a matter of "belief" at all. The cadavers either ramped out from under the seat belts or didn't. This was something visible that Priya could see as well as King and Patrick. He could duck and dodge all he wanted, but I would not let him escape what he had seen and then reduced to writing. I continued, "In 1975 you signed an article that said that seatbelt restraints were considered to be ineffective or result in a *more severe injury* in a rear-end collision." "That's right," he answered. Then Priya decided that there might still be a chance to salvage his position with yet another backtrack: "The authors said it. I had to agree with them at that point in time because I had no experience from the real world." "The very first author listed for this article is you," I retorted. He was forced to respond, "That's right."

There is no greater pleasure for a trial lawyer than a witness who is willing to persist in an untenable position and appear more and more incredible to the jury. Although Priya had seen with his own eyes that cadavers slide out from under their seat belts in rear-end collisions, something easy to see and know based on his own tests, I wanted him to deny the obvious. I pressured him to say whether he agreed or disagreed with what he had published. "It's a very simple question. . . . You say, 'No, I don't agree now'?" "I don't agree with that particular statement anymore," he answered.

If Priya no longer agreed with what he had written, why hadn't he set the record straight in the twenty years since he wrote the article? I challenged: "Have you felt no compulsion to write an article that says, 'Folks, if there's anybody out there who's relying upon this article that I co-authored, you better think twice because this kind of statement isn't accurate anymore and we know better'?" He could only answer, "Yes," which led to my next question: "Have you written such an article?" "I'm writing one," he claimed.

Wow! How naive did Priya think this jury was? Both the jury and I knew he was not writing such an article. My next request was obvious: "Bring a draft of what you have written to court when you return to the stand tomorrow morning." Guess what! The next day Priya returned empty-handed; he had been too busy to retrieve the article. In a parting attempt to rehabilitate himself, Priya said the article he was writing was really unnecessary because there was an abundance of literature stating that seat belts keep people from ramping into the backseat. I had read the existing literature and knew that to be false, so I asked him to name any such article. His attempts to evade my question were useless. I persisted, "My question is very specific, Dr., very, very specific. Do you know of any article or book or literature by anybody who purports to be an expert that says seatbelts prevent ramping?" "I don't know, there may be literature, there may not be," he responded meekly. I then followed with: "There certainly is literature out there, not only yours, but literature through

the years, we saw some of them cited yesterday, written recently, I think 1993, that say seatbelts don't prevent ramping, right?"
"If I write my paper, which will come out in February, that seatbelts prevent ramping," Priya insisted, "you will say that well,
now there is one in the literature. . . . And then you'll start quoting me, that I said that seatbelts prevent ramping." "I'll wait to
read the article before I know whether I want to cite it or not," I
concluded.

Several things now were apparent to the jury. The tests Priya conducted as an unbiased graduate student showed that seat
belts do not prevent ramping. He would have corrected his improper conclusion in the twenty years since he had written the
article if he really believed it to be inaccurate. Priya's claim that
he was in the process of writing an article correcting the error
was an outright lie exposed by the fact that he was "too busy"
to find it when he returned to court the second day. And finally, Priya was not going to publish an article next February that
would contradict his cadaver tests and show him to be an incompetent to his peers.

The positions Priya took on other issues were equally as untenable. Perhaps Ford thought an Ozark jury would not have the
intelligence to see the fallacies in Priya's testimony. Perhaps Priya had successfully sold his story in other venues and thought
he could do it yet again. Perhaps Ford thought a small-town attorney from Southwest Missouri would not do his homework or
lacked the skills to confront and expose a seasoned, evasive expert witness like Priya. Ford was wrong. This highly educated,
obviously intelligent doctor of bioengineering was a fraud, and
the jury knew it.

My personal experience in these years also involved the temptation to settle a client's case instead of gambling on a jury verdict. The lyrics from *The Gambler* said it best:

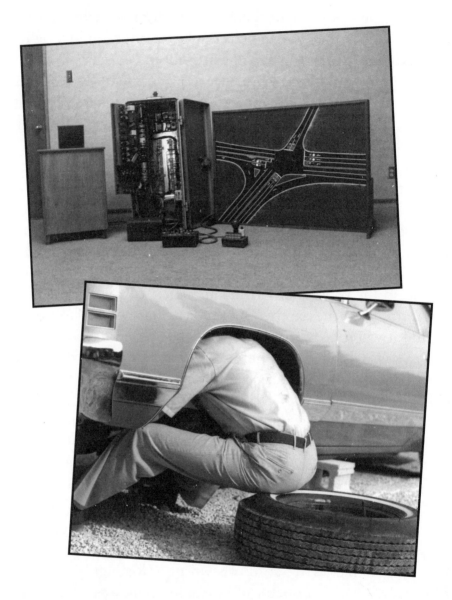

(Top) The controller and model of the Harrison, Arkansas, intersection made by Dr. Richards in Kathy's case.

(Bottom) I assumed my client's position in this case against General Motors for a defectively designed car jack that allowed this car to fall on my client.

(Top) Two died and one was injured in this small plane crash.

(Bottom) We built electric poles and the skeleton of a billboard to help us show how my client came in contact with the defendant's electric wire.

(Top) We built a model of a track drill, including a canopy that would have protected my client from a falling boulder.

(Bottom) This is the hitch that fell on Warren. The "bound" legs are circled.

You've got to know when to hold 'em
Know when to fold 'em
Know when to walk away
Know when to run.

My greatest temptation came in 1980, when I represented a quadriplegic named Lewis. A couple of weeks before the end of a twelve-week trial, my partner told me that Lewis was in the hospital with kidney failure and was not expected to live. At the next conference in the judge's chambers, the defendants offered a few million dollars to settle the case. The offer would have paid us a fee and reimbursed us for our expenses, and there would have been money for Lewis. The defense wanted me on record with my reply so as to embarrass me if I rejected their offer and lost the case—their expectation—or if Lewis died and there was a mistrial. They pushed a pen and paper in front of me and demanded that I respond in writing.

My partner urged me to settle. We had invested thousands of hours and hundreds of thousands of dollars in the case, and here was our chance to come out ahead. Lewis would probably die, so it would not harm him to accept the offer, so said my partner. "I will go to the hospital and get his consent," he said. But other lawyers had done the right thing for the right reason, so why couldn't I? With the pen and paper the opposing attorneys had thrust upon me in my hand, I turned to federal judge Collinson and said, "Your Honor, how do you spell 'shove it'?" If Lewis died, he couldn't care less whether we settled his case. But if he lived, how could we face him if we had persuaded him on his sickbed to settle?

I always hated discussing settlement during a trial. It disrupts the flow of the evidence and is inconsiderate of the jury, who want the trial over in a timely way so they can return to their homes and jobs. To avoid the disruption, I always had my client sign an authorization before the trial began that permitted me to reject any offer that was less than a stated amount. Then when offers came, as they did in Lewis's case, I could politely, but coldly and firmly, reject the offer. Short, frigid, uninterested rebuffs usually were more effective than showing interest, so often more generous offers followed until some cases actually settled in the midst of trial—the "malicious tow bar" case being an example. In Lewis's case, I was frustrated when the defendant refused my oral rejections and demanded a written response in the presence of Judge Collinson—thus my caustic and indignant "How do you spell 'shove it'?" response. Lewis's story had a happy ending. Lewis lived, and our verdict was several times the amount of the offer.

The Inner Circle of Advocates taught me much about the law as well as advanced my legal reputation in the years that followed. Richard Grand, a Tucson, Arizona, attorney, in 1972, conceived the idea of an organization of "highly experienced plaintiffs attorneys who were willing to share information about experts, techniques and whatever it took to be a great trial lawyer." It was limited to one hundred members; while many coveted membership, few were chosen. The Inner Circle carefully evaluates experience, reputation, judicial references, and peer evaluations in identifying the best one hundred trial lawyers in the country.

In 1985, the president of the Inner Circle was W. W. Watkins, a partner in a large Houston, Texas, firm. Like Watkins, almost all members of the circle were from metropolises where large verdicts were common, and successful lawyers were highly publicized. A lawyer from rural Missouri, without widespread media attention, would have had little chance to be recognized, regardless of one's abilities—except for one quirk of fate. Watkins had been born in Clever, Missouri, just thirty miles from Springfield. When it came to his attention that I was obtaining Houston-type verdicts in the small courthouses of Southwest Missouri,

Watkins became curious. After investigating, he and the organization's board decided that I was one of the nation's best one hundred and invited me to join.

Membership was all I expected it to be, and more. Information and ideas were exchanged by mail or phone, before the days of computers and e-mail, on a daily basis about all aspects of our specialty, and a four-day convention was held each summer to help us improve our skills. The mornings of the convention were filled with lectures, nearly always by circle members. We were the best lawyers in the country, we thought, so the best lessons would come from our own members. The afternoons of the convention were devoted to roundtable discussions, where any member could pose a problem and received the thoughts of the circle on how to address it. We did not learn substantive law; we learned trial tactics that we could apply in our practices. I will give you one example, an argument Pat Maloney, of San Antonio, Texas, suggested in a punitive-damage case.

Punitive damages may be awarded if a manufacturer "showed complete indifference to or conscious disregard for the safety of others," in which event the jury may award "an additional amount as punitive damages in such sum as [it believes] will serve to punish defendant and to deter defendant and others from like conduct."[1] The argument, which Maloney suggested, involved a hypothetical case where Clyde was the hypothetical plaintiff and Mega Corporation the hypothetical manufacturer of widgets. It went something like this:

The compensatory damages you award Clyde for his injuries will just reimburse him for his medical bills, lost wages, and pain and suffering. They are built into Mega's cost of production. No one on the top floor of Mega's office building will ever hear of your verdict for compensable damages. Nothing will be done. They will continue to manufacture defective and dangerous widgets because it is cheaper to pay for Clyde's injuries than it is to be a responsible manufacturer. How can you get a message to Mega that it needs to produce a widget that will not kill or maim? The judge, in his instructions, has given you the answer. Punitive damages are the answer! *Punitive damages are the keys to Mega's boardroom.* If your punitive damages award is large enough, someone at the next board of directors meeting will say, "What is going on down there in San Antonio? Why did that jury award 'X' million dollars in punitive damages to this fellow, Clyde? That money will reduce our profits. Part of the dividends I should receive will go to help pay the verdict. Heads are going to roll over this! By the next board meeting, I want to know who has been fired and what has been done to correct the defect in our widgets."

You, ladies and gentlemen of the jury, are the conscience of the community, and you know how to get the attention of the highest echelon of Mega. You have the keys to their boardroom and the means to induce them to produce a safer widget. A year from now you can look back on your verdict with pride and say, "I played a part in people having safer widgets."

I liked Pat's argument and adapted it in a Kansas City trial I had against an insurance company.

On three occasions, I was a presenter at a circle convention. One of my lessons was particularly well received. It went something like this:

In law school I learned a lot about the law, but much of it seemed cold and impersonal. After leaving I found that juries wanted to know more than just the law. Juries are composed of human beings judging other human beings. It was my job to see to it that my clients were warm, trustworthy, likable witnesses, not cold, misleading, or distant. I quickly discovered that a jury would seldom render a verdict for a person they did not like. Thus, I developed what I perceived to be the jury's definition of justice, one not taught in any law school: "We take from those we do not like and we give to those we like," an oversimplification of course, but with a grain of truth.

With my modified and more complex definition of "justice," I set out to never lose a lawsuit because my client was obnoxious, combative, or just plain dumb. I had taken my children to circuses and had seen tricks taught to animals. If a dog can be taught to jump through a hoop, my clients, regardless of their shortcomings, could be prepared to be effective witnesses.

One client with a 78 IQ tested both my theory and my resolve to make him a good witness more than any other. He didn't even know the maiden name of any of his former wives (all of whom probably were quite forgettable). My staff, given the responsibility of preparing him, told me that we dared not put him on the stand. But he was the only person who could tell our version of what had happened to him at the time of his injury. We had to use him. But how could we turn him from someone who could be manhandled on cross-examination by even the most inept lawyer?

It would be a challenge, to say the least, and it would take time and patience, but it had to be done. From the first week of January, we worked with him, examining and cross-examining him, pointing out his inconsistencies, and correcting his misstatements until the morning of trial on July 2. He was on the witness stand for most of two days and was an excellent witness, even under relentless cross-examination. It had taken six months, but we made him into an impressive witness. How could we have done less and slept at night?

Warren, a railroad worker who had his arm pinched off when a fifth-wheel trailer hitch fell on it, presented a different problem. He had given two diametrically opposing statements to the railroad's claims agent, and Jim, the big-shot defense lawyer from Kansas City, was salivating as he waited to cross-examine him. The irreconcilable statements were typical examples of how the Frisco Railroad claims investigators went about building a defense to the legitimate claims of their loyal employees. Warren was called to the claims office, where an agent told him that the railroad appreciated his years of service, sympathized with him for his disabling injury, and said that Frisco wanted to compensate him for his lost income and disability. The agent spoke in a relaxed and friendly way, as he explained that he needed a short, recorded statement from Warren in order to get the payments coming. What the agent did not tell Warren was that any statement he made could be used against him in a court of law and that it might be in his best interest to see a lawyer before answering any questions because his answers needed to be precise and correct on every detail.

More than this, psychologists have conducted experiments to demonstrate how we think we have observed something that we have not observed. One such experiment was to show the audience at a seminar the picture of a house. The picture was then taken away, and the audience was asked how many windows there were on the front side of the house. The responses varied from two to eight. Actually, the house had no windows at all, but the question insinuated that it did. And people expect a house to have windows, so the participants supplied windows that did not exist. Similarly, Warren told the agent what he thought had occurred. There was nothing incriminating in what he said, and if he had not given a second statement, we would not have had a serious problem.

But Frisco knew how the human mind works and knew that no one, even if he had studied what he would say after long contemplation, could relate an occurrence twice without contradicting himself. So a few weeks later, Warren was called back for a second interview. Again, Warren was treated in a cordial way and again questioned about his injuries and what had caused them. Warren answered the questions to the best of his ability, his mind supplying information he did not know, like the people in the window experiment.

At trial we could have lived with either statement Warren had made, but the two of them posed a huge problem. Time and again he had said one thing in one of his statements and the opposite in the other. Whatever Warren testified to, Jim could use something he had said in one statement to show that he had previously said the reverse. It was a lawyer's paradise: Jim would confront Warren with inconsistent after inconsistent statement and accuse him of lying. Juries do not like liars, so we had a serious problem on our hands.

As we prepared Warren to testify, there seemed to be no solution to the catch-22 we faced. If he related one of the versions he had given the agent, neither he nor we could explain why he had said the direct opposite and why both statements were occasionally at odds with the observations of his coworkers. As we tried over and over to find a solution, Warren would sometimes become exceedingly emotional, even to the point of tears. After days of searching, the answer finally came to me in the middle of the night, as answers often did. We did not need Warren to describe how the accident occurred. His coworkers could do that. This, in summary, is what they said: "We needed to lower the hitch, but it was stuck. Warren looked under it and saw that the legs of the hitch had not retracted, so he took a six-pound hammer and struck the leg that seemed to be in a bind. The hitch immediately fell, crashing down on Warren's arm. The edge of the hitch lay on his arm just below his shoulder, crushing it as thin as paper. Warren was white as a sheet and in excruciating pain." This was the truth. Perhaps there was merit in the railroad's contention that Warren was not as careful as he should have been when he hit the hitch's leg without first assuring himself that the hitch could not fall. That was a problem we would have to deal with, but we certainly did not need the additional and perhaps lethal problem of Warren telling two contradictory and somewhat incriminating stories. Adding to our dilemma was the fact that Warren had to be a witness to testify about his medical treatment, physical and mental pain, disability, loss of income, and other topics. But how could we have him testify about these subjects and not about the accident itself? Even if we omitted to ask him, Jim would on cross-examination and paint him as a liar.

Warren's emotions provided the answer, I thought, as I lay awake that night. When my paralegals began preparing Warren, they told him, as they were taught to do, that he must answer the questions propounded to him truthfully, without evasion, explanation, or theatrics. Warren was attempting to follow their instructions as best he could, by suppressing his sometimes overpowering emotions. But what if we could ask the question but not get an answer? Then the two conflicting statements would be of no value to Jim, our salivating opponent.

So I told Warren, "If thinking about how the five-ton fifth-wheel hitch fell on your arm and pinched it off is too much for you to bear and you break down, that is okay. That is understandable." The very thought of reliving the experience—of seeing his arm as thin as paper, of feeling the unbearable pain, of knowing that his right arm would have to be amputated— was enough to make the strongest of men break. We explained to Warren that we must ask him the question, but that if he broke down, we would not press him for an answer. However, and this was most important, if Warren was too emotional to answer my questions, he must be equally emotional and equally unable to answer similar questions Jim would ask! On the witness stand, Warren was the consummate witness: "Warren, tell us what happened when the trailer hitch fell?" Warren broke into uncontrollable sobs. After I had given Warren several minutes to regain his composure, I approached the subject again. "Warren, I know it is very difficult for you to relive this occurrence that has cost you your health and your job, but the jury wants to know what you saw and what you did when this horrible thing fell on you." Again, Warren lost all control over his emotions. I apologized to Warren for imposing on him and said I would go on to other subjects.

Then came the time for Jim's cross-examination, and I held my breath. Twice Jim questioned Warren about the accident, and twice Warren was so overcome with emotion that he could not answer. Jim asked the judge to instruct Warren to answer the question, but the judge wanted no part of badgering a witness. Jim was on his own, and the jury was visibly upset with a lawyer who had no compassion or sensitivity for the plight of a disabled and distraught man. Jim understood, finally, that he was making himself look like Atila the Hun and abandoned the effort. Warren left the stand an impressive witness. Instead of embarrassing Warren, Jim had alienated the jury with his insensitivity.

The "Warren" saga did not end when he stepped down from the witness stand. Each time Warren's coworkers started to describe how Warren hit the impediment beneath the hitch, Warren again broke into sobs. Jim requested that Warren be banished from the courtroom because he could not control himself. The judge agreed and told Warren that he must stay out of the courtroom while his coworkers testified and until he could control his emotions. Thereafter, I noticed the jury glancing at the courtroom door. There was Warren's face,

looking through the window of the door, long, sad, and piti-
ful, wondering what fate awaited him inside.

Jim should have learned something about the juries' (over-
simplified) definition of "justice": "We take from those we do
not like, and we give to those we like." The jury did not like either Jim or the railroad. They did like Warren and made that
perfectly clear by their verdict. I also learned a valuable lesson
from Warren and many other clients and witnesses, both before and after him: there is a solution to almost every problem,
if only I would take the time to be creative enough to find it.

Bill Colson of Miami, Florida, former president of the American Trial Lawyers Association, got the message and told me that
he would never again put an unprepared client on the stand.

Not even exchanges with the Inner Circle prepared me for the
case of *Steven Ganaway v. Shelter Insurance Company*. On November 14, 1981, Steven, a twenty-year-old college student at the
University of Central Missouri, and three friends attended a basketball game, visited a bar, and attended a fraternity party that
extended into the early-morning hours of the fifteenth, before
starting their journey home. Steven was a passenger in a 1980
Honda, driven by his friend Craig Scott and owned by Scott's
mother, Hazel. It was five thirty in the morning, and the effects
of the drinks and the monotony of the road may have caused
Scott to doze at the wheel. Whatever the cause, his Honda collid-
ed with a truck and overturned in a ditch just a few miles from
Columbia, Missouri, where the young men lived. Steven was
thrown from the vehicle and suffered a broken neck. Any chance
for a normal life would now be possible only in his dreams.

Steven's mother sought help from Steven Gladstone, a local
attorney who contacted Scott's insurer, Shelter Insurance Company. Bad news! Scott's liability coverage was a paltry fifty thousand dollars and the medical coverage for passengers a mere five

thousand dollars. Shelter would pay the five thousand toward Steven's monumental medical expenses, but explained that it owed only forty-five of the fifty-thousand-dollar liability coverage because of the last paragraph of part 1 of the policy: "The amount of any payment under [the medical payments coverage] to or on behalf of any person shall be applied toward the settlement of any claim or the satisfaction of any judgment . . . because of bodily injury . . . arising out of any accident to which bodily injury liability (Coverage A) applies."

So the fifty-thousand-dollar liability coverage was partly illusory. Shelter would pay a *total* of only fifty thousand dollars, five thousand under the medical-payments provision and forty-five thousand under the liability coverage because of the reduction stated in part 1. To paraphrase the Good Book, "The insurance company giveth, and the insurance company taketh away." Gladstone was disappointed that so little coverage was afforded by Shelter, but its explanation was compelling. At this point he could have accepted the fifty thousand dollars, charged Steven a fee for his meager efforts, and gone on to the next case. Gladstone, however, was a lawyer with a conscience, a rare combination, some would say. He wanted to be sure that he had left no stone unturned when representing this unfortunate boy who would never father a child, climb a mountain, or hold a job. He did what good lawyers do when they come to a dead end: he consulted a lawyer whom he respected to see if he had overlooked anything. It was in this way that Steven Ganaway's case came to my office on March 4, 1982, and would receive my attention through four legal actions spanning almost nine years.

After twenty-three years of litigating insurance issues, I had reason to be suspicious of Shelter. Insurance companies have two personalities—one when they sell a policy, and the other when they are called upon to pay. When they seek your business, they are full of assurances that they have your best interests at heart: "You can rely on us," "You are in good hands with All-state," "Like a good neighbor, State Farm is there," and "We keep our promises to you" are some of the familiar advertisements we have all seen. Yet when a claim is made, the only thing the client can rely on is the cold, hard reality that he is in the hands of an adversary who does not act like a neighbor and does not keep the promises the sales agent made when he sold the policy. As with lawyer jokes, there is an element of truth in some insurance jokes. For example, "I bought an automobile insurance policy, but the language is impossible to understand. All I am sure of is that after I die, I can stop paying."

As I began to study the Shelter policy, I kept in mind Shelter's duty. An insured has no bargaining power when purchasing an insurance policy. If he asks questions such as "Am I fully protected?" or "Does this policy provide coverage if a claim is made against me?" he will be told he is protected from every conceivable liability. The insurance company is the knowledgeable expert, and the purchaser must either accept the policy as written, go to a different company and buy a nearly identical policy, or be uninsured. Since the law requires liability insurance, the prospect has little choice. The law recognizes this reality and says to the company, in effect, "You wrote the policy, you gave the insured no say in its wording, and you held yourself out to be an expert, so your policy must be understandable and unambiguous. You will not be rewarded for writing an ambiguous policy and then misinterpreting it."

I read and reread part 1 of Shelter's policy. Where did it say that its liability coverage is reduced if it makes medical payments? Nowhere! Part 1 simply provided that medical payments would reduce any *settlement or judgment*. Thus, if Steven obtained a judgment against Scott for forty thousand dollars, Shelter would pay a total of forty thousand dollars, five thousand under the medical-payments provision and thirty-five thousand ınder the liability clause. Steven could not receive a windfall and ecover forty-five thousand dollars for a claim only worth for-y. On the other hand, if Steven obtained a verdict of a hundred housand dollars and that amount was reduced by the five-housand-dollar medical payment, he still would be owed ninety-ive thousand. Shelter would have to pay all of the coverage it ›rovided (fifty thousand dollars' liability plus five thousand nedical), and Steven would have to look to Scott's individual as-ets for the remaining forty-five thousand or be uncompensated or that amount. The only purpose of part 1 was to prevent the ame medical expenses from being reimbursed twice, once un-ler the liability coverage and a second time under the medical-›ayment coverage. Steven's medical expenses exceeded five thou-and dollars many times over, and his claim for personal injury vas worth far more than fifty thousand, so he would not receive ‚ windfall if he was paid the full value of both coverages.

Shelter's refusal to pay a just claim made my blood boil. It was loing what I had seen insurance companies do so many times ›efore—use its size, might, wealth, and self-proclaimed exper-ise to deny a pitifully injured party a deserved recovery. We vould find a way to make Shelter pay for its arrogance. A search ›f the law found no Missouri case construing part 1 of the pol-cy, but there was an Oklahoma case, *MFA Insurance Co. v. Hol-ingshad,* which construed the provision the same way I did.[2] Io make Shelter's action more despicable, it had to have actual :nowledge of the *Hollingshad* case because "MFA Insurance Co." vas the former name of "Shelter Insurance Co." The Oklahoma :ourt had construed this precise provision of Shelter's policy di-ectly contrary to Shelter's present position.

Where there is a wrong, there must be a remedy, I thought. Ne could not sue Shelter directly because we had no relation-hip with it. Only Scott, Shelter's insured, had legal standing to :omplain at this point in time. But Missouri did have case law, still not fully developed, that required an insurance company to act in "good faith" in settling claims. Shelter was acting in bac faith, and we would make them pay. Here was the plan: First, we would give Shelter a chance to pay the fifty-five thousand dollars it owed. Second, if they refused, we would sue Craig Scott for his negligent driving and obtain a judgment against him for more than fifty-five thousand. Third, unless Scott would voluntarily assign his claim for "bad faith" to us, we would force him into bankruptcy and obtain the assignment from his trustee in bankruptcy. Fourth, as an assignee of Scott's claim, we then could sue Shelter for its bad-faith refusal to pay our judgmen against Scott.

By establishing a valuable precedent, we could do a lot o good, not only for Steven but for all future victims of "bad faith" conduct. We gave Shelter several chances to settle but were always rebuffed. On November 18, 1983, Shelter wrote, "On the basis of [the Home Office's] research, they have confirmed tha we are entitled to the medical payments offset as provided in the policy. This of course means that we are willing to pay $5,000 under medical payments and $45,000 under the liability coverage, which would exhaust our coverage."

We replied on December 1, 1983, that our offer to settle for fifty-five thousand dollars would be withdrawn if not accepted by December 15. Our offer was rejected, so on January 12, 1984 we sued Craig Scott for his negligent driving. Then came a surprise from Shelter, which made our four-part plan a five-part plan. On January 12, 1984, Shelter filed an action seeking a judicial declaration that its construction of the policy was correct Apparently, it mistakenly thought that neither we nor the cour would learn of the *Hollingshad* decision or that the trial judge in Columbia, where Shelter was headquartered, would not follow the precedent of an Oklahoma case. It was wrong. Not only did the trial judge find for us, but on July 16, 1985, so did the cour of appeals.[3] Shelter's policy provided fifty-five thousand dollars' coverage, just as we had claimed from the start.

Having been told by the appellate court that it provided coverage in the amount of fifty-five thousand dollars, Shelter then offered to pay that sum in exchange for a release. Too late! When a thief steals money, he cannot avoid punishment by promising to pay it back. Similarly, if Shelter was guilty of bad faith before our offer was withdrawn on December 15, 1983, it could not turn bad faith into good faith by filing and losing a declaratory judgment suit.

Now, implementing part 2 of our plan, on December 5, 1986, after a two-and-a-half-week trial, we obtained a multimillion-dollar jury verdict against Craig Scott. With a verdict exceeding his insurance coverage, Scott had a claim against Shelter for its "bad-faith" refusal to settle Steven's claim, a claim that he could assign to us. Such an assignment, usually made before suit is filed, would benefit both Scott and Steven. It would provide that Steven would not execute on any personal assets of Scott (thus saving him from bankruptcy), and, in return, Scott would assign his "bad faith" claim to Steven so that Steven could sue Shelter. For some unfathomable reason, however, Scott refused to give us an assignment. We had no choice. We forced him into involuntary bankruptcy and obtained the assignment from Kenneth McDonald, his trustee in bankruptcy.

By writing and then misconstruing Scott's insurance police, Shelter had needlessly saddled Scott with a multimillion-dollar verdict, plus interest that was accruing on the verdict. Scott had a right to sue Shelter, claiming it was guilty of bad faith when it refused to settle Steven's claim, and, if successful, require Shelter to hold him harmless by paying the judgment and interest. As Scott's assignee, with all the legal rights Scott once had, now we could sue Shelter for those damages. Our case, *Steven Anthony Ganaway, Assignee of Kenneth L. McDonald, Trustee in Bank-*

ruptcy for Craig Alan Scott v. Shelter Mutual Insurance Company, sought the payment of our multimillion-dollar judgment, plus interest, because of Shelter's "bad faith" conduct. Our optimism was short-lived, however. Shelter filed a motion for summary judgment, which the trial court sustained, and we found ourselves out of court. Not good! After years of frustration, thousands of hours, and tens of thousands of dollars invested in the case, we had failed Steven. Now he would face life as a pauper, with no way to pay his expected future enormous medical bills. When life gives you lemons, make lemonade, they say, so we picked ourselves up and filed an appeal.

Fortunately, the court of appeals saw things our way.[4] When Shelter argued that its interpretation of part 1 of the policy was "fairly debatable," the court held that issue was for the jury to decide. When Shelter argued that its filing of a declaratory judgment action proved it was acting in good faith, the court held that also was a question for the jury. An officer of Shelter filed an affidavit stating that it had a good-faith belief that the five-thousand-dollar setoff was proper, but the court said that was a mere conclusion. Shelter said it was entitled to summary judgment because the people it insured, Hazel and Craig Scott, executed affidavits approving and ratifying Shelter's actions, but neither of the Scotts could have known what evil might have lurked in Shelter's mind when it refused Steven's settlement attempts. Shelter said Craig had not been damaged because he had been discharged from liability by the bankruptcy court, but the court noted that Shelter's own policy provided that "bankruptcy or insolvency of the insured . . . shall not relieve the Company of any of its obligations hereunder." Shelter argued that neither Hazel nor Craig had asked it to settle Steven's claim, but the court said that did not prove Shelter was acting in good faith. Shelter argued that Craig's claim for bad faith was not assignable, but the court held "this point is without merit." The appellate court concluded that Steven was entitled to have a jury decide whether Shelter had acted in bad faith. Hurrah!

At last we were faced with only one more trial and appeal. Depositions were taken, records were obtained, motions were filed, and both parties geared up for a fight to the finish. Shelter now claimed that we had "set it up" by an elaborate scheme. It said we never wanted Shelter to settle. It said Steven would have recovered nothing if Shelter had paid us fifty-five thousand dollars because his medical bills far exceeded that sum; the only way Steven and "his lawyers" could be paid was if Shelter refused our offers. It was the victim of our entrapment, it asserted. Nonsense! Our wishes and desires were irrelevant. We offered to settle for the policy limits and warned Shelter that it would be guilty of bad faith if it refused. What more could we have done? If we had possessed the most sinister intent in the world, we still were at the mercy of the insurance company. It was Shelter and only Shelter that could exercise good faith and accept our offer or bad faith and reject it.

Shelter did not relish facing a jury, some of whom would have had their own unpleasant experiences with an insurance company. As the fateful day approached, Shelter suggested that the trial and its aftermath would be long and expensive, and the ultimate outcome would be in doubt, all of which made settlement attractive: "The company is willing to pay you handsomely for a release, enough to provide for Steven and earn you a substantial fee. There is a good chance we can win a jury verdict, but even if we lose, there will be another appeal and you will not get your money for years. A bird in the hand is worth two in the bush. What do you say?"

At this point I had no desire to be courteous or diplomatic. With more than a touch of sarcasm, I retorted, "Why would I want to settle this case? I have grown to love it and can't bear to see it end. What would I do with my time, without insurance officers to depose, appellate briefs to write, oral arguments to make in an appellate court, and jury cases to try? If we keep at it, the lawyers in my firm will have something to do after I am dead." I made it clear, then and each time settlement was mentioned, that the only way Shelter could avoid facing me before a jury was if it paid every penny of our judgment and every penny of interest on the judgment, not a penny less. I was in no mood, after years of dealing with Shelter's insurance nonsense, to give an inch. Shelter decided that it could not stand the heat, so it gave up the ghost on December 26, 1990, nine years and thirty-seven days after Steven was injured. It paid Steven every cent of his multimillion-dollar judgment and every cent of interest due on his judgment.

I had many bad-faith cases, before, during, and after *Ganaway*, including a bazaar case against a company that insured Robert Berdella, a homosexual who captured, held hostage, raped, and brutalized six young men for up to six weeks before they found peace in death. The cover of Tom Jackman's book about Berdella bore the inscription "Cruel acts of torture and mutilation more brutal than the crimes of Milwaukee serial killer Jeffery Dahmer!" The atrocities of the monster Berdella were exposed when his last victim, Chris, managed to wiggle out of his restraints, jump naked from a second-story bedroom window of Berdella's house, and flee to shelter and aid at a neighbor's home.

John Turner, a Kansas City attorney who represented the parents of one of Berdella's victims, obtained an uncontested judgment against the maniacal demon when his insurance company refused to defend him. Berdella's policy promised that the company would "provide a defense at our expense by counsel of our choice," but had not furnished one, contending that the satanic brute's acts were not covered. John asked me to help pursue a bad-faith suit against the company. We would try to persuade a jury, and then an appellate court, that Berdella's brutal acts were covered by his liability policy. We would argue that Berdella wanted to keep his victims alive, so as to enjoy them, and that their deaths were accidental, not premeditated. If we were successful, we would be making new law. It was a long shot, but it was worth a try.

Only Chris and Berdella could tell us what was in the mind of the beast. We found Chris and enlisted his support. Berdella was next. I established a rapport with the deranged fiend by mail and interviewed him on a few occasions in the only room offered by the staff at the ancient state prison in Jefferson City, a tiny six-foot-by-six-foot cubbyhole, with only two metal chairs for furniture. No guard was present (there was no space for one), and the iron door to the room was closed during our conversations. Chills ran up my spine when a knee of the devil incarnate, accidentally or intentionally, sometimes brushed mine as we sat facing each other.

Despite the favorable testimony of Chris and the monster, the overwhelming evidence seemed to lead to one inescapable conclusion: the beast with no conscience must have known that only suffering and death could result from his demonic deeds. We only had a slim chance to win, but the insurance company did not want to risk a trial and appeal. It wanted to settle, and so did we. It was a sizable settlement, one that pleased our clients, but all the money in the world could not take the place of a son who died a horrible death at the hands of a serial killer. As for Berdella, his life sentence was a short one. He died in his prison cell from what may have been a heart attack on October 8, 1992. Fellow prisoners joked that his screams of pain and cries for help were ignored by prison guards and that his death was preventable, but no one seemed to mourn his passing.

Berdella's insurance company may have had an excuse for its behavior, but there could be none for the conduct of Allstate Insurance Company in a bad-faith case my firm handled. When

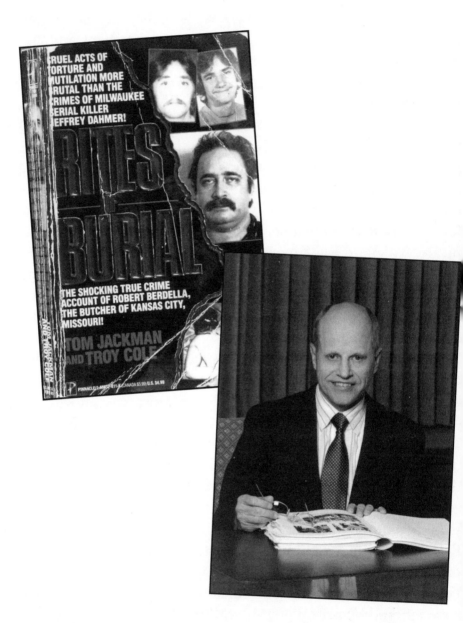

(Top) This book was written about serial killer Robert Berdella, who murdered my clients' son.

(Bottom) At my desk at about sixty years of age.

the court sustained our motion to require Allstate to produce records we believed would disclose a concerted scheme to minimize settlements with injured claimants, it refused. When the judge found Allstate in contempt and fined it ten thousand dollars a day until it produced the documents, it still refused. When the court increased the fine to twenty-five thousand dollars a day, it continued to refuse. By the time the case settled, Allstate's fine totaled more than seven million dollars. Does Allstate now have a greater respect for the American system of justice? Of course not. Was the fine large enough to make it change its behavior? Perhaps a little. One thing is certain: if there are enough brave and resourceful lawyers willing to take on these giants, someday it will pay them to treat policy holders and claimants fairly. Then the public really will be in "good hands."

All good things must come to an end. I had always known that day would come—and when it did I wanted to go out as a class act. I had seen lawyers grow old in the practice, with younger lawyers resenting their ineffective leadership as well as their percentage of the firm's income. Often the senior attorney had been forced out, and frequently bitter lawsuits followed, with each party claiming the other had stolen the firm or money from the firm. The litigation could last for years, with appeals followed by new suits and different theories of recovery. Former close friends and business colleagues became acrimonious and antagonistic, hating each other so much that it gnawed at their guts and made them physically ill. This, above all else, is what I wanted to avoid. I must treat my partners fairly and retain their respect, admiration, and friendship.

More than anything, I wanted to go out when my mind was still quick and my stamina still adequate for the long weeks before and during a trial, when sleep was elusive and emotions ran high. I had seen people in other professions—doctors, fighters, and football players—stay too long or attempt a comeback after they had passed their peak. I wanted to be a trial lawyer who left near the top of his game.

In the winter of 1995–96 I had suffered from a long bout of the flu. In previous years my voice had become weak as a trial had worn on, and that year the weakness persisted after the flu had gone. A trial lawyer without a strong, clear, pleasant voice is no lawyer at all. I saw a doctor, who referred me to a voice pathologist, who prescribed exercises to strengthen my voice and then suggested that I take singing lessens to keep it strong. I was tired and burned out, and my voice was fragile. It was time to pass the baton on to the firm. No one is indispensable. Our clients would be well served by my partners, and I could do other things I had postponed: study history, learn about computers, hike, camp, and float some of our Missouri and Arkansas rivers.

Late in 1996 I told the firm of my plan—I wanted to ease out of the practice over a two-year period and turn the firm over to them. Two years would give Steve, Steven, and Clif time to assume leadership of the enterprise and gain the confidence of our clients. But they protested. They were still in their thirties and not ready to be set adrift. I would have to wait to retire until later, when the time was right. As it turned out, that time would be when the attorney general asked me to represent Missouri in its case against the despicable tobacco industry.

13

THE GREAT TOBACCO CASE

We don't smoke the shit, we just sell it. We reserve the right to smoke for the young, the poor, the black and the stupid.

—The statement of an R. J. Reynolds executive, according to David Goerlitz, the model who represented Winston cigarettes in newspaper and magazine advertising from 1981 to 1988

It was the largest recovery in the history of Missouri litigation! It involved the most intense effort by the largest number of Missouri lawyers, searching the most records, retaining the most experts, accepting the greatest challenge, risking the most personal assets to finance a case, and all this to sue a foe most people still thought unbeatable. It was the case of Missouri against thirteen tobacco companies.

For forty years, lawyers had sued tobacco companies without a victory, eight hundred losses without winning one cent in damages. In 1953, when a scientist at Washington University in St. Louis published a report that tobacco smoke had caused cancer in mice, fourteen tobacco manufacturers reacted in a hurry by publishing a joint "Frank Statement" on January 4, 1954, in four hundred newspapers across the country. A few parts of the "Frank Statement" are worth quoting: "Distinguished authorities point out . . . that there is no proof that cigarette smoking is one of the causes [of cancer]. We believe the products we make are not injurious to health. For more than three hundred years tobacco has given solace, relaxation, and enjoyment to mankind. At one time or another during those years critics have held it responsible for practically every disease of the human body. One by one these charges have been abandoned for lack of evidence."

Despite the cards stacked against them, a few daring plaintiff's lawyers with a committed or insane determination began to sue the evil industry. They were overmatched, opposed by defense lawyers and a bevy of experts who spent 100 percent of their time defending their tobacco clients. Uniformly, the defenses that (1) tobacco is not harmful to smokers, (2) the cancers suffered by the smokers were caused by other factors, and (3) smokers assumed the risk of cancer when they decided to smoke prevailed. The smoking victim died without being compensated, and the lawyer learned that one tobacco case was one too many if he or she wanted to remain solvent.

By the mid-1990s the landscape was beginning to change. Jeffrey Wigand, a tobacco executive, had secreted damaging documents out of the company's building and soon blew the whistle on the megacorporations. Mississippi, followed by Florida, Texas, and Minnesota, filed suit. Now, no longer would it be an individual against unholy tobacco; it would be a state. Indeed, it would be four states lined up one after the other to take on the bully. Now it would be a fair fight.

Missouri's attorney general, Jay Nixon, was cognizant of the growing belief that tobacco might be vulnerable and, in the fall of 1996, called me for my opinion. My view was that the odds of prevailing both before the jury and on appeal were slim, but that tobacco deserved to be sued. Nixon had a political and practical dilemma on his hands. If he did not file suit and other states prevailed, he would have deprived Missouri of funds much needed in the state's coffers. If he sued and lost, he would be embarrassed politically and criticized for spending state funds and manpower chasing an uncatchable rabbit. Nixon needed a way to sue tobacco without spending state funds—and he found it. He would ask private lawyers to represent Missouri in the suit and be responsible for the expenses of prosecution. The question was, would anyone agree to such an outlandish request?

In April 1997, Nixon sent out his "Request for Proposal," seeking lawyers who would work for a contingent fee—if they lost, they would not be paid, and if they won, they would "theoretically" be paid by the state. I say "theoretically" because, while Nixon could enter into the agreement, he could not force the state legislature to appropriate money to pay the attorneys' fee. Anyone who had a finger on the political pulse knew that the legislature would rather do anything than pay "bottom-sucking" lawyers a penny. Any legislator voting for such a fee probably could look forward to being out of office after the next election. Therefore, if we lost, we would not be paid, and if we won, in all likelihood, we still would not be paid. Lawyers ignored the "request" in droves.

But I could not get the case out of my mind. More than 10,700 people had died from tobacco use in Missouri in 1995 alone. Smoking accounted for 70 percent of all cancer deaths in my state. More than 27 percent of Missourians smoked, ranking my state the third-highest per capita smoking state in the nation. Tobacco needed to be sued, and if I wouldn't, who would? I was sixty-five years old and felt that I had another A+ trial left in the tank.

I called a firm meeting and explained the situation. I said I wanted a pound of flesh from the enterprise whose product killed its users. Think of the benefit to society if we could put tobacco out of business. My firm usually followed my lead and agreed, regardless of how wild my ideas were, but this time there was a long silence prior to a discussion that I could not refute. If we took this case, it would make us a one-case firm, they said. It would consume all of our time. We would have to abandon all of our other cases and refuse any new cases that came our way. We would have to advance millions of dollars to hire experts, prepare exhibits, and prosecute the case. Our overhead would continue apace—rent, utilities, salaries for our employees, and so on. We would have no income until the case was over, perhaps five years or more until all the appeals were concluded, and we would be out of business long before then. Even if we survived financially and won, the legislature would not appropriate money to pay our fee. Only a fool would want such a case.

I could not argue the point. The firm was right, and I knew it. But my mind was made up. I would sue the bastards if it took my last cent and my last ounce of blood. So my firm and I reached an agreement. I would submit a proposal to Attorney General Nixon, and, if retained, I would *individually* represent Missouri. The firm's finances and mine would be separated. If I lost the case, it would be my loss, not the firm's. The firm would continue its normal practice, and I would be free to assemble a team of lawyers to bring the suit. I would be the fool. I individually, not the firm, would respond to the attorney general's "Request for Proposal." Only one proposal in addition to mine was submitted by Missouri lawyers, a testament to what all sane lawyers thought of the gamble.

From the summer of 1997 through the summer of 1998, Attorney General Nixon, or his office, discussed the case with me on several occasions. Nixon had filed a "place holding" suit on May 12, 1997, one that would keep his options open until he had to fish or cut bait. That time came on June 8, 1998, when Jimmie Edwards, the trial judge, set a firm trial date of January 24, 2000, and told Nixon he had better be ready. Nixon had been backed into a corner. He had no choice; he either had to dismiss the suit, too large and expensive for his office to handle, or hire outside counsel.

June 15, 1998, is the day Attorney General Nixon told me he wanted just one lawyer, *me*, to be responsible for the prosecution. He wanted to be able to call me day or night and with no runaround. I would have to know all aspects of the case instead of referring him to someone else on the team. Most important of all, I must devote all of my time and all my energy to the case and require all of my team to do the same. I must win the case, if the case was winnable. Then came the discussion about my fee. Most lawyers who were representing other states were retained on a contingent fee of 25 percent, some 15 percent, and one or two less than 10 percent. My contract would be a contingent fee of 7.15 percent, and I would pay all expenses. Nixon, for obvious political reasons, wanted to strike the best deal of any attorney general in negotiating an employment contract. I did not protest the arrangement.

Politics is a way of life in the United States, but nowhere more so than in the "Show Me State." On August 5, 1998, a Republican senator I will call "Senator R," a political opponent of Nixon, sued the attorney general and me, claiming that my employment contract with the state was unlawful. Paul Wilson, an assistant attorney general assigned by Nixon to uphold the contract, argued to the court that "we had to find somebody who was the best trial lawyer in the State of Missouri . . . , who was brave enough to risk ten million dollars of his own money or more, to go against an industry that had never been beaten in the hopes he could beat them, and then persuade the General Assembly in its gratitude to appropriate him a fee. We found one in Tom Strong." Wilson's use of the word *brave* was kind. *Demented* or *totally crazy* might have been more appropriate.

I anticipated that my employment agreement would be challenged even before I was hired, so it was no surprise, nor did I delay my efforts, waiting for it to be filed and prosecuted. I needed a team, and I needed it in a hurry. I would require everyone who joined my team to give 100 percent of his or her effort to the case. Everyone would be available on demand for motions, depositions, conference calls, and organizational meetings. There would be no divided loyalties. If we were organized, if our efforts were coordinated, if we had enough personnel, we could win. All of our eggs would be in one basket, and, like Mark Twain's Pudd'n Head Wilson, we would watch that basket.

On June 29, 1998, I met with the team leaders I had chosen: Ken McClain's firm would be responsible for proving liability. Ken was the first attorney to obtain a court order, which declassified tobacco's documents and was the only experienced tobacco litigator on the team.[1] Jim Bartimus's firm would join the team.[2] Jim was the best-known medical malpractice attorney in the state and would prepare the medical aspects of the case. The firms of Bob Ritter and John Sandberg would review the twenty-five million tobacco documents in the Minnesota depository and others that the court would require tobacco to produce for our inspection.[3] General Nixon wanted Chuck Caldwell's firm to be part of the team.[4] Although no one in Chuck's firm was an acknowledged litigator, it was the most prominent African American firm in St. Louis, where the case was pending. Since a majority of the jury would be African American, Nixon correctly assessed that Caldwell's presence was essential.

These leaders and those in their firms provided forty-nine lawyers to work on our case, up to sixty when needed. Two other lawyers, members of the firms I had retained, were to play an important role in the litigation: Edward D. "Chip" Robertson, who retired from the Missouri Supreme Court, where he had served as chief justice, now would be responsible for pleadings, motions, and briefs. Before it was all over, Chip would be the most dependable and valuable member of the team. Jim Burt, from my firm, with a PhD in economics, would be responsible for providing our Medicaid damage model. Chip and Jim gave our team two members no other state could claim: a former state supreme court judge and an economist with a PhD.

The lawsuit and our team received much attention from the media. In particular, why was I chosen to lead the team? Was I really the best choice, or was Nixon just repaying some political debt he owed me? Of course, I knew Nixon was not repaying a political debt. I had contributed to his opponent, Republican David Steelman, the first time Nixon ran for attorney general in 1992 and had made only modest contributions to his campaigns since. Nixon could have no motive to choose me to sue tobacco other than because he thought I had the best chance to beat the unholy alliance in court. Nevertheless, the subject of Nixon's political debt to me was the object of an investigation by the media, with the results giving me a near-clean bill of health:

> *St. Louis Post-Dispatch, June 30, 1998:* Governor Mel Carnahan praised Strong as an excellent choice, adding that he thinks the fee arrangement is fair and reasonable.
>
> *Springfield News-Leader, June 30, 1998:* Attorney General Jay Nixon appointed the man he considers Missouri's best trial lawyer to lead the state's lawsuit against the nation's tobacco companies. . . . "He is a man of recognized character," Nixon said. "We could not have better representation. . . . I want attorneys who will aggressively litigate and who will recognize and remember their responsibility to the Missouri taxpayers as they enter this potentially lengthy and complex litigation. . . ." Nixon said he wanted a Missouri lawyer with a national reputation to head the team facing the tobacco companies' army of lawyers.
>
> *Kansas City Star, June 30, 1998:* Nixon said he chose Strong, a personal injury lawyer, because he was the best trial attorney in the state. . . . "With Tom Strong's assistance, we will build an aggressive case and will be prepared to face some of the biggest litigators in the country."
>
> *Kansas City Star, July 1, 1998:* On Tuesday, David Steelman, a Republican who lost to Nixon in the 1992 attorney general's

race, defended Nixon by calling Strong the "logical choice" to lead the state's tobacco team. . . . "He's the guy for the job, there's no question," Steelman said.

Springfield News-Leader, July 13, 1998: What colleagues say Strong brings to the court is a perfectionistic approach. Top-notch visual displays. A mastery of minutiae—the results of his sometimes 20-hour days.

Kansas City Star, July 14, 1998: "He's absolutely an over-whelming lawyer," said Fred Wilkins, a partner in Wilkins & Millin in Kansas City. "Tom is as good a lawyer as there is in Missouri—ever."

The newspaper articles made us look good, but they don't win lawsuits. We were well aware that we were facing an uphill battle. Steven F. Goldstone, chairman and CEO of RJR Nabisco, had told the Washington Press Club on April 8, 1998, "The state cases have no merit. Courts in Maryland, San Francisco, Washington and West Virginia have already thrown out these claims. Undoubtedly, where fair tribunals exist, others will follow." Tobacco was welcoming our anticipated fight. One hundred fifty-five attorneys filed their names with the court as lawyers for the various defendants. And for every lawyer listed, we knew there would be several others working behind the scenes.

After forty years of fighting corporations of monstrous size in the courtroom, the braggadocio of the industry and the hoards of attorneys we would be facing did not frighten me as much as some might think. Opposing lawyers would outnumber us a little more than three to one, odds I was used to facing. If we were focused and well organized, we could win. Every week we had a team telephone conference, and every month we met in St. Louis, Kansas City, or Springfield.

Nor were we without some advantages. Our case would be tried in St. Louis, where 53 percent of the population were African American; thus, we would take advantage of a raw nerve other states had ignored. We would emphasize that tobacco had targeted African Americans with their false advertising. Dr. Larry Fields and Dr. Douglas Luke, distinguished St. Louis African Americans who had studied and written about the impact of smoking and the effect of tobacco's advertising on the black community, would be powerfully effective witnesses for us. Tobacco's own records and the statement of one of its executives that "We don't smoke the shit, we just sell it. We reserve the right to smoke for the young, the black, the poor and the stupid" would offend an African American jury who might be black and poor but would not be stupid and would know how to deal with someone who treated them as if they were.

By the fall of 1998, state after state was suing the formerly unassailable foe, and tobacco now was facing dozens of cases filed, not by a person, but by an entity with the talent and resources to challenge it effectively. When the first cases approached trial, tobacco backed down and settled with Mississippi, Florida, and Texas. It went to trial against Minnesota, but chickened out at the close of the evidence and settled with it. General Nixon told us, "Don't even think about settlement." He wanted Missouri's case tried. So did we. We would seek damages of $8.5 billion for reimbursement of Medicaid expenditures and billions more in restitution and penalties under the Missouri consumer-protection law. We had accomplished a lot in a compressed time, and by mid-November 1998 our trial preparations were on schedule. We would be ready.

We had built a strong case under Missouri's Merchandising Practices Act that:

- revealed the industry's targeting of children, the poor, and African Americans in violation of the act

- revealed the lie of so-called low-tar and low-nicotine cigarettes

- created a legal and evidentiary predicate that would allow my team to request crippling civil penalties and restitution against the industry

We had:

- a firm trial date, barely more than eighteen months away

- built a Medicaid damage model that would survive the industry's attacks

- retained more than sixty economic, medical, and liability experts for trial

- identified key tobacco documents and moved to remove the industry's false claims of privilege

- conducted depositions

- accomplished in six months what many states took years to accomplish and some states never accomplished

On November 16, I received a call from Attorney General Nixon. He wanted to meet with the team leaders at his office just two days later. "What's up?" I asked. Obviously, he was not having the major players come to Jefferson City to pass the time of day or to inquire about the progress of the case. Nixon, before always open and candid, was now vague and evasive. "I just want to discuss the case with you," he said in a soft, firm tone, indicating that he wanted no further discussion on the subject.

All of the major players on our team were present at the appointed time as instructed, each with his own guess as to what was in store for us. Perhaps someone had talked to the media, something Nixon had strictly forbidden, and a strong rebuke was waiting. Or perhaps Nixon wanted us to hear some newly discovered evidence that his fellow attorneys general had sent his way. Some speculated that there was a political movement afoot that would require him to nullify my employment with the state and put us all out of work. There was even a thought that he was going to tell us that he had settled our case.

Those with the "settlement" theory came the closest. Some attorneys general had been discussing settlement since last spring, Nixon said. He had attended one of the early meetings but thought tobacco would not deal in good faith. He told that to his fellow attorneys general in no uncertain terms. He wanted no part of such discussions, he claimed, and walked out of the meeting. After that, he was not kept informed (*shunned* might be a more accurate term) about the progress of the negotiations, although he knew they were continuing. Now he was told that a "global" settlement had been negotiated, which each state could join, if it so desired.

The settlement would provide every state that signed it with a payment from the wicked cancer-stick manufacturers as long as the companies sold tobacco, approximately $6.7 billion to Missouri in the first twenty-five years alone, but the remuneration would continue until people quit puffing the death sticks. Perhaps more important, the proposed settlement included eighteen pages of injunctive relief, curtailing tobacco's ability to advertise. No longer would the distributors of the product that caused so much suffering and sorrow be able to post billboards near elementary schools, pass out free samples of their products, advertise in theaters, sponsor sporting events and concerts, or distribute free T-shirts or other merchandise with their logos. Perhaps most important, Missouri would start receiving money now, not several years hence, and a settlement would eliminate the chance of a loss in court, where Missouri would get nothing.

Nixon was on the fence, he said. There were a couple of other attorneys general who were threatening not to sign, and Nixon wanted our thoughts. What were Missouri's chances of winning the case? What would be our recovery if we won? Did we believe joining in the settlement with the destructive giants was the best option? He went around the table, starting with me, to get our responses.

My brain was spinning, as a thousand thoughts raced through my mind. The provision that the base clique could pay for its sins over a period of years made all the difference in the world, giving these iniquitous purveyors of cancer the chance to live to sell another day. A judgment in any of the big states, including Missouri, would be payable immediately in one lump sum and could put the nefarious outfit into bankruptcy. That is what I wanted so badly I could taste it. But Nixon wanted my objective, unbiased opinion, not an emotionally based one, and that is what I was required to give him.

I told him of our work, that we would be ready when the bell rang, and I guaranteed that we would try the best tobacco case that had ever been tried. We were going to hit the destructive syndicate at its soft underbelly, its targeting of African Americans, and we would do it before the most receptive audience possible, an African American jury. I wanted to try the case and do away with the vile industry that was killing tens of thousands of my countrymen each year. Of course, I admitted that no lawyer could guarantee victory—but Nixon knew that.

One by one, Nixon sought the opinion of each person present. Most held my view; all were willing to go to the mat, but one or two, in tone or words, suggested that there were advantages to settlement. It was only Jim Burt who pointed out possible weaknesses in our case and saw advantages to accepting a bird in the hand instead of two in the bush. Nixon listened attentively to each speaker, interposing a searching question here and there.

At the end of the discussion, he thanked us for our thoughts and our willingness to battle the immoral syndicate. He would also need the advice of the governor, leaders in the house and senate, and others, he said, before deciding what he should do. He would attend our monthly meeting in Springfield, scheduled for Friday, November 20, the last business day before the deadline, and tell us his decision. Monday, November 23, was the last day to join the settlement, so he could not procrastinate.

Our monthly meeting attracted more than forty team members who wanted to learn our fate. Somehow, we all knew what the answer would be. Nixon thanked us for our service, complimented us for our labors, but said the feeling in the capitol was unanimous that we should settle. The other two holdout attorneys general had also given in, so the "global" settlement really would be global. With these final three jurisdictions on board, the unsavory alliance had bought peace with every state and territory of the nation. While my taste for tobacco's blood would not be quenched, I understood why Nixon had made the decision he made. He had acted as a responsible servant of the people. Had I been in his shoes, I would likely have ended up coming to the same conclusion he did.

If the settlement was so advantageous that every state was on board, why was tobacco so eager to buy peace? Ernie Pepples, vice president of the Brown and Williamson Tobacco Company, probably said it best in a televised interview the following summer: "I will have to tell you that I misjudged the strength of the attorney general claims. There is the chance that you will end up in the wrong court at the wrong moment and one loss will wipe out an entire industry." That was exactly my hope, that our court would be the wrong court for tobacco, and its loss to us would signal its demise. Now, with the settlement, the poisonous fire sticks would still be on the market killing people. Oh, well! At least the great tobacco case was over. Or was it?

The fact that Nixon had received only two replies in response from Missouri lawyers to his 1997 "Request for Proposal" spoke volumes about their reluctance to take on the nefarious tobacco cartel. What a difference our settlement made! We had brought billions into our state treasury, and now folks were coming out of the woodwork, claiming part of it. We had done the work, but, like the lazy dog, sleepy cat, and noisy yellow duck in the story *Little Red Hen,* many of the lazy, sleepy, and noisy wanted part of the spoils.

Six parties, or groups of parties, filed separate motions to intervene. They included Kansas City, Jackson County, St. Louis County, the City of St. Louis, and more than fifty hospitals, all of whom sought reimbursement for the value of medical care they had provided to Medicaid recipients. A taxpayer alleged that the settlement agreement violated the Missouri Constitution by diverting state money to private attorneys (us). Two citizens attempted to bring a class action on behalf of all Missouri smokers, claiming that the settlement destroyed their right to sue tobacco for their injuries, and one individual wanted to be paid for the wrongful death of his father who died of lung cancer.

In order to ensure that the bounty went where it belonged, to the state treasury, I had to defeat the claims of the attempted interveners three times: in the trial court, then in the court of appeals, and, finally, in the Missouri Supreme Court. Our victory in the trial court came on March 24, 1999, and against the four groups that appealed in the court of appeals on January 18, 2000.

Our state's supreme court had discretionary authority to accept appeals if it so desired or to reject them and let the decisions of the appellate courts stand. Since we had won the cases of the four interveners as well as "Senator R's" claim in the appellate courts, that the attorney general had no authority to hire us, we had hoped that the supreme court would deny all the requests for transfer. Another disappointment! The supreme court accepted the appeal of "Senator R," as well as the four appeals of the interveners.

After more months of writing briefs and arguing the case in the supreme court, we prevailed against both "Senator R" and the interveners. On January 23, 2001, the court's decision became final, and the settlement with tobacco was approved without change.[5] After fighting to protect our settlement in the trial and appellate courts for more than two years, we were the last state to conclude the litigation marathon. There had been challenges in only a few other states and nowhere with such vigor, tenacity, and longevity as here. But we had prevailed, overcoming all obstacles, and at last we could rest. Or so we thought.

Since we had done everything our contract with the attorney general required us to do, we were entitled to 7.15 percent of Missouri's recovery. Assuming tobacco would pay Missouri the projected $6.7 billion, our fee would be more than $479 million. The question that haunted us when we were first hired involved including an item in the state budget to pay us. At this time, the odds of getting such a bill passed were less than zero.

Of course, we could sue the state for our fee. Peter Angelos, who represented Maryland against the unrighteous tobacco tribe, had sued his state for his 25 percent fee and had gained untold denunciation for himself and adverse publicity for the legal profession in the process.[6] I wanted to avoid this kind of scenario at all costs, if possible.

We had an out. The settlement agreement provided that tobacco would pay a fee to the lawyers prosecuting the actions— not the fee that would be paid by their states, but a fee to be determined by agreement or, if the parties could not agree, then by arbitration. In the event of arbitration, there would be three arbitrators, one chosen by tobacco, one chosen by the attorneys for the state, and the third chosen by the first two arbitrators. The arbitration panel would consider the amount of contribution each jurisdiction had made to the cause and make an award that would be paid over a number of years. The decision of the panel would be final—neither tobacco nor the lawyers could appeal. Therefore, if we wished, we could agree with tobacco on a fee or arbitrate and then sue Missouri for the difference between what tobacco would pay us and the amount provided in our contract. I wanted no part of suing Missouri; the thought of it made me sick to my stomach.

It was at this point that the attorney general had another favor to ask. He wanted us to release the state from its contract with us and look solely to tobacco for payment. Such a release would rack up political points for the attorney general and, at the same time, avoid the adverse publicity that would come to our profession if we sued Missouri. It was an easy decision for me, and my team concurred. So it was, on March 30, 1999, well before our difficulties in the courts and with the legislature were over and without any idea as to how much we would be paid by tobacco, that we signed the requested release. Missouri would not owe us a penny, either for our fees or for the millions of dollars in expenses we had already incurred.

Consequently, payment for my forty-nine lawyers who had worked on the case, some for thirty-one months, lay solely with an arbitration panel. The rules for the hearing were simple. Each side was entitled to eleven hours to present its case. When our eleven hours expired, the timekeeper would notify the panel, and we would be stopped in midsentence, if necessary, and told to sit down. With this etched-in-stone limitation, we must plan ahead with our allotment of time. I would have two hours to make the opening statement and final arguments. All of the leaders, except one, would participate. Each would make his or her presentation and then be cross-examined by a tobacco lawyer and possibly the panel. We must be interesting and informative. Graphics would be important. Concise, powerful language would be required. Some humor would be appreciated.

Several dress rehearsals were conducted. We cross-examined and critiqued each other and criticized and suggested ways to improve and condense. Every one of us must conclude within the allotted time. We emphasized the following points:

- We had made a unique contribution to the settlement by showing that tobacco had targeted African Americans with its deceitful and poisonous advertising.

- Our Medicaid damage model was impervious to attack because of our state-specific data, something no other state could claim.

- We were one of only thirteen states with a trial date, and our date was firm. There would be no continuance for us, nor did we want one.

- Our victory over tobacco would be large enough to bankrupt it.

- That Missouri was not at the bargaining table wanting to settle probably influenced tobacco to settle more than those who were there with hat in hand (but we must be very diplomatic with this point).

- We had worked harder over a longer period of time protecting the settlement in our courts and legislative halls than any other state.

Our evidence at the hearing went well, so well that one of the arbitrators complimented our trial team and said he wished we could have tried our case.

Tobacco's evidence and arguments were just what we expected: we were early in trial preparations, had not yet spent much time working on the case, were down to the list of states with a trial date, and, most emphatically, played no part in influencing tobacco to settle. Not one comma, period, or word in the settlement agreement was influenced by anything Missouri did, so argued tobacco.

In the one hour I had for my summation, part of my response to the claim of our insidious opponents that we had not influenced the settlement went something like this:

> Do tobacco's arguments mean that the four years Ken, Jim, Bob, and the rest of the team have devoted to this case were for naught? Do they mean that forty-nine lawyers wasted their time when they agreed to forsake their busy and lucrative practices to devote all of their attention, effort, and sweat to help bring down a corrupt industry? Do they mean that the thirty-four months the team worked after being formally retained so Missouri finally could start receiving tobacco funds in June of this year served no purpose? I certainly hope not.
>
> In thinking about how to properly explain why Missouri is entitled to a full, reasonable fee, I remembered a story as old as antiquity itself. Yes, even older than I. It is the story of a camel. [Here I displayed a picture of Joe, the cartoon camel Chesterfield used in its advertising.] It seems a man loaded a camel with a heavier and heavier burden, until, finally, he added one last straw that broke the camel's back. Philosophers over the centuries have debated: Was it really the last straw that broke the camel's back? Was the last straw any heavier than the first straw? Or the middle straw? Which straw really broke the camel's back? Tobacco says we were late on the scene, the last straw. We disagree, but we need not debate whether we were the first, middle, or last straw. It took all the straws together to form the critical mass that broke the back of Joe Camel.

The decision, handed down on December 27, 2001, awarded us hundreds of millions of dollars less than Missouri would have owed us and would be paid over approximately a twenty-five-year period. We had received our day in court, and due process was served. Now my work on the tobacco case had ended. Or had it?

Since Missouri would not have to pay us either for our fees or to reimburse us for our expenses, I envisioned a grateful legislature, or at least not a hostile one. After all, we had acted professionally, releasing the state from paying us a fee, while at the same time bringing billions of dollars into the state's treasury.

I should not have been so naive. Tobacco had great influence in the halls of our state's capitol, and "Senator R" led the attack. Our fees were, incredibly, dubbed his "number-one priority." When he introduced one of his bills, he passed out buttons with the words *No Obscene Fees* on them. It seemed to make no difference that Missouri would not have to pay our fees or that an industry that had killed thousands in our state would pay them. It didn't even matter that tobacco neglected to complain about paying us and, in fact, was contractually bound to do so by the settlement agreement they had negotiated. The decision was an easy one for the politicians: cheat the lawyers out of a fee and give it to the industry that has no conscience.

In the 1999 session, a senate bill had provided that lawyers prosecuting Missouri's tobacco case could be paid a fee only pursuant to an appropriation by the general assembly. The bill passed the senate by a vote of eighteen to fifteen, but died in joint committee. Naturally, the general assembly would not appropriate money for us, so the intended effect of the bill was to deprive us of a fee.

In the 2000 session, some of the bills would limit the amount we could be paid per hour, restrict the attorney general's right to retain outside legal assistance, levy a 50 percent income tax on lawyers who represent the state in cases that exceed $100 million, and require the attorney general to sever his relationship with the tobacco team.

The attack on our fees continued with even more momentum in the 2001 session. Any imaginable method to deprive us of payment seemed to become a proposed law. Examples of bills offered would require that the state (not my team) receive the fees we were awarded in arbitration, render the settlement agreement that required tobacco to pay Missouri an estimated $6.7 billion null and void, provide that our attorneys' fees be diverted to supplement the salaries of schoolteachers, and provide that our attorneys' fees go to fund the Missouri transportation plan.

In all, twenty-one bills were offered during the three sessions of 1999, 2000, and 2001. In addition, various remonstrances were offered, one condemning the attorney general, another Missouri's tobacco team, and still another former supreme court chief justice Chip Robertson and me, individually.

It was political football at its best, or worst, depending on your perspective. We hired as many as eight lobbyists to help us fight off the political wolves and barely escaped. Some bills came out of committee with a do-pass recommendation, some passed one of the houses, but in the end nothing became law. Sometimes the political scene seemed like a macabre comedy; I felt like the cowboy with an arrow through his chest who said, "It only hurts when I laugh." Why did we have to suffer through three years of political attacks, waste our time, and spend our money when we had just brought billions of dollars to Missouri? Why were we the only state to have so much trouble after the settlement, both in the legislature and in the courts? It didn't seem fair.

What a political ordeal! I had entered the fray with the best possible intentions, hoping to right an incredible wrong, but I learned that the purest of motives can be the object of the vilest attacks by ambitious politicians looking for votes. But at last, now that we had escaped the political wolves, my job was done. Or maybe it wasn't.

When I employed my team, the contracts provided that each firm was to receive a specified amount for its services, but of the 7.15 percent we were to be paid, I retained 1.55 percent (approximately 22 percent of our total fees) to pay those who, in my *sole* discretion, had performed "exceptional service." The retained discretionary fund would be the carrot on the stick that would keep the team motivated to work hard. I did not want to be saddled with dead wood or loafers.

My allocation of the discretionary fees did not please anyone except Jim Bartimus and Chip Robertson. Others thought they had been shortchanged, none more so that Chuck Caldwell. He wanted a judge to redistribute the discretionary fund, but not just any judge in any court. He wanted Judge Edwards to pass on the matter in St. Louis. So he retained a trial lawyer who filed a motion in the now dead tobacco case, seeking relief.

There were fatal flaws in Chuck's legal maneuvers. The case of *Crain v. Missouri Pac. R.R.* held that a dispute concerning attorneys' fees was a separate case, involving different parties and issues than those of the original case.[7] Since Chuck's claim did not involve either Nixon or the tobacco companies or the issues of tobacco's alleged misconduct, *Crain* was authority for the proposition that it must be filed as a new case. But filing a new case is just what Chuck wanted to avoid. If he filed a new case, the statutes said it must be in Greene County, where I lived, not in St. Louis, where he resided. Chuck felt he must avoid Greene County at all cost. I had threatened to reduce his fees if the case went to trial, and Chuck knew that I did not make idle threats. In a different court, he could be in trouble. Seeing that he would have to proceed in Greene County or give up, Caldwell gave up.

So, on November 22, 2002, all the parties I had retained signed a settlement agreement, putting an end to the attorneys' fee issue. Five and one-half years after I had submitted a response to Nixon's "Request for Proposal" and more than four years after I had been formally retained to represent Missouri, after fighting tobacco in the trial court and at arbitration, after fighting "Senator R," the interveners, and a member of my own team in the trial and appellate courts, and after fighting politicians in Jefferson City, finally the case was over. Or was it?

Yes, thank God, finally the case was over.

14

Retirement and Beyond

After the November 22, 2002, settlement was put to bed, I was prepared to fade quietly and gently into retirement. But there was to be one last hurrah! Several days after the June 2006, convention of the Missouri Association of Trial Attorneys, its new president, Tom Stewart, came to my office. I barely knew Tom from casual contacts at MATA functions, and he had just finished losing a lawsuit to my partner, Clif Smart. He was serious as he took a seat in my office. Was he about to complain that Clif had somehow deceived, misled, or mistreated him during the trial?

It was not the trial that was on his mind at all. Tom wanted my reaction to an idea he had been pondering. He said he wanted MATA to present an award to a Missouri trial lawyer who best exemplified what a trial lawyer should be. It would be the start of a tradition, he said; the award would be given every year. Victories in court would be important, but not the only, or perhaps even the main, criteria. Courage to fight the giants, professionalism, unimpeachable ethics, and a sterling character would be major considerations.

Tom had even thought of a name for the award and had consulted several lawyers to see if they agreed. If it was to be the highest honor presented to any lawyer, it should bear the name of the attorney who embodied all the qualities that made the ideal trial lawyer, he reasoned. There were many such courageous, talented, and principled lawyers in Missouri's long history, but Tom had picked the one person who most epitomized the ideal trial lawyer and whose name should be inscribed on the trophy, now and forever. The award should be named "The Thomas G. Strong Trial Attorney Award." Tom had discussed all of this with MATA's officers and staff, and they all agreed that his idea was a good one. Having once obtained the largest verdict in Missouri's history and with only two instances of failing to make a recovery for a client, my record in court was without equal, he claimed, and the example I had set for integrity was an inspiration for all trial lawyers. Everyone he had consulted was enthusiastic that the award should bear my name.

I sat speechless, overwhelmed by the idea that of all the lawyers in the history of Missouri, I had been selected for the honor—but I was also suspicious. Was Tom serious? Was this a practical joke? Was there a catch? Was Tom in charge of raising funds for MATA? When I was cochair of a capital campaign for Missouri State University, naming rights were awarded only in exchange for a contribution. When the dean of the University of Missouri wanted to name the law school "The Thomas G. Strong School of Law," he understandably requested a sizable donation. But Tom never mentioned money. All he wanted was my consent to have the accolade bear my name. Wow! Of course I would allow my name to be on the award.

The first public mention of the award was made in the 2006 fall edition of MATA's magazine. In the president's message, Stewart told of the emotion he felt when reading about the fictional Atticus Finch in *To Kill a Mockingbird:*

> Such courage, integrity, skill and compassion are the very heart of who we are—or should be—when we champion the cause of our clients. We need not rely solely upon Ms. Lee's fictional Atticus for a role model to guide us. We have in our

ranks a number of courageous trial lawyers who have set a standard to which we each can strive. Still, there is one of our number to whom we all owe a debt of gratitude—our very own Atticus Finch, whose verdicts are only eclipsed by the professional integrity with which he led his career. I am pleased to announce the establishment of the *Thomas G. Strong Trial Attorney Award. The Strong Award* will be given each year at our annual summer convention to the trial attorney who most closely exhibits all the attributes by which we have come to know Mr. Strong: skill in the courtroom, integrity in one's professional and personal dealings, compassion for the underdog and respect for the courts and opposing counsel.

Tom and I agreed that the trophy should be extraordinary in order to reflect the honor it represents. After weeks of perusing catalogs and talking to vendors, we decided on a twenty-one-inch, thirteen-and-one-half-pound glass trophy, individually handblown, signed by the renowned Czech artist Jiri Pacinek, and produced by the same company that makes Hollywood's Oscars. MATA's executive director suggested that it be inscribed with headings from the keynote speech I had made at a MATA convention in 1988, and Tom agreed. I enlisted Mary Ann Hall to draw a picture of Missouri's Supreme Court Building, which would adorn the back of the trophy, and it was all put together with the aid of graphic artist Jeff Helder. It was a beautiful trophy of dark glass, which would change color with a change in lighting.

It was customary for the keynote speaker at MATA's yearly convention to be a prominent person, usually from out of state. In 2007, however, I was invited to fill that slot, as I had a few times before. It would be my last farewell, so I typed the speech, a rarity for me, and memorized it—a first. A couple of weeks after the convention, Spencer Farris, a lawyer I never recall meeting, sent

me a copy of a nationally syndicated column he had written for
the *St. Louis Daily Record* newspaper. It stated, in part:

> I had another run-in with a giant this month. It was at our
> state trial lawyers' convention. My law partner, outgoing pres-
> ident of the organization, created an award to acknowledge
> the qualities that separate the best in our profession. Trial tal-
> ent, speaking ability and hard work are standard, but there is a
> magical something else that defines the truly great. This award
> is named after a truly great trial lawyer, Tom Strong, and he
> came to speak in honor of the inaugural presentation.
>
> Perhaps the best part of the new award was Mr. Strong's
> speech. He stopped lecturing when he retired, thinking that
> no one wants to hear his war stories. I can tell you that no one
> who heard him that night agrees with his assessment. I hap-
> pen to think I work with three of the very finest trial lawyers
> around, and I am not easily impressed. Mr. Strong impresses.
>
> In the dewy eyed early days of my practice, I was deeply
> moved to hear Mr. Strong speak. . . . His diction is unusual,
> and his tiny frame does not bespeak the powerful presence
> he possesses. His speech was modest, yet we felt his love for
> our profession. I was once again inspired to do good work
> from his telling of tales. My mind whirled trying to imagine
> the courtroom warrior that has since retired, the giant bend-
> ing down to speak to us.
>
> We all know giants and legends of giants. . . . These men and
> women represent the very best, and the mastery of the craft
> that we aspire. And each time we mention the giant's name,
> his legend takes another breath.

From beginning to end, the trial award represented one pleasant experience after another. No defense lawyer opposed me,
found fault with my evidence, picked apart my arguments, or

criticized me for failing to call a witness. I was recognized as someone who had made a positive contribution to society in general and to my profession in particular. It was absolutely the perfect end to a wonderful career.

Later, on January 1, 2008, profound changes came to the Strong Law Firm, my firm in name only since my retirement. Clif Smart had been retained the previous month as the in-house attorney for Missouri State University, Steven Harrell had decided to open his own one-man office, and Steve Garner and the rest of the attorneys began a new venture at 415 East Chestnut Expressway in a building I had helped build and occupied as part of the Farrington, Curtis, and Strong firm forty years before.

Steve asked me to be in the new firm, which he wished to name Strong-Garner-Bauer, PC, and said he would give me a free office plus a small yearly stipend. Presumably, my name and presence might still attract some business, but Steve's overriding consideration undoubtedly was to be charitable to a long-time friend and professional associate. Steve asked me to think about his proposal and give him an answer the next day, if possible. I needed no time to think. Steve was the best trial lawyer in the state, in my opinion. No one worked harder, had more talent, or represented an injured plaintiff with the right motives more than Steve. This would be my opportunity to remain close to a dear friend as well as to retain some exposure to a profession I love.

Now, after four years in the new firm, with seven lawyers, counting me, five paralegals, two nurses, a bookkeeper, a receptionist, three secretaries, and a handy man, business is booming. I look forward to coming to my beautiful, commodious office every morning and to see the pleasant, loyal lawyers and staff who make it the best law firm I know.

Now, in retirement, I look back on my life in court. It was a satisfying life, pursuing a dream some are unable to pursue because of health or circumstances beyond their control. I had no excuse to fail. I was healthy, with a supportive family, and from the start I had the opportunity to try cases. More important, I had the perfect background to be a successful trial lawyer. I had always graduated near the top of my class and along the way had learned much about public speaking, persuasion, and analyzing and simplifying issues. Even more important was what I had learned about life in those formative years—working productively and hard from the summer after my seventh grade forward on the farm, as a laborer building a highway, as a clothing salesman, as a gas station attendant, as part of a congressman's campaign for office, and as an agent in the Counter Intelligence Corps. I had associated with people from all walks of life and had learned some of life's great lessons: work hard, save money, apply yourself, never shrink from a challenge, and never think that second place is good enough.

I had the desire and ambition, plus the physical and mental tools, to be a winner, and I knew I would outwork any adversary. I had not even taken a vacation the first three years of my practice. My main enemy throughout was sleep or rather the lack of it. When something was on my mind, as an upcoming trial often was, I had trouble sleeping for more than three or four hours a night; on rare occasions sleep did not come at all. I often kept a tablet and pencil on the floor by my bed in order to make notes of things that invaded my mind during the night, possible solutions to a weakness in my case, or ways to cross-examine an opposing witness effectively.

I am often asked, "What was the most interesting case you ever had?" or "What was your favorite case?" or "What was your most important case?" My answer to these and similar questions was always something like this: "Every case I accepted was like one of my children, so every case was my favorite. Everyone's case, big or small, was the most important one in the world to my client, so every case was the most important case to me as well, at the time I was working on it."

I was twenty-three years old when I became a licensed attorney, twenty-five when I began practicing in Springfield, and seventy-three when the last fragments of the tobacco case were put to rest. From my very first case, which resulted in a twenty-four-hundred-dollar verdict for my injured client, to the tobacco case, which resulted in the largest recovery in Missouri's history, there was never a dull moment. The thrill of victory was what I lived for, the thought that I had played a part in giving hope to a person with a critical need. Still, my greatest motivator remained the agony of defeat, or fear of defeat, and the desperate need to avoid it, which drove me to the point of exhaustion.

There have been dramatic changes in my profession since I walked, with wonder, fear, and excitement, into Tate Hall to attend my first law school class in 1952. Any college graduate could enter a state-supported law school then. "Come, but don't expect to graduate," I was told, "because only a third of you will receive that coveted degree." Now there are LSAT examinations and grade-point requirements. It is difficult to be admitted to most law schools now, but once you are there, you will graduate if you apply yourself. After all is said and done, I don't know that law school graduates are any better qualified now than then. Some are competent, some not, just as it has always been.

Trial lawyers are different now than two generations ago. Then nearly every attorney thought himself able to try a case. And since it was trial by ambush, where you had no idea what your opponent had waiting for you, there was little preparation—E C Curtis once had eight-five insurance defense files in the two file drawers he kept in his office. Many who tried cases, with little self-confidence, interest, or talent, were resigned to blunder through and hope for the best. Yet there were a few gifted lawyers who excelled. With little television and outside entertainment, audiences often came to watch the unfolding excitement in the courtroom. Some attorneys would play to the crowd as much as to the jury, with exaggerated gestures and flowery language. Trials often were like spontaneous plays, with the script written as the plot unfolded. The lawyers who won were smart, quick witted, articulate, and persuasive speakers. They were the few who would become famous. This was the stage I stepped onto, and to which I quickly adapted.

Most of today's trial lawyers, particularly those from the huge firms, are of a different breed. I call them "paper lawyers" because their expertise is filing motions, briefs, and other documents by the ream. They are persuasive writers with the aim of excluding your witnesses, limiting your evidence, and disposing of some or all of the issues without a trial. They do not covet trying the case. They are paid to avoid it. As a result, their trials are few and far between. Many of them are not gifted speakers and are out of their element once they have to face a jury. Their trials tend to be long, tedious, repetitious, and boring. Their opening statements and closing arguments are written, and they speak without passion or conviction. There is no doubt that these advocates know more about their case than the lawyers of old, but many lack their spontaneity and jury appeal. Who would win if some famous lawyer of the past faced some famous lawyer of today? I would bet on Clarence Darrow of a century ago against any of them.

Cases were settled as often when I practiced law as they are now, but by different means. Today, mediation and arbitration, which became popular only at the end of my career, are common ways to arrive at a compromised settlement. Before, lawyers settled cases by talking to each other—what a unique idea—not in the sterile, impersonal atmosphere of a hearing where lawyers talk to a mediator and the mediator talks to the opposing side. I hated mediation and usually avoided it unless the court ordered it or the client demanded it. My approach to settlement was different from any lawyer I know. Defense lawyers sometimes seemed to want to settle cases immediately before trial, perhaps in order to work more hours and charge a larger fee. After I had established a reputation as a person not afraid of the courtroom, I advised my opponents that if they wanted to settle their case, it must be done at least thirty days before trial. "I am not going to live through the agony of the final throes of preparation, only to miss the excitement of trial because of a last-minute settlement," I asserted. At first, opponents thought I was making an idle threat. "Tom, I finally have authority to pay your demand," they would say on the eve of the opening day. "Sorry," I would reply, "but that offer expired a month ago. If the case settles, it will be during trial for more than my previous offer." The word spread, and my cases either settled at least a month before trial or went to court, except in the rare instance when my client got cold feet and demanded that I relent.

When was justice more often served, in the days of trial by ambush or today? "Today" is the indisputably correct answer in my field of practice. In the era of "trial by ambush," there was no way to discover what was in the records of the manufacturer of a defective product. And it is in those records where the "smoking gun" is found that unveils the sins of the manufacturer. It is there that complaints of other victims, admonitions from employees, tests that disclose its danger, and other incriminating evidence are found. An injured plaintiff, without access to defendant's files, has little hope of victory. Changes in discovery and substantive law have resulted in more conscientious manufacturers and safer products. Manufacturers can no longer secrete their records as they once could, so they are vulnerable to being exposed when they have placed profit ahead of safety.

Juries also are under attack by some who want their cases decided by judges. I hope that never happens. No judge is as smart as the combined intelligence of twelve conscientious jurors and has twelve times the chance of being prejudiced. Thomas Jefferson had it right when he said, "I consider trial by jury as the only anchor ever yet imagined by man, by which a government can be held to the principles of its constitution." The American system of justice is not perfect by any stretch of the imagination, but it is still evolving and is better than whatever comes in a distant second.

Of course, there is life outside the courtroom, and, in reflection, mine has been lived at frantic pace, with handball, racketball, snow and water skiing, scuba diving, horseback riding, farmwork, and hiking filling my spare time.

In one activity, I nearly pushed the envelope too far. After climbing Wheeler Peak, Mount Elbert, Mount Massive, and Mount Whitney, my son Jack and I needed a bigger challenge. Mount Rainier, a massive, 14,411-foot glaciated volcano in the state of Washington, had been our target in 1980. There, at Paradise Inn, a small 1916 vintage hotel at 5,400 feet, cousin Tim Gaines, Jack, and I sat in a group of about a dozen climbers waiting to be told what was in store for us. "This is an exhausting and demanding climb," the guide said in solemn tones, "and not all of you will reach the summit. We will leave the dropouts in sleeping bags and pick you up on the way back, but no one will stay with you. You will be on your own. People die on this mountain, an average of about two a year, more than on any mountain in the United States so you must stay with the group. Ice falls, crevasses, which are not visible because they are covered by a thin layer of ice or snow, and foolhardy decisions are the major causes of deaths. If you are not in excellent physical condition and don't have the guts to persevere when the going gets tough, don't start the climb."

I glanced around the room and saw only young, lean, strong-looking men—no females. We appeared to be the weaklings in the group, and, of course, I was by far the oldest. After the session was over, Tim, Jack, and I discussed the guide's dire warnings and opined that they were undoubtedly mostly hype, calculated overstatements designed to dramatize the adventure and perhaps put a little fright in those who were not committed to it. We would have no trouble.

The climb would take two days. We were to leave early in the morning and by seven or eight in the evening arrive at Camp Muir, an unheated little stone hut at 10,188 feet, with bunks where climbers could rest. At midnight we would leave the hut, climb the rest of the night, reach the summit about dawn, and return to Paradise Inn late in the afternoon of the second day.

We reached Camp Muir on schedule, but resting was a different matter. It was bitterly cold in the tiny hut—the stones between us and the outside glacier felt more like blocks of ice than rocks—so we spent the next four hours shivering and counting the minutes till midnight when we could start moving again. I soon learned that the next 3,000 feet of elevation would tax me to the limit. Before long I was dragging one foot behind the other, thinking I would puke and fall over with the next step. Then, one by one, some of the young, athletic-looking men gave up and were left alone as promised, in their sleeping bags to be picked up on the way back. If they could quit, why couldn't I? I was forty-eight years old! But every time I asked myself the question, the answer came back—I could not let my son see me fail. I would keep going as long as I could stand. Somehow, after what seemed like an eternity of agony, we ended up on the summit, cold and shivering. "Avoid dehydration," we were instructed. "Drink some water." I had kept my water bottle between my goose-down coat and a heavy sweater I was wearing, but it was frozen solid. How could it be so unbelievably frigid *inside* my coat? I asked for a drink from Jack and Tim, but their water also was frozen. "Let's get off of this mountain!"

Once down, I confessed to Tim and Jack that I had thought about giving up, particularly after seeing others drop out. They conceded that they verged on collapse but would not quit since I had not. All three of us had reached the summit because we knew we would forever hear from the other two if we had quit. The warnings we had received before the climb no longer seemed like calculated overstatements, designed to dramatize and frighten. The climb was as demanding as alleged. Young, strong-looking men did give up, as promised. Nor were the dangers overstated. In 1981, the year after our assent, eleven people died on the Ingraham Glacier of the massive mountain.

Rainier had been an unforgettable experience. It proved that mental determination can force the body to perform unthinkable feats, and it whetted Jack's and my appetite for the even more strenuous sport of rock climbing. I needed to get in great physical shape if I was going to tackle climbs more formidable than Rainier. Part of my preclimb routine was to ascend the stairs of a ten-story building ten times, for a total of one hundred stories, with a backpack filled with seventy pounds of sand to duplicate the average weight of our packs on our trips. The Springfield newspaper of March 25, 1983, carried a picture of me on the stairs with an article that stated, in part, "Trim at 51 years of age. Strong tries to get four or five workouts a week of different activities. . . . Three to four months before climbing, Strong builds up his legs by borrowing the stairs of the ten-story Plaza Towers building."

While accepting complete and total exhaustion as part of our adventures, we almost got more than we bargained for on Wolfs Head, a rock-climbing peak in the Wind River Range of Wyoming. After establishing a base camp and resting, we started our assent at three in the morning, reaching the summit and returning to camp by late afternoon, totally spent. But there would be no rest. At camp we were met by swarms of relentless mosquitoes thirsting for our blood. We decided to press ahead, knowing that we were facing an additional nine-hour march over hills, fallen trees and boulders, through mud and creeks, and across rough terrain of every description before we could expect to arrive at our van. And, of course, we would be toting nearly seventy pounds of gear on our backs. The nine hours of torture was without a pause. We knew if we sat down, we would not have the strength or willpower to pick ourselves up and move on.

Our guide called the twenty-eight-hour ordeal the equivalent of a death march, and perhaps for me it nearly was. As I fell onto the floor of our van at the end of the nightmare, my heart was beating like a machine gun, and my legs below the knees were swollen, my ankles twice their normal size. After returning to Springfield, a doctor friend said I had suffered congestive heart failure.

Humpty Dumpty sat on a wall,
Humpty Dumpty had a great fall;
Threescore men and threescore more,
Cannot place Humpty as he was before.

Mountain-climbing deaths too often are the result of monumental lapses of judgment. That was nearly so at Sam's Throne, near the tiny town of Mount Judea (pronounced "Mount Judy" by the locals), in middle Arkansas. The throne is an outcropping of rock, plus a circular column of "Ozark granite." It is a popular climbing destination in the Midwest because it offers pitches of all difficulties, from the easy to difficult 5.13 overhangs. Jack and I had made frequent visits there.

The fateful day occurred on December 20, 1986, at the end of a cliff Jack and I called the "chicken head" wall. We had been on the wall several times, with one of us belaying the other during the climb. On this particular day, for a reason I will never understand, I told Jack not to belay me (a technique of using friction on a climbing rope to prevent a climber from falling). But this day I needed one. I have no memory of falling, or of much of the rest of the day for that matter, because of a head injury I received. I fell almost forty feet in Jack's best judgment, landing on a boulder, as Jack watched helplessly below. There is a rock-climbing saying that a fall of twenty feet is serious injury, and forty feet is death. If that is true, I may have dodged a bullet and disappointed the grim reaper.

My lacerated scalp received numerous stitches at the hospital later that day. My lower left leg was placed in a cast, followed by surgeries in 1987, 1989, and 1992. The injury left me with a permanently impaired knee. I could still walk, however, so Jack and I have hiked over some beautiful territory, including the Buffalo River trail and the 168-mile Ozarks Highland Trail.

Nonlegal activities were not confined to the physical. I was a member of the Junior Chamber of Commerce, Kiwanis Club, YMCA board, Wilson's Creek National Battlefield Foundation, and the National Center for Tobacco Policy at various times in my life. Yet no extracurricular activity compared to my involvement with the college that has become Missouri State University. Three generations of my family have received an education there, beginning with my mother who enrolled in 1918, myself in 1949, and all three of my children, who attended Greenwood, the university's laboratory school. My family has been associated with and benefited from the school in all except the first sixteen years of its existence. It is because of the education Mother received there that she was able to support our family during the Great Depression, and it is because of my education there that I was able to live at home, earn money for college and law school, and still graduate in three years. Son Jack now is a professor there. Friends and associates have also been closely connected with the institution, as students, as staff members, or on the faculty. Clif Smart, my law partner for fifteen years, now serves as its president.

Feeling a deep debt of gratitude, I have remained active at the school ever since returning to Springfield, as president of the Alumni Association, charter member and president of the Papa Bears (basketball) booster club, president of its board of governors, cochair of its first comprehensive fund-raising campaign, vice chair of the search committee for president of the university, president of its foundation, and currently cochair of its second comprehensive campaign.

I had no title, however, when I participated in an exhausting several-year effort to obtain a new name for our institution. We had been Southwest Missouri State University since 1972 and felt that we were now Missouri State University except in name. We deserved the name. Shakespeare once claimed that names are of little importance. "What's in a name? That which we call a rose by any other name would smell as sweet," his Juliet asserted. Those of us who tried for nineteen years to influence the Missouri legislature to change the name of our institution, however, considered the issue to be of monumental importance; there was much more at stake than just a name.

In the four years before we finally obtained the nom de plume we craved, I was in Jefferson City, wooing politicians for the university. I talked to every senator and representative of either party who would grant me an audience, hosted fund-raising events at my house for members of both parties, and contributed tens of thousands of dollars to the war chests of those who committed to help bring us the new moniker. Democrats listened because they considered me to be one of them, Republicans because they pretended to favor a new name, and everyone because I was helping fund their campaigns. Finally, in 2005, all the hard work paid off. On August 28 of that year, when the name became official, a party, complete with fireworks, lasted far into the night. What's in a name? Well, Juliet, in our case, a lot. A new name for our university is a big deal indeed!

After the battle for a new name had begun, but before it had ended, the tobacco case was winding down, and it was time to repay the university for what it had done for my family. What it had given my family was priceless. So, in 2002, my family and I gave the university the largest gift it had received at that time: two endowed chairs for professors and several scholarships for students. In appreciation, on May 17, 2002, the board of governors voted to rename the Public Affairs Building, first occupied in 1998, "Strong Hall." The building is an impressive 150,000-square-foot structure located at the west end of the school's main mall and houses the College of Humanities and Public Affairs, KSMU radio (the National Public Radio station) and Ozark Public Television.

In late 2005, university president Mike Nietzel called. Did he have a new assignment or a question in mind? Or did he wish my advise or my financial support? It could be any of the above, but it never was just to pass the time of day. When he eventually found me at my cabin at the lake on a workday, a call he placed personally, obviously, he had gone to a lot of trouble to track me down. Mike wanted to tell me that I had been chosen to receive the "Bronze Bear Award," given to those who have exhibited "extraordinary achievement and/or outstanding support" for the university. The university had given three generations of my family an education. Now it was giving me this high honor. What a humbling experience!

Into every life some rain must fall, they say. My association with politics and politicians has been much less than satisfying. In the 1950s and '60s I was impressed by the teachings of Walter Judd, Everett Dirksen, Barry Goldwater, and Ronald Reagan. I saw Judd speak in Springfield and can paraphrase his message on the evils of too much welfare. "I can do my daughter's homework for her, but I don't; not because I don't love her, but because

The Strong Law Firm, 2001 (nine lawyers and staff).

I do." Dirksen stood on a table in a driving rain in Springfield's Phelps Grove Park and talked about our nation's lack of fiscal responsibility. "A billion here, a billion there, and pretty soon you're talking about real money," he said in an era when a billion dollars *was* "real money." "Government is not the solution to our problem. Government is the problem," said Reagan. Small government, fiscal accountability, and individual responsibility were messages that appealed to me, so I served on the Greene County Republican Central Committee as a young lawyer and worked for Barry Goldwater when he ran for president in 1964.

But talk is cheap, they say, and when the Republicans gained office, they did not practice what they had preached. Our national debt increased by $832 billion when Reagan was president and by a whopping $1.3 trillion during the administration of George W. Bush. Welfare fraud continued unchecked, and small government was still an illusion regardless of the party in power.

(Top) Jack on a 5.10d pitch at Yosemite.

(Bottom) Yours truly, at seventy-nine years, doing my yoga.

Strong Hall, at Missouri State University.

Republicans had lost credibility with me. Even worse, they had sold out to several interest groups.

Some of those groups directly and brutally affected my clients; they included insurance companies and manufacturers who were lobbying for "tort reform" to obtain immunity from lawsuits or to limit the amount they must pay to the people they injured or killed. The money of those organizations began to pay political dividends nationwide in the mid-1980s as they invested more and more in Republican candidates for office. The "reformers" had a distinct advantage. The sick and injured were not organized, had no lobby, and had no voice in the Missouri legislature when tort reform came to Missouri in 1987. Only the Missouri Association of Trial Attorneys was willing to be their advocates. Seeing firsthand the plight of the victims of negligence, trial lawyers, I included, increasingly became politically active. This fight was personal.

The "reformers" knew what would sell and what would not sell:

- First, they defined the issue as one for "reform." Who could be against reform? The very term indicated that something needed to be fixed and that they were the ones to fix it.

- Second, they did not identify the giant companies that were backing them financially, namely, insurance companies and corporations that were reaping huge profits while manufacturing unsafe and dangerous products.

- Third, they avoided attacking the innocent, vulnerable, injured victims of their wrongful conduct and, instead, attacked trial lawyers. "Trial lawyers were getting wealthy by filing frivolous, meritless lawsuits that cost society millions of dollars to defend," they argued.

There was little logic behind the frivolous-lawsuit argument, if people paused to think about it. "Frivolous lawsuits," by definition, are lawsuits without merit. Why would any trial attorney file a meritless lawsuit? Before a lawyer can win a case, he or she must prevail three times: first, obtain a jury verdict; second, persuade the trial judge to affirm the verdict; and third, convince the appellate court that the verdict was justified. Any case that is won three times is not "frivolous." Frivolous lawsuits are dismissed before they ever see the courtroom or are thrown out by the jury, trial judge, or appellate court. That is not to say that frivolous suits are never filed. Silly lawyers do silly things. But trial lawyers who want to earn a living do not file suits they think they will lose. Most trial lawyers work for a contingent fee and are paid only if they win. Filing a few frivolous lawsuits is a sure way for a lawyer to become personally acquainted with bankruptcy court.

When the argument of the "reformers" was pierced to its nub, it was clear that it wasn't the frivolous lawsuits they feared. It was the legitimate suit with the potential to reduce the dividends they could pay their stockholders. As vice president of MATA in 1987, I was assigned the job of resisting the proposed legislation. I decided that Ernie Hubble, a Kansas City attorney, and I should go straight to Governor John Ashcroft. As an attorney, he would know that the Seventh Amendment to the United States Constitution guarantees that "the right of trial by jury shall be preserved, and no fact tried by a jury, shall be otherwise re-examined in any Court of the United States, than according to the rules of the common law." He would recall that one of the "injuries and usurpations" addressed by our Declaration of Independence was the act of the king of England in "depriving us in many cases, of the benefits of trial by jury." We would remind him that our forefathers of the eighteenth century cherished their unfettered access to our courts and filed more lawsuits per capita than we file today. In fact, many involved petty disagreements between neighbors that today's reformers would think frivolous.

Ashcroft would see the fallacies of the bill and the logic of letting the judiciary deal with judicial problems. He could end this attempt to deprive victims of their rights. Ashcroft, who had practiced law in Springfield and had taught business law at Missouri State University, was a friend of mine. I had supported him in every race he had run, so he would listen to me. When Ernie and I entered the governor's office, I expected that the first few minutes would be spent in pleasantries. Once a rapport had been established and we were relaxed, we could discuss the pros and cons of the tort reform bill, I thought.

The meeting was a disaster from the start. There would be no pleasantries or a chance for Ernie and me to state our case. The governor greeted us by saying that tort reform was high on his priority list, that the judicial system was broken, and that frivolous lawsuits were driving up the cost of defending lawsuits. He cited the examples of a man who sued when he injured himself while using his power lawn mover to trim his hedge and the man who sued Winnebago for his injuries when he put it on cruise control, as he was driving on an interstate highway, and walked to the back of the driverless vehicle to get a soda. We attempted to tell the governor that his examples, widely circulated by "reformers," were the blackest lies out of the deepest depths of hell, but he was in no mood to listen. Tort reform must be passed this session, he said. Instead of resisting the inevitable, we should work to craft a bill that would bring meaningful reform to Missouri. Ernie and I were ushered out of Ashcroft's office before we could say three words about the dangers of the pending legislation. When we returned to the MATA office, Linda Simon, MATA's executive director, asked how we had fared. "On a scale of one to ten, it was a minus four," I admitted.

As I talked to the Grand Old Party members of the Missouri General Assembly, I began to realize that they really knew nothing of the pros and cons of tort reform, nor even understood what the bill they were supporting would do, if passed. They had cashed the political contribution checks of the "reformers" and believed their lies, as had the governor. Their sole objective was to please constituents who had donated monstrous sums to their campaigns by passing a "tort reform" bill—almost any tort reform bill. Just having personally witnessed the complete lack of understanding of the governor, I figured that if we could agree to a bill that appeared to give something to them but did not really give much, all might not be lost. Some bill apparently was going to be passed, and it would not be wise to dig in our heels and resist an irresistible force.

We planned our strategy. MATA would arrange a meeting of the two warring parties that would satisfy the "reformers" as well as MATA. The meeting was near the end the session, when things were always hectic beyond description. Even under ideal circumstances, the general assembly passes or rejects bills it has not read and does not understand. In the last days of the 1987 session, our opponents were in a panic, desperate to pass "tort reform," nearly any bill that would allow them to look good to their donors. I told the "reformers" that their prefiled bill was unacceptable, that we would fight it to the death, and that they could expect a filibuster unless they were willing to compromise. Back and forth the negotiations went, later and later into the night. Finally, it was time for me to propose our "final" compromise, a bill I had previously written but had kept under wraps until the time was right.

The reformers wanted an end to joint and several liability,[1] and my bill addressed the issue in a way that would have no effect on most lawsuits and little effect on the rest. I played the part of a beaten warrior, telling the reformers that we had given them the world with a fence around it. But if we were to weaken joint and several liability, we must have a concession for the deal to fly. The concession was "prejudgment interest," which would allow plaintiffs 9 percent interest on the final judgment from the time they had offered to settle, if their offer was less than the verdict they later obtained. Most of the reformers did not appreciate the impact prejudgment interest would have, but more than anything else, it was the lateness of the night that caused them to cave. The session ended with the passage of something the reformers could claim as "tort reform," but it gave defendants little or nothing in the ordinary case, and prejudgment interest gave plaintiffs something significant they had craved and deserved for years. The sick and injured gained more than they lost in the legislative session of 1987, but they did lose something and any loss is too much. Little by little the victims of the rich and powerful, without the wealth to finance an influential lobby of their own, have lost more and more of their rights.

Starting in the 1980s, Republicans saw that attacking trial lawyers as the root of many evils could win them votes. By 1992, it was part of the presidential debates, with George H. W. Bush asserting that Bill Clinton was supported by "every lawyer that ever wore a tasseled loafer." In the 1994 congressional campaign, Newt Gingrich and his allies included "tort reform" as one of the ten planks of their "Contract with America," promising to limit punitive damages and prevent "frivolous lawsuits." Just a decade ago, as we saw in "The Great Tobacco Case," "Senator R." led a three-year attack against my profession. Trial lawyers typically are not shrinking violets, and we fought back. How could I support a political party that was attacking my profession and attempting to restrict the rights of my clients?

It wasn't only tort reform that chilled my enthusiasm for the GOP. The banking industry, Wall Street, and the National Rifle Association had too much influence in the party to suit me. Then when George W. Bush became president in 2000 and plunged us into an unnecessary and ill-advised war in Iraq, my alienation was nearly complete.

Two individuals also played a major role in my becoming more friendly with Democrats. In 1988, when Democratic lieutenant governor Mel Carnahan, a lawyer and friend, said he was going to run for governor in 1992 and wanted my support, he got it in a big way. He won, and Wilma and I were among his first guests to stay in the Truman Bedroom in the Governor's Mansion after the election. Mel was a governor with the right principles, and I was proud to support him. Unfortunately, he died in a plane crash while he was campaigning against John Ashcroft for the US Senate in 2000, before being elected posthumously to the office, resulting in his wife, Jean, serving in his place.

The second Democrat to gain my support was Jay Nixon, whom I grew to admire as I worked with him in the tobacco case. In 2010, Nixon, then governor, appointed me to serve on Missouri's Coordinating Board for Higher Education. It was an important board, responsible for overseeing Missouri's 13 public four-year colleges and universities, 17 public community colleges, 25 independent colleges and universities, 120 proprietary schools, and 39 specialized independent schools. I was almost seventy-nine and flattered to think that Nixon believed that I could still be an asset on a major state board. But members of such boards are subject to confirmation by the Missouri Senate, usually just a formality. I was different, however, and a GOP senator mounted an attack against me. He did not assert that I was unqualified for the position and would not energetically fulfill my duties or that others would have been a better choice. The senator, salivating to block my appointment, had only one complaint—that I was a Democrat and had lied when I stated in the filing papers that I was an independent.

But I was an independent. I had learned the hard way that if you are a member of a political party, you are expected to believe and behave in a certain way, something I was not prepared to do. In the presidential election of 1992, I had voted for third-party candidate Ross Perot as a protest against both parties. As time passed, I supported candidates from both parties, more Democrats than Republicans, based on my faith in their desire and ability to serve the public rather than promote their personal careers. I found being independent to be an asset, as when I worked with both parties to obtain the name change for Missouri State University. There was merit in the statement of young Albert Einstein: "How an intelligent man can subscribe to a party I find a complete mystery."

It is true that I no longer was a Republican, but that did not automatically make me a Democrat, a concept the attacking senator refused to accept. Even stanch Republicans who vouched for me, including Senator Bob Dixon, my sponsor at the confirmation hearing and my advocate with his senate colleagues, and former Republican state senator Norma Champion, for whom I had held a fund-raiser at my home, could not quench the rebellious senator's thirst for my blood. Of all the important work Missouri's senate could have done that session, too much of it took a backseat to arguing about whether I was a Democrat in disguise. I refused invitations to say I was a Democrat, and the session ended without a vote on my confirmation.

I still arrive at the office between six and seven in the morning, but now I am busy looking after business interests and serving on civic boards and committees. To the extent possible, afternoons are reserved for studying history and other subjects of interest, playing duplicate bridge in local tournaments, doing aerobic exercises, lifting modest weights, performing yoga in my workout room, singing a solo at Grace Methodist Church, or having a brief role as a Confederate officer in the new interpretive film of the Civil War Battle at Wilson's Creek, which is now showing at the park's visitors' center.

Most satisfying of all retirement pleasures, however, are the trips I have taken. When I was a child it never occurred to me that I might travel outside the United States. Neither of my parents, none of my grandparents, and no one in my family had, except as members of the armed forces in World War II. At a family reunion when I was a teenager, it was lamented that a distant relative, who had lived to be one hundred, had never realized her dream to journey beyond Greene County to see the father of waters, the Mississippi River. My father, commenting on the ease of travel in the 1930s, talked of the time when a journey from the Marshfield farm to St. Louis, before the days of Route 66, took three days. But wanderings to other countries, not just another city in Missouri, were something else. In the 1960s and '70s, my time was too precious, the world too big, the boats too slow, and the financial commitment too great for journeys abroad.

Retirement has allowed me to travel to about sixty countries: from Angkor Wat, Cambodia, to Paris, France; to Halong Bay, Vietnam; to Macchu Pichu, Peru; to the Great Wall in China. More impressive than the magnificent structures man has built and the natural wonders that have filled my mind with awe are the people of every race, color, and belief I have met. In essence, most of them are very much like most of us in Springfield: they want to make a living, to be left alone with family and friends, and to live in peace. Yet wars come, and peace-loving people fight for their country against other peace-loving people who fight for their country. Why can't a civilization that is smart enough to build the Great Wall or send a man to the moon be smart enough to avoid the killing and insanity that come with war?

The fondest of all my reflections, of course, are of my mother. After eighty years of life, she still influences my values, thoughts, and actions more than any other person. She was the ultimate child psychologist, from a mother's instincts rather than from a formal education. She knew exactly what to say to encourage her two sons, challenge them, and build their self-esteem. But the greatest of all lessons was not what Mother said but who she was, what she did, and the example she set. She worked her fingers to the proverbial bone, supported a family of four during the greatest of all depressions, had the character of a saint without flaunting it, maintained a wonderful sense of humor through it all, and faithfully taught school until a few days before she died. Through all the adversity, poverty, and pain while cancer ravaged her body, she never complained, seldom mentioned her deadly affliction, and never acted as if life had dealt her a bad hand. If there ever was a model for what a mother should be, she was it. It has been sixty-two years, but I still recall as a seventeen-year-old what Mother said in her hospital room just a few hours before she died. She was so weak she could barely speak, but I could hear her plainly: "You can make a difference, Tommy, if you do your best." Too often I have not done my best. Too often, I have not made much of a difference.

Lives of great men all remind us,
We can make our lives sublime,
And, departing, leave behind us
Footprints on the sand of time.[2]

The poet was only partially correct. All of us, not just the great, leave footprints. Whether we like it or not, whether we are great or small, mean or gracious, givers or receivers, we all leave footprints. Every life—good, bad, or mediocre—affects someone for better or worse. Nothing will ever be quite the same after we are gone.

NOTES

Chapter 1

1. Henry Wadsworth Longfellow, "A Psalm of Life."

Chapter 3

1. *A. J. Industries, Inc. v. The Dagon Steel Foundry Company,* 394 F.2d 357 (1968).

Chapter 6

1. Charles Mackay (1814–89), *No Enemies?*
2. *Coffman v. St. Louis\-San Francisco Ry. Co.,* 378 S.W. 2d 583 (1964).
3. *Bine v. Sterling Drug, Inc.,* 422 S.W. 2d 623 (1968).
4. *Leathers v. Coca Cola,* 286 S.W. 2d 393 (1956).
5. *Gustafson v. Benda,* 661 S.W. 2d 11 (1983).
6. *Firestone v. Crown Center Redevelopment Corp.,* 693 S.W. 2d 99 (1985).
7. Punitive damages are not to compensate a plaintiff for a loss, but to punish a defendant who has shown a complete indifference to or conscious disregard for the safety of others.
8. *State of Missouri, at the Relation of Robert J. Smith, Administrator of the Estate of John Galt, Deceased, Relator v. The Honorable Douglas W. Greene, Judge of the Circuit Court of Greene County, Missouri, Respondent,* 494 S.W. 2d 55 (1973).
9. The NBA and ABA merged in 1976.

Chapter 7

1. *Roberta J. Ward v. Penn Mutual Life Insurance Company*, 352 S.W. 2nd 413 (1961).

Chapter 8

1. Trial transcripts are not prepared for cases that are not appealed, so references to the statements of the lawyers and the testimony of witnesses are based on my best recollection.

Chapter 9

1. Jack's heart condition was diagnosed as Wolff-Parkinson-White syndrome when he was twenty-eight and was corrected by surgery at the Cleveland Clinic in 2009, when he was fifty.

Chapter 11

1. *Brown v. United States*, 356 US 148 (1958).
2. Edna St. Vincent Millay, "Renascence."

Chapter 12

1. *Missouri Approved Instructions*, 10.05.
2. *MFA Insurance Co. v. Hollingshad*, 483 P.2d 330 (Okla. 1971).
3. *Shelter Mutual Insurance Company v. Ganaway*, 694 S.W. 2nd 521 (1985).
4. *Steven Anthony Ganaway, Assignee of Kenneth L. McDonald, Trustee in Bankruptcy for Craig Alan Scott, v. Shelter Mutual Insurance Company*, 795 S.W. 2nd 554 (1990).

Chapter 13

1. Humphrey, Farrington & McClain, Independence, Mo.
2. Bartimus, Kavanaugh, Frickleton & Presley, Kansas City, Mo.

3. Gray & Ritter, St. Louis, Mo.

4. Caldwell, Hughes & Singleton, St. Louis, Mo.

5. *State of Missouri, ex rel. Jeremiah W. (Jay) Nixon, Attorney General v. American Tobacco Co., Inc., et al.,* 34 S.W. 3d 122 (2001).

6. *State of Maryland, et al. v. Maryland State Board of Contract Appeals and Law Offices of Peter G. Angelos, P.C.,* 773 A 2d 504 (2001).

7. *Crain v. Missouri Pac. R.R.,* 640 S.W. 2d (Mo. App. 1982).

Chapter 14

1. Joint and several liability allows a plaintiff to recover all the damages from any of the defendants who are liable, regardless of their share of the liability. That defendant or defendants found liable then may claim contributions from other responsible parties for their share of the liability.

2. Henry Wadsworth Longfellow, *A Psalm of Life.*